HEINEMANN INTRODUCTORY POLITICS

US Government & Politics

ANDY WILLIAMS

Heinemann

Heinemann Educational Publishers
Halley Court, Jordan Hill, Oxford OX2 8EJ
a division of Reed Educational & Professional Publishing Ltd

MELBOURNE AUCKLAND FLORENCE PRAGUE
MADRID ATHENS SINGAPORE TOKYO SÃO PAULO
CHICAGO PORTSMOUTH NH MEXICO IBADAN
GABORONE JOHANNESBURG KAMPALA NAIROBI

First published 1996

99 98 97 96
10 9 8 7 6 5 4 3 2 1

British Library Cataloguing in Publication Data
A catalogue record for this book is available from the British Library

ISBN 0 435 33155 8

Designed by Jackie Hill at 320 Design, Kent
Cover design by Aricot Vert Design
Cover illustration by Aricot Vert Design
Typeset by Books Unlimited (Nottm), NG19 7QZ
Printed and bound in Great Britain by The Bath Press, Somerset

Acknowledgements

The publishers would like to thank the following for permission to reproduce copyright material. Associated Examining Board for the questions on pp. 66–7, 102, 137–8, 153, 168–9; University of Cambridge Local Examinations Syndicate for the questions pp. 36, 45, 66, 81, 102, 119–20, 137, 153, 168; University of London Examinations and Assessment Council for the questions on pp. 36, 45, 66–7, 81–2, 102–3, 119–20, 136–8, 153, 168–9; University of Oxford Delegacy of Local Examinations for the questions on pp. 36, 45, 66, 119, 137, 153.

The publishers have made every effort to trace copyright holders. However, if any material has been incorrectly acknowledged, we would be pleased to correct this at the earliest opportunity.

Contents

Introduction v

1 **An historical introduction** **1**

The colonization of the 'new world' 1
The foundations of federalism 8
The 'era of good feelings' 10
Jacksonian democracy 11
American expansion and seeds of civil war 12
Reconstruction 16
A new century 17
The 1920s and the Depression 19
The New Deal 20
Postwar America 22

2 **The constitution** **28**

Introduction 28
The Articles of Confederation 29
The constitutional convention 30
Dispute resolution in the constitution 32
Ratification 34
Changing the constitution 34

3 **Federalism** **37**

The Founding Fathers and Federalism 37
The structure of state and local government 38
The powers and functions of state governments 38
The federal–state relationship 39

4 **Elections** **46**

The number of elections 46
Presidential elections 47
Congressional elections 62

5 **Political parties** **68**

Introduction 68
The party system 69
Third parties 71

Party competition 73
Party structures 74
Functions of political parties 76
Party fightback 79
Conclusion 81

6 The presidency 83

Perceptions of the president 83
The Founding Fathers and the presidency 84
Constitutional powers 85
Operating within constitutional constraints 89
Operating outside constitutional constraints 98
Too much or too little power? 101

7 The federal bureaucracy 104

The executive branch of government 104
The origins of the US bureaucracy 105
The growth of the federal administration 106
The structure of the federal administration 107
Methods and problems of co-ordinating the executive branch 114

8 Congress 121

Introduction 121
Congress and the constitution 122
Functions of Congress 123
Congressional performance 126

9 The Supreme Court 139

Introduction 139
The structure of the federal courts system 140
Judicial independence 141
The power of the Supreme Court 144
Limits to the Supreme Court's power 152

10 Pressure groups 154

Introduction 154
Types of interest group 155
Pressure-group power 159
The targets of pressure-group activity 160
Perspectives on pressure-group activity 167

Appendix 1 170
Appendix 2 174
Appendix 3 176

Sources 192

Index 193

Introduction

In the past, many politics textbooks have been written in an attempt to straddle two stools: the A level student and undergraduate. As a result the A level student has been required to wade through a mass of material, some of which is relevant to their course and some of which is not. In the classroom, teachers have been there to guide and help, but outside the classroom they have been required to distinguish between fundamental, useful and merely interesting material with very little help.

US Government and Politics has been written with only A level students in mind. It offers a thorough grounding in the processes, institutions and policy areas of the American political system whilst making comparisons with the equivalent institutions in the UK.

Comparisons with the UK political system are made to encourage students to keep thinking about the British system whilst studying its American counterpart. However, this is not a comparative politics text and the comparisons are only intended to spark further thought rather than to provide an in-depth analysis of rival political systems.

The book combines description, explanation and analysis – the three levels of understanding required of A level students. The basic workings of the institutions and processes are described to ensure that all students understand how, for example, a bill passes through Congress and how the presidential primaries work. However, relatively little space has been allocated to simple description. The quality of written work at A level depends on a student's ability to explain and to analyse the American political system. Therefore the greater part of the text is devoted to explanation of the political institutions and processes and analysis of their effectiveness.

The approach to American politics employed in this book is not historical. After all, this textbook is designed to introduce students to analysis of American politics rather than its historical development. However, whilst most of us have an approximate knowledge of British politics and society and so take some knowledge for granted, this is not the case with American history. Therefore, in an effort to quickly familiarize the student with the main points of American political, social and economic development, a very brief sketch of American history is included as the opening chapter. This is necessarily a cursory glance at around five centuries of history and only claims to identify a few highlights of the country's development.

The American political system differs from its British counterpart in that its entire development stems from one key event – the framing of the American constitution. In Philadelphia in 1787, the 'Founding Fathers' of American democracy laid down a blueprint for the construction of the political system, and so each chapter takes the ideals of those men as its starting point before analysing the state of the institutions and political players today.

Every effort has been made to bring this text as up to date as possible. However, any textbook becomes dated even before it reaches the printing presses. Therefore it is important that students use newspapers, radio and television to keep track of the most recent developments in American politics.

The aim has been to cover all of this material in a manner that will be easily accessible to students and will leave them with a clear understanding of the American political system. However, politics, like chemistry, physics and economics, has its own technical terminology. American politics in particular has its own vocabulary. Terms like log-rolling, pork-barrel, sound bites, spin doctors and iron triangles are not merely jargon designed to make the subject more complicated. The terminology forms the language of politics which students need to understand and to use in their written work. To emphasize the importance of the language and to help students become familiar with the terminology the key words have been listed at the beginning of each chapter and then highlighted in the text.

1 An historical introduction

The colonization of the 'new world'

Modern America is a nation of immigrants. The English, Spanish, French, Germans, Irish, Italians, Japanese and Africans have all added to the population of the 'new world' over the last three hundred years. However, the original inhabitants of the Americas were also immigrants, crossing from Asia over the Bering Straits approximately 15–20,000 years ago.

Early settlers

These early settlers developed advanced civilizations – the Mayas in Central America, the Aztecs in Mexico and the Incas in Peru. Some or all of these had developed societies with advanced language and number systems, impressive architectural structures and administrative systems that covered a wide area. In North America, although there were no 'great' civilizations, there was considerable diversity amongst the tribes, over 200 languages and most had developed farming and, or, fishing. When European explorers arrived in North America at the end of the fifteenth century the native population numbered around two million and roamed over most of the continent. So, America was a 'new world' strictly from a European perspective.

Spain

The first explorers to reach the 'new world' were from Spain. The Pope drew a line of demarcation between the overseas empires of Spain and Portugal in 1493, from the north to south poles to the West of the Cape Verde Islands (off the West African coast). Spain was granted the rights to the 'heathen lands' to the west of the line and therefore concentrated its efforts on the region, with such explorers as Christopher Columbus, an Italian, sponsored by King Ferdinand and Queen Isabella of Spain; Amerigo Vespucci (who gave his name to the continent); Vasco de Balboa (crossed Panama and reached the Pacific Ocean in 1513); Ponce de Leon (landed in Florida in 1513); and Ferdinand Magellan (circumnavigated the globe, 1519–22).

Spanish conquistadores soon began to colonize and plunder the new world for its precious metals. Hernando Cortes defeated the Aztec empire in Mexico (1520), Francisco Pizzaro conquered Peru (1531), Hernando de Soto colonized the Mississippi region (1539–42) and Francisco Vasquez de Coronado pushed Spanish territory beyond the Rio Grande (1540). However, the rule of the conquistadores was soon supplanted by direct rule from Spain and by 1575 the Spanish empire stretched from the southern regions of North America down to the southern-most tip of South America.

France

However Spanish settlers did not have it all their own way at this time. The French and the Dutch were soon on the scene. The French in particular established their presence in Quebec, along the St Lawrence and Mississippi rivers in the sixteenth century. As a result, French territory extended from New France (modern-day Canada) down through Louisiana to the Gulf of Mexico.

The English colonies

Explorers under the patronage of the English Crown had begun to explore the North American coast in the fifteenth century. However, it was not until the defeat of the Spanish fleet in 1588 that the English navy became predominant on the high seas. And the accession to the throne of James I in 1603 brought more support for overseas adventures – both as a means of weakening France and Spain, and of solving some of the domestic problems with which England had been beset since the fifteenth century.

The discontented

Many of the settlers who migrated from England to North America were discontented with their lot in England. Religious dissenters, whether Puritan or Roman Catholic, sought to be free of the diktat of Church of England bishops. Many peasant farmers had been dispossessed by the spread of the enclosures, as large landowners took over great tracts of arable and common land, upon which the peasants were reliant for their livelihood, turning it over to pasture. These peasants sought a new life in the lands of the 'new world'. Some settlers were leaving debts or a criminal record behind whilst others were seeking new outlets for their wealth. The availability of funds to be invested in the Americas allowed the monarch to make grants of land to individuals (proprietorships), which required no investment from the Crown, but created a source of raw materials and a market for English goods.

Virginia

The first English colony to be established was Virginia (1607). After an uncertain start it began to prosper under royal patronage. By 1660 there were 40,000 settlers in the colony, with the best lands divided amongst the wealthiest inhabitants, who also dominated the politics of the colony. 'Bacon's Rebellion' was an attempt to wrest control of the colony from the rich landowners, but it failed and proved to be the only serious challenge to royal authority until the American Revolution itself.

Puritans and Calvinists

The colonies of New England (Massachusetts, New Hampshire, Connecticut and Rhode Island) were initially settled by Puritans and Calvinists. The Puritans wished to reform the Church of England, leading it away from any practices not mentioned in the bible and the influence of the Roman Catholics. Calvinists followed the teachings of Swiss theologian John Calvin, believing in an omnipotent God, hard work and piety.

Quakers

William Penn founded Pennsylvania in 1681 in order to create a 'holy experiment'. He aimed to create a community governed by the principles of the Society of Friends, or 'The Quakers' – pacifism, plainness in manners and dress and democracy in their worship. In order to reap a return on his investment Penn encouraged settlers to come from all over Europe, creating a multi-cultural community of English, Germans and Scandinavians, amongst others.

New York was originally the Dutch colony of New Netherland. It was captured by the English in 1664 and given to the Duke of York by his brother Charles II. The Dutch momentarily regained control in 1674 but were ultimately pacified by the promise of religious and cultural toleration.

In the south the colony of the Carolinas was created in 1660. The northern half was populated by farmers of smallholdings; those in the southern half concentrated on producing goods for export. Ultimately, holding these halves together proved impossible and they were divided in 1729. The final English colony to be created was Georgia, in 1732, and this was primarily for military reasons. The English feared attack from the Spanish colony of Florida, and populated Georgia with only the most reliable settlers. Roman Catholicism and slavery were banned, the size of holdings was restricted and the import of rum was prohibited. However, these rules were rapidly relaxed as it became difficult to recruit settlers.

Carolinas

Georgia's problems were familiar to most of the other colonies. Even after they had been established, the colonies faced problems of declining populations and falling migration rates. Consequently, many of the rules initially adopted were abandoned in the search for new recruits.

Problems

The economies of the colonies developed according to the assets of each region. New England suffered from harsh winters and poor land and so concentrated on fishing, small-scale manufacturing and overseas trade. New York, Pennsylvania and Delaware benefited from better soil and so agriculture prospered and they became major suppliers of wheat to the rest of the colonies. The economy of the southern colonies came to be dominated by large-scale agriculture – the plantations; Maryland, Virginia and North Carolina all produced tobacco. By the middle of the eighteenth century Maryland and Virginia were producing 50 million pounds of tobacco per year. South Carolina exported 500,000 pounds of rice per annum.

The economies

The need for a large labour force on the plantations lay at the root of forced immigration into the colonies – slaves. Although the majority of workers were drawn from the poor white communities, in 1700 there were 25,000 slaves throughout the whole of the colonies, with perhaps half in Virginia, and by 1760 there were 300,000.

Slaves

Aside from slaves from Africa, settlers also came into the English colonies from Germany, Scotland and Ireland. German groups tended to settle in Pennsylvania, although they were also found in the southern colonies. Similar patterns of migration were followed by the Irish-Scots, who had initially colonized Northern Ireland but left due to religious persecution.

Other settlers

The battle for supremacy in North America

From the end of the seventeenth century for almost a century, the attitudes of France and Britain to their American lands were largely determined by the intensity of their struggles for predominance elsewhere. France possessed great areas of North America, known as New France, from Montreal down to the Mississippi. However, the population of these areas was little more than 75,000, located mainly around isolated trading posts. As a result they were forced to ally themselves with local Indian tribes in order to defend their territories.

French lands

The English colonists coveted control of the fur trade and the Ohio–Mississippi basin and feared losing control of the Atlantic fishing ports. As a result of this competition the eighteenth century was punctuated by periods of war and uneasy peace. However,

English expansion

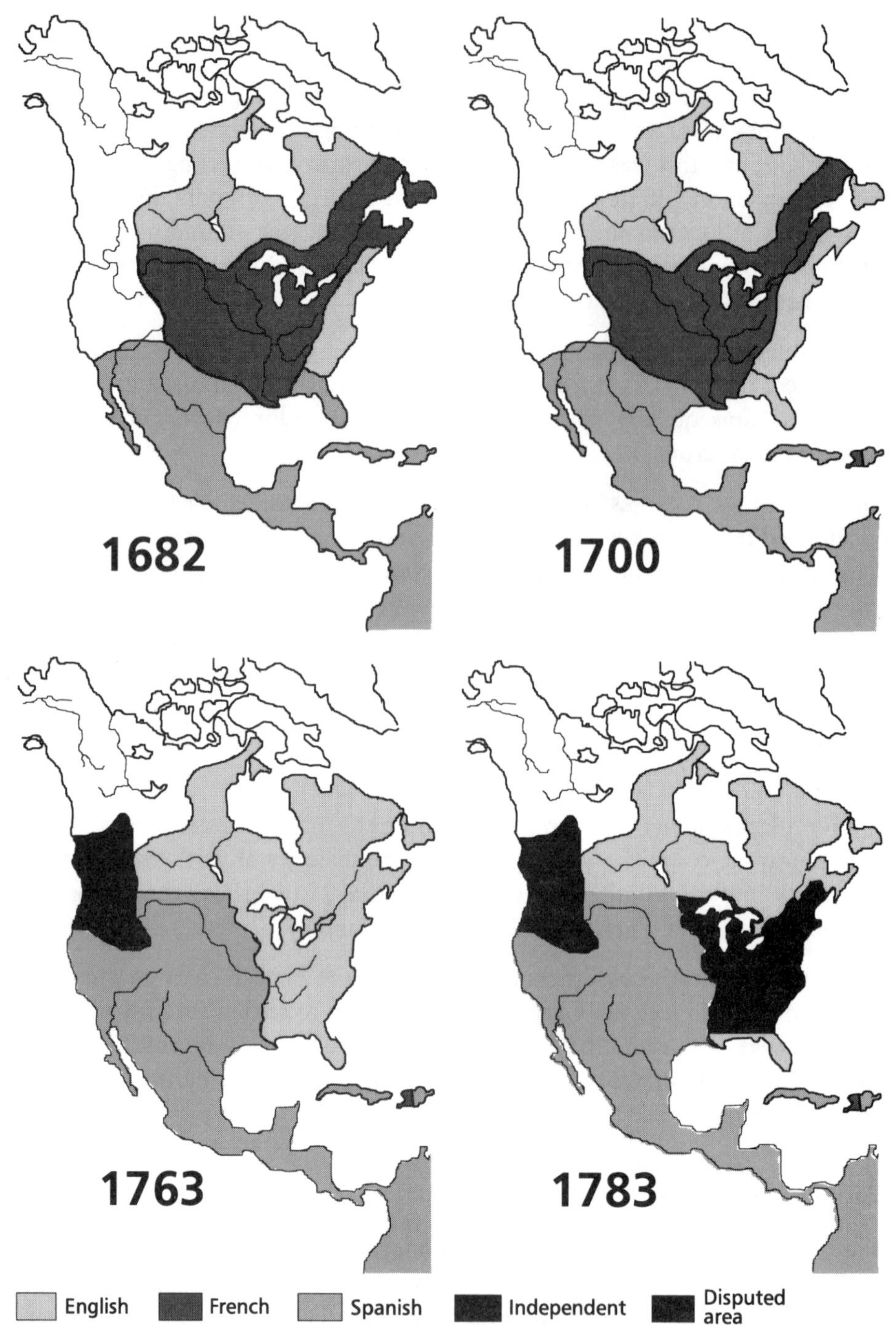

Figure 1.1 The Ownership of North America, 1862–1783

the British forces prevailed, taking the capital of New France, Quebec, in 1758. The Paris Peace Treaty (1763) saw Britain gain all French lands to the east of the Mississippi (except New Orleans), Canada and Florida, which was taken as compensation from Spain in exchange for Cuba and the Philippines. Spain gained all

French lands to the west of the Mississippi and New Orleans. French influence in North America was therefore reduced to its holdings in the West Indies.

The English colonies and imperial administration

The victory over France had been achieved at great cost to the British government and many in the British government believed that the colonists had not contributed sufficiently to the cost of the war. They therefore moved towards imposing greater restrictions on them.

Mercantilism

A regime of control and restriction was nothing new to the English colonists. Whether under rule by the monarch, James I, Charles I and, following the restoration of the monarchy, Charles II or under Parliament the American colonies were always governed directly from England. The colonies were viewed as a valuable source of raw materials and as a market for finished products and as such they could help England build considerable trade surpluses with which it could then purchase precious metals. According to the economic theory of *mercantilism* the level of precious metals accumulated determined a country's wealth.

Revenue from the colonies

With this in mind Parliament passed a series of acts designed to maximize revenue from the American colonies. These included the Navigation Acts (1651 and 1660), the Enumerated Commodities Act (1660), the Staple Act (1663), the Duty Act (1673) and the Enforcement Act (1696). The Navigation Acts required all goods entering English ports to be carried on ships owned and largely manned by British subjects. The Enforcement Act introduced tough measures to enforce the Navigation Act. All English and colonial ships were to be registered and customs officials were given the power to search ships and warehouses.

However, in Britain there were demands for these laws to be tightened to prevent the colonists avoiding the Navigation Acts and to increase revenues from the colonies so that the burden of the national debt on the British taxpayer could be reduced.

New legislation included the Sugar Act (1764), the Currency Act (1764), the Stamp Act (1765) and the Quartering, or Mutiny, Act (1765). The Sugar Act reduced the tax on molasses that had been introduced in 1733 but increased the duty on sugar and a range of new taxes on imported goods. The Currency Act forbade the printing of further paper money in the colonies. This prevented colonists taking advantage of the inflation to repay their debts at a depreciated rate. The Stamp Act required all legal documents in the colonies be taxed and furthermore that they be given an official stamp to prove the taxes had been paid. Finally the Quartering Act sought to reduce the cost of lodgings for British troops by forcing colonists to offer soldiers a billet if existing barracks proved inadequate.

Colonial protest

This new legislation led to protests in the colonies. The more radical opponents of the measures, calling themselves the Sons of Liberty, organized demonstrations and terrorized tax collectors. More widely, the legislation served to unite the disparate colonies in opposition against British rule.

Whilst the British government was aware of the unrest in America its decision to repeal the Stamp Act and to reduce many of the duties was the result of falling trade between the colonies and Britain. However, the relaxation of control was short-lived. Under Prime Minister William Pitt, the Chancellor of the Exchequer, Charles Townshend, attempted to reassert Britain's control over the colonies' trade. Duties were introduced on glass, lead, tea and paper in 1767; in the same year the New York legislature was suspended for failing to comply with the Quartering Act and a similar fate befell the assemblies of Massachusetts and Virginia for writing a letter calling for resistance to parliamentary taxation.

Boston Tea Party

Colonial resistance was rekindled by the new legislation and by a series of incidents between British troops and colonists, including The Boston Massacre (1770) and the attack on the British ship *Gaspee* (1772). The cargoes of three ships were dumped into Boston harbour in response to the Tea Act which had given the East India Company a monopoly on the sale of tea in the colonies. This became known as the Boston Tea Party (1773).

Continental Congress

The British Parliament then passed a series of Coercive Acts, known as the Intolerable Acts in America, in an attempt to restore control over the colonies. These provoked a new round of united resistance to British rule. Representatives from all but one of the colonies (Georgia) met in Philadelphia in 1774 for the Continental Congress. Here they agreed to form the Continental Association which would boycott trade with Britain.

The American Revolution

To the American colonists the actions of the British government appeared oppressive and designed to remove their liberties. All British legislation was imposed without reference to colonial governments and in some cases colonial government had been suspended completely. For example, all officials of Massachusetts were to be

The Declaration of Independence

'...We hold these truths to be self-evident, that all men are created equal, that they are endowed by their Creator with certain unalienable rights, that among these are life, liberty and the pursuit of happiness. That to secure these rights, governments are instituted among men, deriving their just powers from the consent of the governed. That whenever any form of government becomes destructive of these ends, it is the right of the people to alter or to abolish it, and to institute a new government, laying its foundation on such principles and organizing its powers in such form, as to them shall seem most likely to effect their safety and happiness ...'

The Declaration was drawn up in 1776 by a committee of five, although Thomas Jefferson is credited with drafting almost all of it.

It begins with a justification for breaking from the rule of a tyrannical king. This is largely based on the ideas of *John Locke*. It then goes on to catalogue the king's abuses and the colonists failure to gain redress.

(For full text see Appendix 1)

appointees of the Crown and public meetings without permission of the Governor were banned. However, the majority of colonists hoped for a softening of the British position rather than independence.

'Olive Branch'

With this in mind the Second Continental Congress (1775) sent an 'Olive Branch' message to King George III in an attempt to fend off war. But by this time British troops and the Massachusetts Minutemen had clashed at Lexington and Concord, where the British suffered 1000 casualties. The Congress therefore laid its own plans to raise an army, appointed George Washington as commander-in-chief and attempted to build an alliance with France.

To an extent the British Prime Minister, Lord North, attempted to take a conciliatory position by offering to stop Parliament taxing the colonists, except in cases where tax was designed to regulate trade, if colonial assemblies would raise their own taxes to support the Crown in their colony. But this was rejected by the Congress. Shortly afterwards it became known that the king had not accepted the 'Olive Branch' petition and considered the colonies to be in rebellion. In 1775 Parliament passed the Prohibitory Act, which closed all American ports.

Declaration of Independence

Reluctantly the American colonies declared independence from Britain in 1776 in a document composed largely by Thomas Jefferson. The Declaration fulfilled different purposes: it was a statement of the reasons for separating the colonies from Britain and served as a political pamphlet to win over any colonists who might be undecided.

War

The war which followed was marked by the inept leadership of the British forces and the skill of George Washington. Washington's deployment of the small American army prevented its destruction by the British and, once in alliance with France, took it to

Key Battles of the Revolution

Trenton (1776)	Washington surprises British forces and takes 1000 prisoners.
Princeton (1777)	Early in the new year British forces were defeated again, illustrating that they were not invincible.
Saratoga (1777)	British General Burgoyne defeated and surrenders 5000 prisoners. It prompted France to forge an alliance with colonists in 1778.
Savannah (1778) Charleston (1780) Camden (1780)	The British shifted their attentions to the south where they expected to find greater support. A string of victories was followed by Lord Cornwallis's retreat to the north for supplies and reinforcements.
Yorktown (1781)	Cornwallis was defeated by combined American and French forces. No more offensives were launched after this defeat.

victory at Yorktown. The Peace of Paris, signed in 1783, brought an end to the revolutionary war.

The foundations of federalism

New constitution

After a period as a loose confederation of states a new constitution was framed in 1787. This created a new system of government which was based on the separation of powers both between the federal government and the state governments as well as between the institutions of the federal government.

The compromises that were made between the various factions at the constitutional convention in order to achieve the ratification of the final document have by no means brought an end to disagreements over the role of the central government and the power of its institutions. Indeed, much of the development of the United States over the next two hundred years has concerned the relative power of its branches of government.

The first presidential administration, under George Washington, faced a number of problems including the national debt, estimated to be $54 million, not including a further $25 million estimated to lie with the individual states; the need to establish US dominance over its boundaries; and the need to establish the boundaries of the federal government's own authority.

Finance

Alexander Hamilton, Washington's treasury secretary, sought to deal with the national debt by honouring all debts in full. As part of his strategy he proposed a system of taxation; that the federal government should take responsibility for some of the debts

Alexander Hamilton (1755–1804)

Alexander Hamilton was born in the British Windward Islands but grew up on St Croix in the Danish Virgin Islands. He grew up in difficult circumstances, providing for himself from the age of twelve and relying on friends to fund his attendance at King's College (now Columbia University). During the War of Independence he served as George Washington's secretary and aide before becoming a Wall Street lawyer.

A firm advocate of strong federal government, he was a prime sponsor of the Annapolis Convention, which called for the constitutional convention in Philadelphia. He was a delegate to the Philadelphia Convention from New York, a signatory to the Constitution and a co-author of *The Federalist Papers*.

He believed that to survive, the United States would need to establish its credentials with the wealthy capitalists and so he attempted to put the country on a sound financial footing. He also refuted the idea of a pure democracy, believing it would lead to 'mob rule'. Instead he favoured a 'balanced' government on the British model, consisting of Commons, Lords and monarchy.

Hamilton was killed in a duel with a political opponent, Aaron Burr – who was also the vice-president of the United States.

Jefferson and Madison

Thomas Jefferson (1743–1826) was the author of the Declaration of Independence, the first secretary of state, the second vice-president and the third president of the United States.

Many historians regard him as a philosopher politician, a strong advocate of the separation of powers and limited government. In 1962 John F Kennedy, when dining with that year's Nobel Prize winners, said: 'I think this is the most extraordinary collection of talent, of human knowledge, that has ever been gathered together at the White House – with the possible exception of when Thomas Jefferson dined here alone.'

Nevertheless Jefferson was an extremely astute politician. He is considered to be the founder of the American party system with both of today's parties tracing their roots to him; he used the powers of the office of presidency to the full to make partisan appointments and wined and dined congressional leaders in an effort to secure the passage of his legislation.

James Madison (1751–1836) was the chief architect of the constitution and the country's fourth president. He was instrumental in calling for the constitutional convention, creating a national government and achieving the ratification of the finished product as a co-author of *The Federalist Papers*.

Initially a Federalist he gradually moved away from the party of Jefferson and Madison to lead the Democratic-Republicans with Jefferson. He spent the early years of the republic as a major congressional leader. As president he was less successful and during the 1812 war with Britain the White House and the Capitol were burned down.

of the states; that a national bank should be created; and that American industry should be fostered by high protective tariffs. Although his proposals would help reduce the national debt, they would also serve to strengthen the position of the federal government over individual states, and so all were the subject of heated controversy in Congress. James Madison led the opposition in Congress, often with the support of Secretary of State Thomas Jefferson.

Growth of federal power

Deep divisions over Hamilton's economic strategy and its implications for the balance of power between the federal and state governments laid the foundations of an emerging party system in the United States. Those who favoured a strong federal government coalesced around Washington and Hamilton, calling themselves the Federalists. Those favouring a weaker federal government rallied around Thomas Jefferson, who had resigned from Washington's second Cabinet, and James Madison – they were known as the Republicans or the Democratic-Republicans.

The first peaceful, democratic transfer of power in the new republic was achieved in 1800 when, led by Jefferson, the Democratic-Republicans took over the presidency.

Judicial review

It was during the presidency of Jefferson that the third branch of the federal government – the Supreme Court – entered the political fray over the power of the federal government. In a famous case, *Marbury* v. *Madison* (1803), Chief Justice John Marshall established the right of the Supreme Court to review the actions of other branches of government. This was a fundamental extension of the power of the Supreme Court and by implication of the federal government – a development to which Jefferson was opposed. It is perhaps worth noting that Jefferson, like many presidents, including Abraham Lincoln, did not believe he was obliged to enforce all of the decisions of the Court, and that the executive's responsibility to enforce decisions allowed him discretion.

The presidencies of Jefferson and his successor, Madison, can be considered successful in that they continued during the crucial period of political party development, when a breakdown could have occurred in the political system. Jefferson and Madison avoided the conflicts that had characterized the Washington/Hamilton administrations and created bi-partisan support on a range of issues. However, they were not able to avoid a renewed war with Britain. They had hoped to avoid it through diplomacy but, in the face of growing insults from the European powers, the United States was eventually pressured into war in 1812.

The 'era of good feelings'

The Treaty of Ghent (1814) brought an end to the war with Britain and led to a period of revitalization in the United States. The American economy developed and party battles were subdued under President James Monroe.

A national economy

The war with Britain had shown up the inadequacies of the inland transport system in the United States and so public and private funds were allocated for its improvement. As the infrastructure developed, so the economy began to move from a group of largely self-sufficient states to a system of inter-related economies, each becoming increasingly dependent on the others. In other words a national economy was developing and with it came renewed attempts to create a Hamiltonian system of national finance. A second Bank of the United States was created in 1816, which was instrumental in provoking a major economic crisis in 1819.

In an effort to prevent rapid increases in prices the Bank of the USA attempted to reduce the amount of printed currency in circulation. In doing so it caused a massive deflation of prices, particularly in the south, which led to bankruptcies and job losses. This in turn led to renewed party divisions over the economy and the power of the central government (seen by many as having provoked the crisis).

James Monroe had been re-elected in 1820 with only one dissenting vote in the electoral college. However, the presidential election of 1824 caused much bad feeling and the beginning of a new party system.

1824 election

Three candidates stood for the presidency in 1824: Andrew Jackson (Tennessee), Henry Clay (Kentucky) and John Quincy Adams (Massachusetts). Jackson, the hero of the 1812 war with Britain, won a majority of the popular vote but failed to win over 50 per cent of the electoral college. This left the House of Representatives to choose the new president. Henry Clay threw his support behind Adams and was named secretary of state (considered at the time to indicate succession). Jackson believed he had been robbed of the presidency by a political bargain and almost immediately began to mobilize support for the next election. A coalition of support formed around Jackson and became known as the Democratic Party. The 'era of good feelings' was over.

Jacksonian democracy

Jackson eventually came to the presidency in 1828 at the head of the Democratic Party facing a Republican opposition in disarray. The Democratic Party believed in a return to the principles of Jefferson and Madison, so on his election to the presidency Jackson set about dismantling the strong federal government that had been established by the Monroe and Adams administrations.

Economic opportunities

Jackson believed in greater democracy, more economic opportunities for the 'common man' and less federal regulation of the economy. In 1832 the Bank of the United States became a focus of Jackson's hostility in what became known as the 'Bank War'. The bank needed to renew its charter in 1836 but its president, Nicholas Bibble, pushed for a renewal prior to the election of 1832. Jackson took the opportunity to use the charter as an election issue. He vetoed the bill passed by Congress and created the impression that the bank was a threat to the very independence and liberty of Americans. Jackson's re-election in the same year saw an attempt to destroy the bank by withdrawing all federal government deposits. This was eventually carried out by the secretary of the treasury, Roger Brook Taney. The bank responded by reducing lending and increasing interest rates and an economic recession followed in 1833.

Doctrine of Nullification

Jackson's desire to decentralize also led to an unexpected crisis in South Carolina. The economy of South Carolina was heavily dependent on cotton which, by the 1830s, was in abundant supply. As a result the economy of the state began to deteriorate and with it the standard of living – a fact which many plantation owners blamed on the protectionist tariff of 1816 which increased the cost of imported goods. Despite his image of being a supporter of greater rights and freedoms for individual states Jackson upheld the idea of a protectionist tariff, albeit at a lower rate. In 1832 South Carolina's state legislature called a convention in an attempt to declare the federal tariff null and void. The idea that states had the right to overrule acts of the federal government became known as the Doctrine of Nullification. Jackson responded by denouncing their actions and in 1833 called on Congress to authorize the use of military force to ensure compliance with federal law. This crisis over South Carolina only signalled the problems that would resurface in coming years.

Whigs

Jackson's policies galvanized the opposition into the creation of a new political party, the Whigs. They believed in slow, careful growth of a national economy, a strong national financial system and social reform. The Whigs remained a relatively weak force in national politics until the election of 1840, which was won by their candidate, William Henry Harrison. The Whigs had found it relatively easy to defeat Jackson's hand-picked successor of 1836, Martin Van Bueren, who had presided over a financial crash and economic recession. However, Harrison died only five weeks into his term of office and was succeeded, for the first time in United States history, by his vice-president, John Tyler.

States' rights

Tyler, a southerner who believed in states' rights, was brought onto the presidential ticket for political reasons and was not a great supporter of Whig legislative proposals – he vetoed many of the proposals put before him by the Whig Congress. His policies were pro-southern rather than Whig or Democrat, which cut across established party lines and contributed to the north–south divide that culminated in the civil war.

American expansion and seeds of civil war

Louisiana Purchase

Early in the life of the republic, boundaries were expanded as the population grew. During Washington's presidency Vermont (1791), Kentucky (1792) and Tennessee (1796) were all admitted to statehood. At the beginning of the nineteenth century President Jefferson's emissaries negotiated the Louisiana Purchase from France. The territory of Louisiana was huge, stretching from the Missouri river in the north and the Rocky Mountains in the west to the Mississippi river in the East and the territory of Orleans in the south. The territory cost $15 million and was ceded to the United States in 1803.

Population growth

In the early years of the nineteenth century the United States experienced rapid population growth – from 5.3 million to 9.6 million. This led to demands for the borders of the United States to be pushed further west. The migration to the west was fuelled by its abundance of fertile land. By 1820 almost 25 per cent of the population

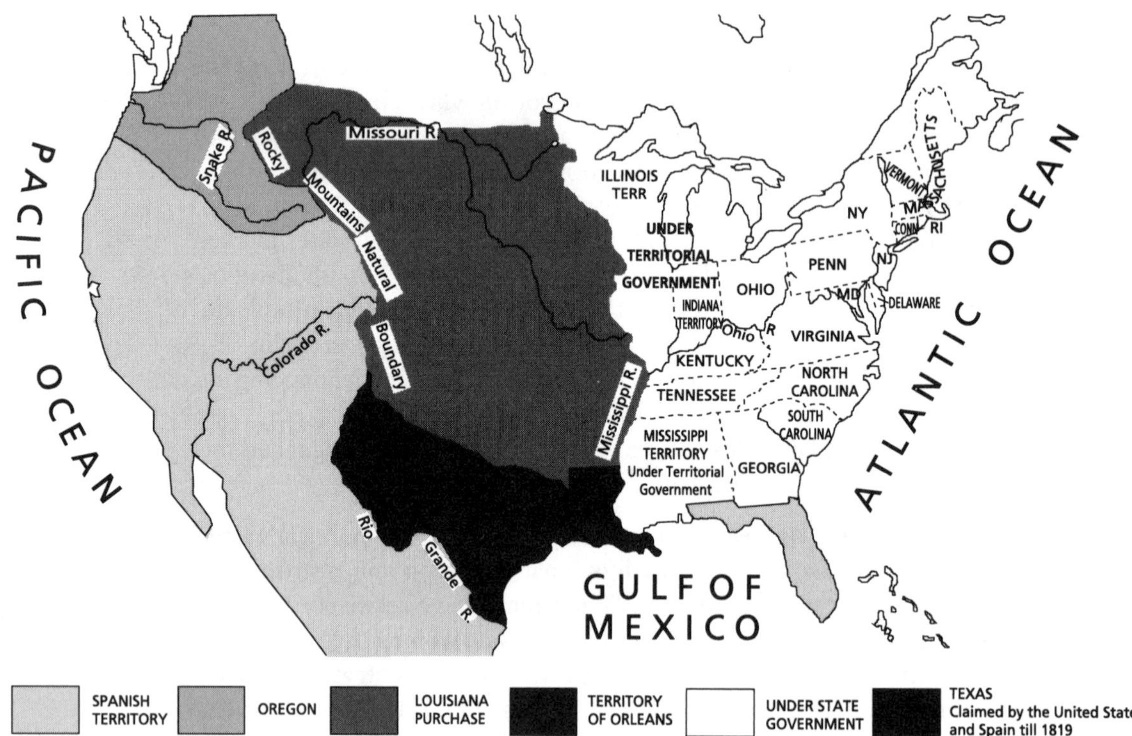

Figure 1.2 The United States after the Louisiana purchase

lived to the west of the Appalachian Mountains and six new western states joined the Union. They were Louisiana, Indiana, Mississippi, Illinois, Alabama and Missouri.

In 1845 a journalist, John L O'Sullivan, wrote that it was America's 'manifest destiny to overspread the continent allotted by Providence for the free development of our yearly multiplying millions.' This summed up the feeling of many in the United States. In Texas Americans migrated into the Mexican province in large numbers, causing disquiet in the Mexican government that eventually ended in war between the United States and Mexico and the admission of Texas to the Union in 1845.

Pacific states

The war with Mexico also resulted in the capture of California and New Mexico, which took United States territory across to the Pacific seaboard. They were finally secured by treaty in 1848. In the north-west, meanwhile, the settlement of the Anglo-American differences over Oregon brought the region into the Union in 1846.

Immigration

The rapid population growth at the beginning of the century was quickly outstripped in subsequent decades. The population grew to 12.86 million in 1830, 23.2 million in 1850 and 31 million in 1860. These dramatic increases were caused, at least in part, by an influx of immigrants who accounted for 12 per cent of the population by 1850. They came from poor working conditions in Great Britain, famine in Ireland and economic depression and political turmoil elsewhere in Europe.

Slavery

In the southern states, slavery dominated the economy. The large-scale production of tobacco, rice, sugar and cotton relied on the use of forced labour. However, in the 1830s elements of public opinion in the tobacco-producing states of the south began to question the institution of slavery. But the cotton-producing states remained committed to it and to the extension of slavery into the new states in the south-west. In Mississippi the slave population grew from 32,000 in 1820 to 436,000 in 1860. In view of the importance of slavery to the southern economy and in opposition to the growing pressure for the abolition of slavery from the north, most southern politicians were forced to defend the south and in doing so defended slavery.

Free states

The need for southerners to defend slavery combined with the rapid westward expansion of the United States led to an obvious area of conflict: should the new states be slave states or free states? In fact the issue was by no means new but it had been kept at bay by the recognition that, to keep the Union together, there needed to be a balance between its free and slave states.

Missouri Compromise

When Missouri had applied for statehood in 1812 a compromise had been reached by which slavery would not be allowed above a latitude of 36° 30″ throughout the territory of the Louisiana Purchase. The acquisition of the new territories led to renewed debate about the extension of slavery because the Missouri Compromise did not stretch to the Pacific. In 1850 another compromise was cobbled together to cope with the expansion westwards. California was admitted to the Union as a free state, the slave trade was banned in Washington DC, a stricter law regarding fugitive slaves was to be passed by Congress and Utah and New Mexico would be free to decide for themselves, according to the principle of popular sovereignty, if they were to be admitted to the Union as free or slave states.

Popular sovereignty

However, as expansion continued – fuelled by economic interests – the issue raised its head again over the admission of Kansas and Nebraska, both being outside the range of the Missouri Compromise. Senator Stephen A Douglas of Illinois introduced the Kansas-Nebraska Act in 1854, which abolished the Missouri Compromise and enshrined the principle of popular sovereignty as national policy. This meant all new states would be allowed to decide for themselves whether or not they would be free, which depended on whether or not they were settled by abolitionists or those in favour of slavery. The rush to settle Kansas turned the state into a battle-ground referred to as 'bloody Kansas'.

The Republican Party

The Kansas-Nebraska Act proved extremely divisive. It was supported by southern Whigs and Democrats and opposed by members from the north. The northern coalition of opposition to the expansion of slavery formed the basis for the new Republican Party. The issue of the expansion of slavery then became a fight between the Republicans in the north and the Democratic Party, dominated by southerners.

The presidential election of 1856 illustrated the extent to which north–south battle lines were being drawn. James Buchanan, the Democratic Party's candidate won with only a slight majority. In fact, had the Republican candidate, General John C Frémont, won Pennsylvania and Illinois, where the Democrat margin of victory was small, he would have taken the presidency without winning a single southern state.

The Taney Court

In 1857 the Supreme Court entered the dispute over the extension of slavery by ruling on the case brought by a slave. The case, *Dred Scott* v. *Sandford*, further divided the Congress and the country. It was welcomed in the south but denounced in the north as evidence of a slave-owning conspiracy that controlled government (five of the nine Supreme Court justices were from slave states).

The Dredd Scott Case (1857)

Dred Scott, a slave living in Missouri with his master, had been taken by his master to Wisconsin – a northern part of the Louisiana Purchase that was free from slavery due to the Missouri Compromise. Whilst in the free state Scott sued for his freedom.

The Court ruled that a slave or a descendant of a slave had no right to bring a case before the Supreme Court. Furthermore it ruled that the federal government had no right to remove a man's property – the property being the slave – whether the master and slave were resident in a slave state or not. Chief Justice Taney went on to proclaim that the Missouri Compromise had been unconstitutional all along.

Lincoln

By the time of the 1860 presidential election the country was sufficiently divided to see two separate contests for the presidency. In the north Abraham Lincoln fought Douglas; in the south John C Brekinridge from Kentucky fought John C Bell from Tennessee. Although Lincoln only won 40 per cent of the votes he won a majority in the electoral college, without winning a single southern state, and became president. His party, the Republicans, also took control of the House of Representatives.

Abraham Lincoln (1809–1865)

Abraham Lincoln was born in Kentucky. A lawyer by training he served several terms in the state legislature of Illinois before being nominated as the Republican candidate for the Senate in 1858. In accepting the nomination Lincoln put forward his view on the slavery issue: 'A house divided against itself cannot stand. I believe this government cannot endure permanently half slave and half free. I do not expect the union to be dissolved; I do not expect the house to fall; but I do expect it will cease to be divided. It will become all one thing, or all the other.'

During the campaign he took on the Democratic incumbent, Stephen A Douglas, in a series of debates, which received national publicity. Although he lost the election in 1858 the campaign began the momentum towards his nomination as the Republican candidate in 1860.

Lincoln opposed the extension of slavery but, for his time, his views were considered moderate. In his inaugural address he told the states that had seceded: 'In your hands, my dissatisfied fellow countrymen, and not in mine is the momentous issue of civil war. The government will not assail you. You have no conflict without being yourselves the aggressors. You have no oath registered in heaven to destroy the government, while you have the most solemn one to "preserve, protect and defend" it.'

Nevertheless civil war did break out and Lincoln led the Federal or Unionist forces to victory, emancipating the slaves along the way. His address at Gettysburg in November 1863, although only 272 words, has become one of the most famous speeches in political history.

Five days after the surrender of the Confederate forces at Appomattox on 9 April 1865, Lincoln was assassinated by John Wilkes Booth.

In 1959, on the 150th anniversary of Lincoln's birth, the American poet and Lincoln biographer, Carl Sandburg, began a speech to both houses of Congress with these words: 'Not often in the story of mankind does a man arrive on earth who is both steel and velvet, who is as hard as rock and soft as drifting fog, who holds in his heart and mind the paradox of terrible storm and peace unspeakable and perfect.'

Southern withdrawal from the Union

Secession

The Republican victories led, almost immediately, to South Carolina's decision to secede from the Union. Soon after, six other states (Mississippi, Florida, Alabama, Georgia, Louisiana and Texas) followed suit. The cause of their withdrawal was not only the issue of expansion of slavery but also the more fundamental issue of states' rights. The southern states feared that a Republican president and House of Representatives could destroy their way of life by forcing them to abolish slavery and to accept economic measures such as a high protective tariff, which the south had always opposed.

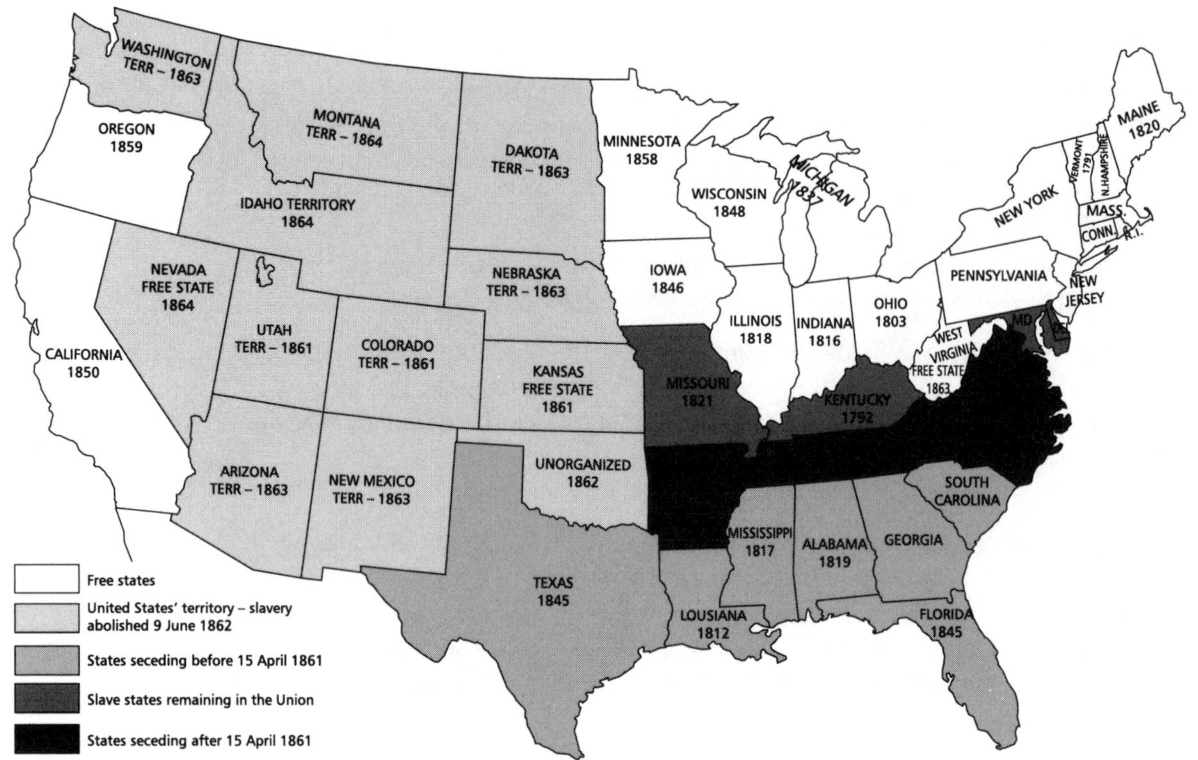

Figure 1.3 The United States in the Civil War

In February 1861 the seven secessionist states formed the Confederacy and chose Jefferson Davis as their president. They seized federal government property and only Fort Sumter and Fort Pickens remained in the hands of the federal government.

On assuming office President Lincoln declared the secession to be illegal and he moved to re-supply Fort Sumter. However, he could not prevent its fall to the Confederacy on 15 April 1861. Lincoln called on the free states to raise troops to defend the Union. This rallied the northern states to his side but Arkansas, Tennessee, North Carolina and Virginia seceded. The Civil War had begun.

Reconstruction

States' rights and slavery

The Civil War ended in 1865 having, in the bloodiest way possible, clarified two issues unclear from the Constitution: the position of individual states within the union and the morality of 'human property'. The war established that individual states did not have the right to secede from the Union and that the idea of slavery should be removed from the American system forever.

White backlash

However, the end of the war did not bring an end to controversy about the position of former slaves in American society or the position of ex-Confederate states within the Union. The period of reconstruction saw the federal government attempting to recreate southern society along more equitable lines, with confiscated land being given to former slaves, and former male slaves being registered as voters and participating in

The Course of the Civil War

The main army of the Unionist forces, the Army of the Potomac, was commanded by a string of generals as Lincoln sought to defeat the main army of the Confederacy, the Army of Northern Virginia, led by General Robert E Lee.

1st Battle of Bull Run (July 1861)	Unionist forces attempting to seize Richmond are defeated.
Shiloh (April 1862)	General Ulysses S Grant advanced into the South and withstood the Confederate onslaught at Shiloh, Tennessee.
Antietam (September 1862)	Lee forced to retreat after bloodiest single-day battle of the war (4500 killed).
Vicksburg (July 1863)	Grant proceeded from Shiloh to lay siege to the port of Vicksburg for six weeks until Confederate forces surrendered.
Gettysburg (July 1863)	General George G Meade commanding the Army of the Potomac forced Lee to retreat from Pennsylvania. It was a major turning point in the war.
Atlanta (September 1864)	Unionist General Sherman led his army across Georgia taking the important communications centre, Atlanta.
Wilderness Campaign (1864)	Grant moved relentlessly towards the Confederate capital, Richmond. It fell in April 1865.

General Lee surrendered the Army of Northern Virginia to Grant at Appomattox Court House on 9 April 1865. A few weeks later the surrender of General Joseph E Johnston to General William Tecumsah Sherman in North Carolina brought the war to an end.

new elections to the legislatures. However, many white southerners turned to organized terrorism to retain control of their political systems and to intimidate the black population into retreat. Most famous of these groups was the Klu Klux Klan.

In the rest of the country public opinion was turning against the idea of reconstruction. They were experiencing a period of unmatched prosperity and wanted to put conflict in the south aside. By 1876 southern Democrats had regained control of all but three states (Florida, South Carolina and Louisiana) and the period of the Republican vision of reconstruction was over. For former slaves this meant that their hopes of a new future were dashed and in many parts of the country they remained second-class citizens.

A new century

The beginning of the twentieth century saw fundamental changes in American society and in the American economy. Industrialization, population growth and urban development brought new problems to the government.

Industrialization

The end of the nineteenth century saw a period of rapid industrialization in the United States and for the first time agriculture began to take second place. From 1880–90 the value of manufacturing output in the US rose from $3,748 million to $5,406 million (44 per cent), whilst the agricultural output rose by only 20 per cent. Over the same period the urban population grew by 71 per cent whilst the farm population grew by only 13 per cent. It was at the turn of the century that the main urban centres, so familiar today, took off. The population of New York grew from 1.9 million in 1880 to 4.7 million in 1910; over the same period Los Angeles grew from 11,000 to 319,000.

Mechanization

This industrialization was fuelled by the mechanization of many industries including agriculture and textile production. Innovations of the time included the steam engine, the electric motor and the internal combustion engine. The mechanization reduced costs and improved productive capacity as well as allowing the large-scale movement of goods as transport improved. Indeed, machinery production and transport became industries in themselves.

All of this was made possible by the availability of capital for investment. Investment funds became available as banks grew up to handle the money deposited by the increasingly wealthy population.

Immigration

A renewed period of immigration began at the end of the nineteenth century and the beginning of the twentieth century. Unlike previous waves of immigrants who had come from northern Europe, the new arrivals came from eastern and southern Europe. Between 1901 and 1920, 3 million immigrants came from Italy, 2.5 million from Russia and almost 4 million from elsewhere in eastern and southern Europe.

These immigrants were ideal workers, filling industries' need for more labour; they were used to a much lower standard of living in their countries of origin and so were prepared to work for low wages.

Organized labour

The period of industrialization brought prosperity to many segments of the population but for many others it brought appalling working conditions and poverty. Trade unions began to be active in this era and the labour leader Eugene Debs ran for the presidency four times on behalf of the Socialist Party. Unions encountered a great deal of resistance from business-men who organized private guards and the police to suppress strikes. Also the union movement was divided between those, such as Samuel Gompers, who preferred to confine union demands to economic issues such as wages and conditions, and others, such as Debs, who sought more fundamental changes in capitalism. By the beginning of the twentieth century the Gompers perspective had won out.

Progressive reform

Whilst the workers were fighting for better conditions the middle classes also sought reforms in American society. Social, governmental and economic reforms were all on the agenda as Americans sought to impose order on their domestic world, just as they had imposed order on the rest of continent through expansionism in the nineteenth century, and on other parts of the world (Hawaii, the Philippines, Cuba and Panama) at the beginning of the twentieth century.

Results of this reform movement included the introduction of regulatory commissions, the extension of the franchise to women, the beginning of a movement for greater civil rights for the black population, and prohibition.

Economic reform

Economic reform was designed to counter the detrimental effects of the growth of business. Regulatory commissions were set up and powers of existing commissions were enhanced during the presidencies of Theodore Roosevelt and William Taft. Most important was the Interstate Commerce Commission, which was given extra powers to ensure free trade between the states and to prevent the monopolistic practices pursued by large corporations. New commissions included the Industrial Relations Commission.

Voting rights

In Wyoming, women had been given the franchise since 1869 but by 1900 only three states had followed their example. By 1919 twenty-nine states had given women the right to vote but it was not until the 19th Amendment to the constitution (1920) that women across the United States had the complete right to vote.

Civil rights

Although the progressive movement largely emanated from the white middle classes, members of the black population, such as Booker T Washington and W E B Dubois, also began to become more active in the movement for reform. In 1909 the National Association for the Advancement of Colored People was formed to fight for greater civil rights.

Prohibition

The reform movement was concerned not only about rights and liberties but also the moral fibre of the United States' population. Perhaps the greatest victory for the reformers was the ratification of the 18th Amendment in 1919 which prohibited the manufacture and sale of alcoholic drinks in the United States. Prohibition did not end until 1933, when it was repealed by the 21st Amendment.

The 1920s and the Depression

Republican dominance

By the 1920s disillusionment about progressive reform had begun to grip society. The Republican Party turned its back on further reform as the right wing of the party took control. Their aim was to allow business to follow its own course, free from regulation, in the belief that this would lead to greater prosperity. The Republicans dominated the 1920s as Warren Harding, Calvin Coolidge and Herbert Hoover served terms in the White House. They believed in the value of private enterprise, hard work and individualism.

Prosperity

For the most part the 1920s was a decade of economic prosperity. The United States' gross national product grew by 40 per cent and the government and people grew complacent about America's underlying economic problems. These included a boom in real estate speculation helped by a banking system that was all too prepared to grant easy credit. Through property deals many saw their wealth escalate but this was based on market prices which were far in excess of the real value of the property. Similar speculation occurred on the stock market with market prices rising rapidly without any thought for the real value of the shares being traded.

Over-production

Throughout the 1920s industrial production increased. Industrialists increased their manufacturing capacity and goods poured out of factories. However, many of these goods were priced beyond the reach of most consumers who, even with wage increases, were still on very low incomes. As a result many firms could not sell their output and began to lay off workers or go bankrupt.

Agriculture

The weakest sector of the American economy was agriculture. Farmers had rapidly expanded production during World War I by borrowing heavily. At the end of the war their over-production caused prices to plummet leaving farmers unable to repay debts.

The Crash of 1929

Despite the weaknesses in the United States economy, speculation on the stock market continued until 1929 when investors began to be insecure about the economic boom. Panic-selling set in at the end of October and by mid-November $30 billion had been wiped off the value of shares. The effect of this downturn was to encourage businesses to cut back production, which further deepened the economic depression.

Economic collapse

Between 1929 and 1932 industrial output fell by 50 per cent, over 100,000 businesses were declared bankrupt, and national output fell by almost 50 per cent. By 1933, 5,500 banks, unable to collect their loans, had closed and almost 15 million workers (40 per cent of the working population) were unemployed. Those that remained in work faced wage cuts of up to 60 per cent.

The New Deal

Franklin Roosevelt

In 1932 Franklin Roosevelt, the governor of New York for two terms, sought and won the Democratic Party's nomination for the presidency. He campaigned on the basis of a programme of federal reform to bring an end to the Depression. Roosevelt won 57 per cent of the popular vote in the election and the Democrats won massive majorities in the House of Representatives and Senate.

In his inauguration speech of 1933 Roosevelt pledged 'a new deal for the American people.' Since then his proposals for economic recovery have been known as the New Deal. On assuming office Roosevelt summoned Congress on 9 March and it sat for '100 days' in order to enact the provisions of the New Deal. Roosevelt's proposals included banking reform to improve confidence in the financial system; farm relief in the form of cash payments to stop the over-production and price controls to halt the decline; poor relief to enable states to provide welfare for the unemployed and homeless; and a series of public works programmes, under the supervision of the

The New Deal Legislation

1933	Emergency Banking Relief Act Civilian Conservation Corps Act Federal Emergency Relief Act Agricultural Adjustment Act Tennessee Valley Authority Federal Securities Act National Employment System Act Home Owners Refinancing Act Banking Act of 1933 Farm Credit Act National Industrial Recovery Act Civilian Works Administration
1934	Farm Mortgage Refinancing Act Civil Works Emergency Relief Act Home Owners Loan Act Securities Exchange Act Federal Communications Commission Act Federal Farm Bankruptcy Act National Housing Act
1935	Emergency Relief Appropriations Act Resettlement Administration Rural Electrification Act National Youth Administration National Labour Relations Act Social Security Act Banking Act of 1935 Public Utilities Holding Company Act Bituminous Coal Conservation Act
1936	Government Contracts Act Farm Tenant Act
1937	National Housing Act
1938	Agricultural Adjustment Act Food, Drug, and Cosmetics Act Fair Labor Standards Act
1939	Food Stamp Plan

National Recovery Administration, all designed to get more people back to work and to put money into circulation to enable consumers to start buying goods again.

Conservative opposition

Roosevelt's proposals did not meet with unanimous approval. Conservatives believed that Roosevelt was relying far too much on the power of the federal government and was taking the country towards socialism. The Supreme Court also objected to the extent to which the federal government was interfering in the affairs of the states and struck down a number of New Deal programmes as a result, including the National Recovery Administration in 1935.

In 1935 and 1937 the second and third New Deals followed. These broadened the aims of the original New Deal by addressing social reform as well as economic recovery. Trade union power was increased, a system of social security was established and loans were provided for slum clearance.

From 1932 to 1939 federal aid had increased from $218 million to $5 billion but the Depression was not over. Indeed, it did not end until war broke out in Europe and the American economy began producing weapons for the war against Hitler and for America's subsequent entry into the wars with Germany and Japan.

Post-war America

World leader

At the end of World War II the United States found itself in a new role – leader of the 'Western World'. As the strongest of the western allies it fell to the United States to counter the apparent aggression of the Soviet Union. The result was a war of words between the superpowers which frequently spilled over into military conflicts, usually fought by proxy.

Cold War

However, the 'Cold War', as it became known, had a serious impact on domestic politics as well as international relations. Whilst both superpowers attempted to gain the upper hand abroad they also used propaganda techniques against their own populations in an effort to secure their support. Therefore many Americans were brought up to believe in and fear the threat of communism from the Soviet Union. To an extent this fear, at its height, was paranoic.

In the 1940s and 1950s American politics was dominated by this level of anti-communism. National problems were blamed on communist subversion, civil servants were forced to take an oath of loyalty and restrictions were placed on suspected communist sympathizers. Congress began to hold investigations into the activities of suspected communists through the House Un-American Activities Committee. Richard Nixon first made his name in the committee hearing concerning Alger Hiss, a State Department employee suspected of spying for the Soviet Union, and in the 1950s Joseph McCarthy began to hold similar hearings in the Senate.

Aside from fears of communism the post-war period saw undreamed-of prosperity in the United States. American industry that had been geared up for military production now turned its attention to consumer goods and flooded the market with an array of products that the American people, after years of war, were only too pleased to buy. Policy-makers and industrialists avoided the excesses of the 1920s that had led to the Depression and the economy expanded rapidly.

The civil rights movement

Whilst the white population benefited from the post-war boom the black population of

America was still largely viewed as a second class of citizens. Black attitudes to their position in society grew more hostile in the 1930s and during World War II. In the Depression many blacks had moved from the south to urban areas in the north, where their standard of living improved, albeit marginally, and they began to consider their place in society rather than mere subsistence. Also in the north blacks were treated better than in the south, where racial attitudes had changed little since the Civil War. Finally, in World War II blacks had been treated as equals by the Europeans, if not by their own army, and they sought to maintain this attitude at home.

The Brown case

President Truman proposed civil rights legislation as early as 1948 but the Congress, dominated by white southern Democrats refused. As a result he used his executive authority to desegregate the military and the federal administration. However, it was left to the Supreme Court to declare racial segregation in schools unconstitutional in *Brown* v. *Board of Education, Topeka, Kansas* (1954). Nevertheless segregation remained and resistance to it grew.

Peaceful resistance

In 1955 blacks in Montgomery, Alabama, organized a bus boycott in protest at

Martin Luther King (1929–1968)

Martin Luther King was born in Atlanta, Georgia, the son of a Baptist minister. Whilst at college he developed an interest in the passive resistance policies employed by Gandhi in the liberation of India from British colonialism.

King became a Baptist minister himself and came to prominence as a leader of the Montgomery bus boycotts. As a result of the national prominence he gained at the time he created the Southern Christian Leadership Conference which was the basis of his activities until 1968.

King organized a number of marches including the March on Washington in 1963. At the end of this march he addressed the crowd from the Lincoln Memorial with his 'I have a dream' speech. His influence over the Kennedy and Johnson administrations resulted in the Civil Rights Act (1964) and the Voting Rights Act (1965).

Despite his success King was never free from challengers from within his movement who felt that his strategy of non-violent resistance was outdated and that he was too willing to compromise with white decision-makers. King was also criticized for not paying enough attention to the economic plight of the black community outside the southern states.

Outside the black community he lost the support of the Johnson administration after denouncing American involvement in Vietnam and was under almost constant attack from the FBI under J Edgar Hoover.

On 4 April 1968 King was assassinated in Memphis, Tennessee. Riots broke out in 125 American cities and lasted for more than a week as King's death provoked blacks to lash out against their oppressors.

segregated seating on public transport. The boycott lasted a year and ended only when the Supreme Court declared such segregation unconstitutional.

A prime leader of the boycott was a Baptist minister, Martin Luther King. King became a pivotal figure in the civil rights movement, speaking eloquently for rights and organizing peaceful resistance to inequality.

Reluctantly President Eisenhower supported the *Brown* decision in Little Rock (1957) by using the National Guard to escort black children to a white school. However, politicians in general were reluctant to get involved in such a controversial issue. With a relatively small proportion of the black population registered to vote the political fortunes of presidents and members of Congress depended largely on the white vote. By and large whites were worried by advances in civil rights for economic as much as racist reasons. They felt that any advances in black well-being would necessitate a decline in their own.

De jure and de facto

In the 1960s, as Congress enacted civil rights legislation, the nature of the civil rights movement began to change. Although legal, or de jure, discrimination had been abolished, in practice, or de facto, discrimination remained in the hearts and minds of many whites all over America. This led to a radicalization of the movement and the development of more extreme groups such as the Nation of Islam and the Black Panthers. Malcolm X, a leader of the Nation of Islam in New York, preached black separatism whilst the Panthers, originating from California, condemned racism as an integral part of American society.

In an effort to deal with de facto discrimination legislators turned to affirmative action, or positive discrimination, programmes. These programmes continue today and are intended to give members of the black community a head start at school and college, at work and to an extent in voting, in an effort to integrate the black community into American society.

President Johnson's Great Society

Lyndon Johnson came to the presidency in 1963 after the assassination of John F Kennedy. A southern Democrat, he may have been expected to be more conservative than his predecessor but surprised many by launching a programme of civil rights legislation and social reform known as the Great Society.

In 1964 the programmes included the Civil Rights Act and a number of job training programmes including the Job Corps. The following year Congress enacted Medicare (social security for the elderly), Medicaid (social security for the poor), the Voting Rights Act and federal aid for education and housing provision for the poor. Reforms continued throughout his presidency along with an economic stimulus package, including tax cuts, in an effort to reduce poverty through economic growth.

Despite his achievements in domestic policy Johnson will probably be remembered for American involvement in the war in Vietnam.

Vietnam

President Kennedy was responsible for escalating early involvement in the Vietnam War, although he was personally opposed to using combat troops in South-east Asia.

Great Society Legislation

1964	Civil Rights Act Urban Mass Transportation Act Economic Opportunity Act Wilderness Preservation Act
1965	Elementary and Secondary School Act Medicare Voting Rights Act Omnibus Housing Act Department of Housing and Urban Development National Endowment for the Arts National Endowment for the Humanities Water Quality Act Air Quality Act Higher Education Act
1966	National Traffic Safety Act Minimum Wage Increase Department of Transportation Clean Water Restoration Act Model Cities Act
1967	Public Broadcasting Corporation
1968	Open Housing Law Omnibus Crime Act Federal Housing Act Scenic Rivers Act

When Kennedy came to office there were only 900 American advisers in Vietnam; when he was assassinated there were 16,000. It was President Johnson who moved the Vietnam War from a minor intervention in a civil war between North and South Vietnam to a war between North Vietnam and the United States.

When Johnson became president in 1963 he devoted much of his energies to his domestic programme. However, there was a fundamental difference between Johnson's attitude to the war and that of his predecessor: Johnson believed that commitment of American forces could defeat the communist Viet Cong from North Vietnam. Johnson therefore sought to escalate the war.

Gulf of Tonkin

Unsure of his ability to win congressional support for the war Johnson used an incident in the Gulf of Tonkin in 1964, in which he claimed American ships had been subjected to an unprovoked North Vietnamese attack, to gain congressional approval for retaliation and escalation – the Gulf of Tonkin Resolution. Johnson did not escalate the war immediately due to the impending election but early in 1965 he ordered American troops into Vietnam. By the end of the year the number of American combat troops in Vietnam jumped from 25,000 to 184,000.

Escalation

Over the next three years the number of American troops increased dramatically: 1966 – 385,000; 1967 – 485,000 and 1968 – 536,000. Despite their heavy commitment the Americans seemed to make little headway against the Viet Cong – although government made claims to the contrary. This was confirmed in 1968 when the North Vietnamese launched the Tet Offensive. 'Tet', the Vietnamese new year holiday, was an attack against 116 cities which took the Americans by surprise. Although the attack was repulsed it proved that the Viet Cong had the strength and the capability to attack American forces at will. It was a major turning point in the war.

'Tet'

'Tet' had a tremendous impact on America as it was covered by television crews without restriction. Not only was it disturbing to watch, but it indicated to the American people that the imminent destruction of the Viet Cong was exaggerated. This, combined with the increasing American dead (9378 in 1967; 14,592 in 1968), resulted in mounting opposition to the war.

Lyndon Johnson (1908–1973)

Lyndon Baines Johnson was born in Texas. He was brought up in a political family – his father had served in the Texas legislature – but his initial training was as a school teacher before he entered politics as an aide to a member of Congress.

Johnson was first elected to the House of Representatives in 1937, in which he served for eleven years. He ran for the Senate in 1941 but was defeated. However, he ran again in 1948 and was successful amidst accusations of ballot-rigging in the Democratic primary.

In 1953 he became minority leader of the Democrats in the Senate and majority leader two years later when the Democrats resumed control. He was an effective Senate majority leader pursuing a policy of co-operation with the Eisenhower administration.

He harboured ambitions to run for the presidency in 1960 but was unable to win the Democratic nomination. Instead, he accepted the call to be Kennedy's vice-presidential candidate. However, his time as vice-president was difficult. He was given little or no power and resented his treatment at the hands of the Kennedy clan.

On Kennedy's death in 1963 Johnson became president and proceeded to push forward an ambitious programme of social reform, second only to Roosevelt's New Deal. After winning a landslide victory in the 1964 presidential election, however, Johnson became increasingly distracted by the Vietnam War. Oppositon to the war grew to such an extent that he chose not to run for the Democratic nomination in 1968.

In retrospect Johnson's administration presided over great achievements in domestic policy, but in Vietnam it came up against the limitations of American power. Even in the sphere of domestic affairs, Johnson's Great Society probably laid the groundwork for the conservative backlash that persists today.

The opposition initially took the form of student protests but soon incorporated middle-class voices and even dissent within the administration. Anti-war marches took place all over the country, the largest being in Washington DC, New York and San Francisco.

Democratic divisions

The Democratic Party split over the war and the 1968 presidential election was won by the Republican candidate, Richard Nixon. Nixon sought to end the war by encouraging the South Vietnamese to undertake their own defence. This was known as the 'Vietnamization' of the war. Nixon began the withdrawal of American troops in 1969 but escalated the bombing of North Vietnamese positions and cities and extended it to include Cambodia. At the same time Henry Kissinger, Nixon's National Security Advisor, pursued peace talks with the North Vietnamese in Paris.

However, Nixon's policy simply outraged domestic opinion further. Congress repealed the Gulf of Tonkin Resolution and eventually all American troops were withdrawn in 1972, with a peace treaty signed in 1973.

Post-Vietnam

The Vietnam War was a key event in United States politics. The post-war era had begun well, with American victories in Europe and the Pacific. The American economy was stronger than ever before and Johnson had sought to ensure that all sectors of American society could benefit from this prosperity. But by 1974 America had suffered an ignominious defeat in South-east Asia, in a war which many Americans believed was pointless. Furthermore their president, Richard Nixon, had used the war and the protests at home as an excuse to expand the powers of the presidency beyond all recognition, culminating in impeachment charges being brought against him. This became known as Watergate.

All subsequent presidents have suffered from the damage inflicted on the American political system, and the confidence of the American people in that system, by the Vietnam War and by Richard Nixon. The post-Watergate presidents have also found it more difficult to work with Congress and most have found it difficult to project American power abroad.

In terms of policies the disillusionment that followed the late 1960s and early 1970s has pushed Americans into a prolonged period of conservatism in domestic policy. All holders of the presidency, whether Democrat or Republican, have been relatively conservative and the victory of the Republicans in the 1994 mid-term elections is one more step to the right.

2 The constitution

Questions to be answered in this chapter

- What are the origins of the US constitution?
- What are the main elements of the US constitution?

Terms to know

- Amendments
- Antifederalism
- Bill of rights
- Codified
- Confederation
- Constitution
- Democracy
- Electoral college
- Executive
- Federalism
- Founding Fathers
- Interdependent
- Interpretation
- Judiciary
- Legislature
- Monarch
- President
- Ratification
- Separation of powers
- Sovereignty
- States

Introduction

Constitutional convention

The Constitution of the United States of America was framed in Philadelphia in 1787. The convention began on 25 May and ended on 18 September. During those months 55 delegates from the thirteen ex-colonies drew up the **constitution**, a ten-page

Constitutions

A constitution is a set of broad rules and principles by which a state is governed. It is important that the rules should be broad because a constitution must allow a political system to develop over time.

Constitutions can be either written or unwritten. The former are **codified** in a single document, whilst the latter may be drawn from a variety of sources.

A constitution should contain rules regarding the three main elements of a political system: the relationship between central and local government; the relationship between the institutions of central government; and the relationship between the government and the governed.

document which has been the basis of government in the United States for over 200 years.

Originally their brief was to revise the Articles of Confederation, which had been in existence since America had won its independence from Britain in 1781. The **Confederation** had been a very loose grouping of **states** with a weak central government.

The Articles of Confederation

After the Declaration of Independence in 1776 all thirteen colonies drew up constitutions for themselves. Common features of these constitutions included popular **sovereignty**, the supremacy of the legislative branch of government, a weak executive branch and limited government.

Popular sovereignty

Popular sovereignty was important to the colonists given their grievances against the British government. They believed that the British government had attempted to rule the colonists without reference to their rights and liberties, and were anxious to avoid any repetition of this. The Georgia Constitution (1777) stated that: 'We, therefore, the representatives of the people, from whom all power orginates and for whose benefit all government is intended, by virtue of the power delegated to us, do ordain ... that the following rules and regulations be adopted for the future government of this state.'

In all the new states the legislative assembly carried most power, being able to determine policies but, in some cases, to elect state governors and judges. In all states except New York, the executive branch was reduced to a supporting role with few administrative powers and often a term of office of only one year.

The branches of government

Every system of government needs to be able to make law, ensure that everyone is aware of the law and to enforce the law. In modern political systems these functions are carried out by the three main institutions of government: the legislature, the executive and the judiciary.

The **legislature** is responsible for law-making. In democratic societies this is usually an elected assembly. In the United States this function is carried out, at central government level, by Congress.

The **executive** is responsible for implementing, or executing, laws. It puts policies into practice via administrators. In contemporary societies executives are also responsible for initiating many policy ideas which are then put before the legislature. In the United States this branch is headed by the president, who co-ordinates the work of the bureaucracy.

The **judiciary** applies law in court. Judges are responsible for interpreting the meaning of law and assesing the extent to which law is relevant to particular cases. In the United States the judicial branch is headed by the Supreme Court.

Federalism

As well as the branches of government at the centre of a political system most states have a second tier of government made up of a number of smaller units based in regions of the country. These local governments enable policies to be made and implemented with reference to a local community.

In America the 'regions' began as colonies and subsequently became independent states. However in 1787 they came together to form a larger unit known as the United States. In doing so they gave up some of their power to the central government but retained the ability to make laws relating to some issues, independent of the central, or federal, government. Such a system is known as federalism.

Bill of rights

The constitution of Virginia went further than the other twelve and in doing so it laid down a framework that many other countries, including the United States, would follow in the future. At the beginning of this document was a **bill of rights**, which outlined the rights and liberties of its citizens and so created a government that was limited in its authority over the people (see Appendix 2).

Articles of Confederation

In 1776 the Congress had been asked to draw up a plan to bring the ex-colonies together in an association. Eventually, after some conflict, these plans were adopted in 1777 as the Articles of Confederation. They came into effect in 1781.

The Articles merely created a very loose league of states who would co-operate with each other to a limited extent. Each state retained its sovereignty and the Articles could not be amended unless there was unanimous agreement. The Articles created a congress with a limited role for government in society.

Limits on federal government

The states were so anxious to retain their independence that Congress could not raise taxes, control trade between the states or with other countries and could use its limited powers only against states, not against their citizens. The weaknesses of the Articles led to problems immediately after the Revolution. Some states printed excessive amounts of currency in an effort to ease debt problems, others imposed tariffs against trade with other states, and most failed, to a greater or lesser extent, to meet their financial obligations to the Confederation. As a result a movement for a new constitution was organized and a convention was called to meet in Philadelphia on 14 May 1787.

The constitutional convention

State delegates

The delegates to the convention were chosen by the state legislatures. The largest came from Pennsylvania and included Benjamin Franklin, James Wilson and Gouverneur Morris. The most prestigious group, however, came from Virginia, and included George Washington, James Madison and George Mason. Thomas Jefferson, who was serving as Minister to France at the time, did not attend. Rhode Island was the only state not to send delegates.

Virginia plan

When the convention eventually convened a number of state delegations put forward their own plans. The Virginia plan included the creation of a bicameral legislature, with both houses being apportioned according to population; an elected national executive and a system of national courts. It also gave the legislature the power to disallow state laws that contravened the constitution and to use armed force against states of the Union.

New Jersey plan

Subsequently New Jersey produced its own plan that elaborated on the powers of the legislature. These powers were to include raising import duties, the regulation of interstate commerce and the appointment of an executive which in turn would be responsible for appointing federal judges. According to the New Jersey plan the laws of Congress would be the supreme laws of the land.

Great Compromise

Many of the provisions of the New Jersey plan were rejected as the battle lines between large and small states were drawn. A particularly thorny issue was the apportionment of seats in the legislature. Whilst the large states supported allocation according to the relative populations of the states, the smaller states refused to accept this provision for fear that the national government would be dominated by their larger neighbours. The result of this conflict was the Connecticut, or Great, Compromise. According to this the lower house would be proportioned according to population whilst the upper house would give equal representation to all of the states.

In the end, the delegates declined to give the sweeping powers favoured by Viginia and New Jersey. Instead they drew on the original Articles of Confederation and some of the state constitutions to enumerate specific powers for Congress.

Executive

However, a much more controversial issue was the allocation of power to the executive branch of government. A relatively strong executive was created, based on that of New York, and the idea that the president should be elected by the legislature was rejected. They proposed instead that he should be chosen by an **electoral college** that gave disproportionate weight to the smaller states (see page 61).

Judiciary

The convention had agreed on the need for a national judiciary at an early stage. Judges were to be appointed by the president with **ratification** from the upper house. They also proposed that Congress should have the power to create inferior courts if it so wished. However, the final element of the New Jersey plan – supremacy for federal law over state law – was adopted and state judges were instructed to uphold national law when in conflict with state laws.

After being in almost continuous session for four months the final draft of the constitution was signed by 39 of the 55 delegates and was sent to Congress, which distributed it to individual states. It had been decided that specially elected delegates in each state would discuss the document and decide whether to ratify or not. Only nine states were required to ratify for the new constitution to come into operation.

Federalists v. antifederalists

There followed a period of intense lobbying in the press for and against the new document. The supporters became known as the federalists; the opponents as the antifederalists. For the former, Alexander Hamilton (see page 8), James Madison (see page 9) and diplomat and jurist, John Jay, wrote a series of articles, that became known as *The Federalist Papers*, for the New York press. The case for **antifederalism**, on the other hand, was put forward by Richard Henry Lee in *Letters of the Federal Farmer*.

Dispute resolution in the constitution

National identity and liberty

The first challenge for the framers of the constitution, known as the **Founding Fathers,** was to forge a national identity for their new country without undermining the independence of the states or of individuals. Many felt that a strong central government would have the potential to interfere with states' rights in the same way that the British government had done before the Revolution. This group became known as the antifederalists. They opposed the move to federalism, preferring states to retain their powers under the Articles of Confederation.

Within the federalist grouping there were divisions. Thomas Jefferson and James Madison preferred a central government constrained by significant checks on its powers, whilst Alexander Hamilton and George Washington favoured a very strong national government.

The result was a constitution which attempts to combine both a strong central government with state and individual liberties. The states have their own powers, and the principle of federalism recurs throughout the document. The **president** is elected on a state-by-state basis; the Senate is made up of two elected representatives from each state, regardless of the state's size; the House of Representatives is composed of groups of congressmen elected from individual states; and the constitution can be amended only with the approval of 75 per cent of the states. In fact the presidency is the only nationally elected office in the United States.

The separation of powers

As we have seen, the system of federalism divides power between the central government and the state governments. However, the framers of the constitution went further and divided power within the central government. Their aim was to avoid tyrannical rule and to ensure that no individual or group would be persecuted.

Dispersed power

No single institution of the federal government is sovereign; they are all independent and **interdependent**. The president has specific powers, all of which are checked by Congress and the Supreme Court. Congress has perhaps the most power but it too is

Comparison

The main tenet of the British constitution is *parliamentary sovereignty*. In other words, Parliament holds the supreme power within the British political system and all other institutions of government are subservient to it.

This principle results in local government that lacks constitutional independence and the power to make its own law, an executive that is dependent on Parliament and can be brought down by a vote of no confidence, and a judicial system that has no power to assess the constitutionality of Parliament's actions.

checked by the Supreme Court and the president. The Supreme Court has developed the power to interpret the constitution and review the other branches of government but it cannot enforce its own decisions and its membership is determined by the other two branches.

Elections

The Founding Fathers also guarded against a single group taking possession of all three institutions at the same time by creating a system of staggered elections. Members of the House of Representatives have a two-year term of office and are, therefore, closely in touch with public opinion. The president has a four-year term of office. Senators have a six-year term of office and are elected on a two-year cycle, with one third of the Senate coming up for re-election every two years. Members of the Supreme Court are not elected at all. They are appointed by the president and ratified by the Senate. They hold their offices for life. Such a system is designed to prevent a populist group gaining the upper hand in all three institutions on one election day.

Democracy

The newly independent Americans were fresh from the experience of undemocratic rule from England and were adamant that their new government should be democratic and republican. They therefore chose a president rather than a **monarch** and set terms of office for each institution, with the exception of the Supreme Court.

House of Representatives

Despite the creation of systems of election for choosing members of the government, the degrees of democracy in operation varied widely. The House of Representatives was elected from districts, each with approximately the same population, within each state. It was, as its name implies, intended to represent the people.

Senate

The Senate, on the other hand, was not. Each state sends two senators to Washington regardless of the size of each state's population. Therefore smaller, less populous, states receive disproportionate representation. In addition senators were not elected directly by the people until the 17th Amendment was passed in 1913. Prior to this change they had been chosen by the state legislatures.

Electoral college

Even the president is not elected in a simple 'one person, one vote' contest. The Founding Fathers created the electoral college, which consists of delegates from each state who are charged with selecting a president on behalf of the people. Again this results in the smaller states being over-represented.

State power

The departure from the principles of one person, one vote can partly be explained with reference to federalism and to the importance of the states in the American system. Another explanation is that the Founding Fathers were taking into account the levels of illiteracy prevalent at the time and the poor methods of communication. As a result elections were best confined to local communities from which delegates could be despatched to select national officers.

Economic motives

In 1913 Charles Beard, an American historian, offered an alternative explanation. He argues that: 'it is an economic document drawn with superb skill by men whose property interests were immediately at stake' (*An Economic Interpretation of the Constitution of the United States*, 1913). The Founding Fathers were hoping that the intermediaries between the people and the president and the Senate would prevent populist, radical candidates being successful, thereby securing their own economic privileges.

Ratification

By May 1788 Delaware, New Jersey and Georgia had unanimously approved the constitution; Maryland and South Carolina with large majorities; and Connecticut and Pennsylvania by narrow margins. Debate in the remaining six states was intense. In Massachusetts it was ratified when supporters agreed to propose antifederalist **amendments**. In New Hampshire federalists narrowly avoided defeat in January but were successful in June, after an adjournment, followed rapidly by ratification in Virginia. Antifederalists in New York seemed likely to be successful until news of the New Hampshire and Virginia decisions turned the tide and the state voted to ratify on 30 April 1789. In November 1789 North Carolina also ratified the constitution but Rhode Island did not do so until one year later.

Changing the constitution

The US constitution is a written, codified document and has survived for over 200 years. This has been possible because it has changed and adapted to take into account developments in American society. (For the full text of the constitution and its amendments see Appendix 3.)

Comparison

The British constitution is unwritten; in other words it is not contained in a single codified document. It is made up from a number of sources including historical documents, statute law and conventions. As a result the British constitution is relatively easy to change, for example by passing a new law through Parliament or by changing a normal pattern of behaviour – changing a convention. There is no formal amendment procedure – it is considered a flexible constitution.

Amendments

The Founding Fathers laid down two procedures for proposing amendments to the constitution. The first requires Congress to call a national convention at the request of two-thirds of the states – along the same lines as the original convention in Philadelphia. This procedure has never been used, although in 1911 the support of one more state would have required Congress to call a convention regarding the direct election of senators. The second method requires a two-thirds majority in both houses of Congress.

Once proposed, an amendment needs to be ratified by three-quarters of the states. This can be done either through a vote in the state legislatures or by special state ratifying conventions. The latter has been used only once, for the 21st Amendment in 1933.

Although over 10,000 amendments have been suggested only 40 have ever been

The Bill of Rights

In 1789 James Madison proposed a series of seventeen amendments to the constitution that had been promised to the antifederalists. All were approved by the House of Representatives but the Senate rejected the first two and the last five.

The First Amendment prohibits the establishment of a state church and guarantees freedom of speech, worship, press and the right to peacful assembly.

The Second and Third Amendments reflect concern about a standing army and soldiers being housed in private homes. The Second lays down the right to bear arms and the Third prevents billeting of soldiers in private homes in peacetime.

Amendments Four to Eight concern the protection of life, liberty and property. They prevent unlawful searches of property, an individual being tried for the same crime twice, and a defendant being forced to give evidence against themselves. They also lay down rights concerning arrest and trial.

The Ninth Amendment assures citizens that the list enumerated in the Bill of Rights is by no means exhaustive.

The Tenth Amendment was designed to limit the power of the federal government. It acknowledged many of the fears of the antifederalists by stating that any federal government powers not specified or implied by the constitution should lie with the states or the people.

approved by Congress and only 27 have been approved by the states. This is because the procedure was deliberately made difficult by the Founding Fathers in an effort to preserve political stability.

The proposed Equal Rights Amendment

The ERA was the proposed 27th Amendment which grew out of the women's liberation movement of the late 1960s. Introduced in 1972, it stated that: 'Equality of rights under the law shall not be denied or abridged by the United States or any state on account of sex.'

It quickly gained overwhelming support in both houses of Congress and seemed destined to be ratified with ease. However, after being approved by 22 states opposition began to take shape.

Conservative opposition was based on the fact that it would make women eligible for draft into the army and combat duty. In addition many felt that it was unnecessary because the 14th Amendment already prevented discrimination. President Reagan threw his weight behind the opposition movement.

The final deadline for ratification was March 1982 by which time it had only gained 35 of the 38 states required by the constitution. The amendment therefore died.

Judicial interpretation

However, the constitution has been kept up to date through judicial **interpretation.** The Supreme Court has the power to interpret the constitution and in doing so has been prepared to ignore precedent and overturn previous judgements. Key interpretations include *National Labor Relations Board* v. *Jones & Laughlin* (1937); *Brown* v. *the Board of Education, Topeka, Kansas* (1954); and *The United States* v. *Richard Nixon* (1974).

Questions

Short questions

1 **a** What were the main features of the proposed 27th Amendment [Equal Rights Amendment]?
b Why has it not been ratified?
(ULEAC, January 1992)

US questions

1 Why has it proved so difficult to amend the US constitution? (UCLES, June 1994)

2 How flexible is the American constitution? (UODLE, June 1993)

Comparative questions

1 'Constitutions are becoming increasingly unreliable as guides to political reality.' Discuss. (Illustrate your answer with reference to at least two countries.) (ULEAC, January 1995)

2 Do constitutions really matter? (Illustrate your answer with reference to at least two countries.) (ULEAC, June 1993)

3 'It is not only the constitution that is important; it is the extent to which rulers respect it.' Discuss. (Illustrate your answer with reference to at least two countries.) (ULEAC, June 1991)

3 Federalism

Questions to be answered in this chapter

- How is local government structured in the United States?
- How is power distributed between the federal and state governments in the US?
- How has the distribution of power changed since 1787?

Terms to know

- Bicameral
- Block grants
- Board of Supervisors
- Categorical grants
- City council
- City manager
- 'Commerce clause'
- Concurrent jurisdiction
- Concurrent powers
- Confederation
- Constitution
- Co-operative federalism
- Creative federalism
- Denied powers
- Doctrine of Nullification
- Dual federalism
- Enumerated powers
- Federal government
- Flexible funding
- Governor
- Grants-in-aid programmes
- Great Society
- Inherent powers
- 'Layer-cake' federalism
- Legislature
- Line-item veto
- 'Marble-cake' federalism
- Mayor
- New Deal
- New Federalism
- Non-partisan
- 'Picket-fence' federalism
- Reserved powers
- Revenue-sharing
- Separation of powers
- State government
- States' rights
- 'Swaps'
- Veto

The Founding Fathers and Federalism

When the framers of the **constitution** met in 1787 no single issue divided them more than the role of the central government in relation to the state governments. At the extremes were those who wanted the complete abolition of the states in favour of one nation, whilst others favoured the loose **confederation** of 13 states that had been in place since 1781. Eventually a compromise solution was found with both the **federal government** and **state governments** having their own powers and each checking the other.

Since 1787 the relationship has been in a state of flux with power waxing and waning between the federal and state governments. On balance the federal government has come out on top.

The structure of state and local government

Like the national government, each state government has a constitution which lays down the relationship between the governmental institutions at state level. All have a system of **separation of powers** between the three institutions of government.

Governors

The executive branch of government at state level is headed by a **governor**. How much power the governor has varies from state to state. Most governors serve for four years and can run for re-election an unlimited number of times. Most have the power to **veto** legislation and even have a **line-item veto**, which presidents have envied. Most governors have considerable powers of appointment and have the power to formulate the state's budget.

State legislature

Each state has a **legislature** and in every case, except Nebraska, it is **bicameral** (made up of two houses). However, beyond that similarity they vary widely. Most have lower houses which are elected for two years and upper houses which are elected for four years. But in twelve states, members of the upper house serve for only two years and in four states the lower houses serve for four years.

State legislatures tend to function along the same lines as Congress. Both houses have representative, legislative, investigative and financial functions and much of their work is carried on through a system of standing committees. However, not all state legislatures meet every year. Some meet only in alternate years.

State judiciary

In addition each state has a judicial system which can apply state laws and some federal laws. The major difference between the state and federal system concerns the way judges are selected. Judges in federal courts are nominated by the president and ratified by the Senate. In most states, judges are elected for periods which vary from four to fifteen years. This is a means of keeping judges in touch with the democratic process. Many such elections are **non-partisan**.

Local government

Within each state there are numerous units of local government. The two main categories are municipal government and county government. The former covers cities, towns and villages. Most cities elect a **mayor** or **city manager** and a **city council** plus an independent judiciary. A city government is the largest unit inside the state and is usually administered by an elected **Board of Supervisors** along with certain elected officials such as sheriff and treasurer.

The powers and functions of state governments

The constitution does not make any reference whatsoever to federalism. Nevertheless it has become a dominant principle of American government, with governmental powers being distributed between the states and the federal governments.

The constitution outlines the division of powers between the states and the central government. However, it is only the vaguest of outlines and the interpretations have, at times, been controversial.

Federal powers

Article I of the constitution gives Congress the power to make laws on specific matters, including defence and currency. They are known as **enumerated powers**. The federal government is also considered to have **inherent powers**, which can be realistically carried out only by a national government. Obvious areas of national responsibility include foreign affairs and war. Article I of the constitution also gives Congress the power to: 'make all laws which shall be necessary and proper for carrying into execution the foregoing powers.' The Supreme Court has interpreted this to mean that Congress has the power to make any laws necessary to effectively carry out its enumerated powers.

Denied powers

Restrictions are placed on the federal government as the constitution denies certain powers to it. These are known as **denied powers**. Congress is not allowed to apply taxes to exports nor is it allowed to create titles of nobility.

Comparison

Britain is a unitary state. As such, political power is concentrated with central government. Local government has no constitutional independence in Britain and only has as much power as the central government chooses to give it.

State powers

State governments have fewer powers specifically given to them by the Founding Fathers. It would be easy to interpret this to mean that the state governments were considered to be less important than the federal government. However, it is more likely that the precise allocation of the powers of federal government was designed to be a restriction on it, to the advantage of state government. Many of the Founding Fathers believed that all powers not expressly given to the federal government would automatically reside with state governments. This idea was formalized as the 10th Amendment to the constitution which states that: 'the powers not delegated to the United States by the Constitution, nor prohibited by it to the States, are reserved to the States respectively, or to the people.' These **reserved powers** include regulating their own commerce, running elections and providing for public safety. In addition the federal government and the state governments share certain powers. These are known as **concurrent powers**. For example citizens are subjected to both central and state government taxes.

This constitutional division of powers has resulted in states having a wide range of responsibilities. Their direct responsibilities include the provision of public education and health care; transport; and law enforcement. Each state makes its own laws concerning marriage and divorce, and voting and drinking ages. Indirectly states take a wider range of responsibilities through their finance of local government. Included in this category are public health and subsidized housing.

The federal–state relationship

The framers of the constitution were divided over the degree of power to give to the central government of the United States. In fact it was this issue that gave rise to the beginnings of the party system in America. The Federalists believed in a strong central government whilst the Democratic-Republicans believed in a limited central government and more power to the states.

States' rights

Jefferson and Madison believed so strongly in the rights of the states and the limits on the federal government that they argued in favour of each state's ability to determine for itself what was, or was not, constitutional. Jefferson wrote that each state has: 'delegated to that [the federal] government certain definite powers, reserving, each state to itself, the residuary mass of right to their own self-government; and that whensoever the General Government assumes undelegated powers, its acts are unauthoritative, void, and of no force ...' (*The Writings of Thomas Jefferson*).This became known as the **Doctrine of Nullification** and it held considerable weight in the states, particularly those in the South until after the Civil War (see page 11).

National supremacy

Supreme Court

It fell to the Supreme Court to be the arbiter of the federal versus state contest. Its actions at the beginning of the nineteenth century, under Chief Justice John Marshall (1755–1835), soon put an end to the belief that the states would remain independent entities, immune from central interference. Marshall believed in a strong central government and used the Court to enhance the position of the federal government.

Marshall Court

In *Fletcher* v. *Peck* (1810) the Supreme Court declared a state law unconstitutional for the first time. This was followed by *McCulloch* v. *Maryland* (1819), which established the 'implied powers' of the federal government based on Article I of the constitution.

In 1824 Marshall pushed the powers of the federal government still further by adopting a broad interpretation of the **'commerce clause'** of Article I of the constitution, which gives Congress the power to: 'regulate commerce with foreign Nations, and among the several States, and with the Indian Tribes.' In *Gibbons* v. *Ogden* (1824) the Court declared that the federal government was within its rights to regulate the New York to New Jersey ferry because this provision allowed the federal government to take responsibility for all navigable waters, even those within a state.

Dual federalism

The appointment of Roger Brook Taney as Chief Justice of the Supreme Court, in 1836, helped the pendulum to swing back towards **states' rights**. The Taney Court avidly defended the states' rights to preserve slavery. In doing so it overruled a federal law for only the second time, in *Dred Scott* v. *Sandford* (1857). This case is seen as an important milestone on the road to civil war. The Taney Court was made up of seven justices, four of whom were southerners. Therefore the politicians of the North were reluctant to heed the judgement of such a 'biased' court.

Civil War

It is often asserted that the Civil War began over the issue of slavery but in fact the war was about the rights of individual states. Firstly, because the southern states believed that the North had no right to impose an anti-slavery policy on the whole country they decided to secede. Secondly, the constitution made no provision for secession by individual states so a war was fought to prevent the Confederacy leaving the Union.

The victory of the Unionists ended talk of the right to secession but it did not end the debate regarding states' rights (for more detail, see pages 12–22).

'Strict constructionists'

After the Civil War the Supreme Court was made up of 'strict constructionists' (see page 150). They were determined to restore the authority of the Court after Lincoln had refused to accept its condemnation of his suspension of habeas corpus (an individual's right to be brought before a court after arrest). The Court continued to restrict the ability of the federal government to interfere in the affairs of state governments.

Segregation

Although the 13th (1865) and 14th (1868) Amendments had abolished slavery and had given all citizens equal protection under the laws, the Court took a fairly conservative view of these amendments. In *Plessy* v. *Ferguson* (1896) the court upheld racial segregation, so long as it was equal. This meant that separate institutions or facilities for both black and white citizens were constitutional so long as they were of equal quality. In addition it acted to restrict the federal government's ability to interfere in the industrial policies of the states, despite the fact that the post-Civil War era was perhaps the greatest period of industrialization in America's history.

The Supreme Court's refusal to allow the federal government to interfere in the industrialization process in individual states illustrates the doctrine of **dual federalism,** which was the dominant interpretation of federalism at the time. According to this view the federal and state governments had been given separate areas of jurisdiction by the constitution and the two should not merge. The principle was elucidated by the British historian and ambassador to the US (1907–13), James Bryce: 'The characteristic feature and special interest of the American Union is that it shows us two governments covering the same ground yet distinct and separate in their action. It is like a great factory wherein two sets of machinery are at work, their revolving wheels apparently intermixed, their bands crossing one another, yet each doing its own work without touching or hampering the other.' This conception of dual federalism is sometimes known as **'layer-cake' federalism.**

Co-operative federalism

Opposition to New Deal

Dual federalism continued to be the predominant doctrine regarding federal–state relations up to and including Franklin Roosevelt's **New Deal,** which involved intervention in the economy on a scale never before experienced in America (see pages 20–22). Initially the Supreme Court ruled against a number of the policies collectively known as the New Deal. In *Schechter Poultry Corporation* v. *United States* (1935) the Court ruled that the National Recovery Administration which had been established by the National Industrial Recovery Act (1933) was an unconstitutional expansion of presidential authority. The Court found that the industrial code the Schechter corporation was accused of breaking amounted to interference with intra-state commerce. In addition Chief Justice Hughes stated that: 'Extraordinary conditions may call for extraordinary remedies. But ... Extraordinary conditions do not create or enlarge constitutional power. The constitution established a national government with powers deemed to be adequate, as they have proved to be both in war and peace; but these powers of the national government are limited by the constitutional grants.'

Change of step

However, by 1937 the Supreme Court had decided that to continually challenge the authority of the president was taking it out of step with public opinion. It began to adopt a more relaxed view of the president's policies. *National Labor Relations Board* v. *Jones & Laughlin* (1937) is considered a turning point in federal–state relations. For the first time the federal government was given the authority to intervene in state affairs.

Concurrent jurisdiction

The New Deal brought with it a new conception of federalism – the doctrine of **concurrent jurisdiction**, or **co-operative federalism**. Under this doctrine both the federal and state governments are considered to be part of the same governmental system and as such they are expected to co-operate with each other.

The need for the federal and state governments to work together has resulted from the greater responsibilities government has taken on in the twentieth century. The first is in the field of economics. The development of Keynesian economics, which preached state intervention on a large scale, has given government cause to take responsibility for the state of the economy. Large-scale intervention needs to be planned on a national level but implemented at the state and local levels; co-operation therefore becomes necessary. In the 1960s the American government also took responsibility for social welfare issues. President Johnson's **Great Society** involved an increased welfare provision through Medicaid and Medicare as well as greater government interest in civil rights issues (see page 25). All of these programmes cost money and only the federal government was able to provide it. Again, planning and funding often came from the central government whilst implementation was carried out locally.

Creative federalism

Indeed President Johnson encouraged decision-making on the Great Society programmes to take place on all levels of the political system in an effort to gain greater co-operation between the various layers. He called it **creative federalism.** Perhaps the best example is the Demonstration Cities and Metropolitan Development Act (1966) through which the Johnson administration attempted to work with local government institutions and bypassed state governments.

Federal spending

Along with the key Supreme Court decisions, finance has been a major impulse towards greater co-operation between the different levels of government. So long as the federal government lacked the power to raise an income tax its financial means were limited. As a result so was its ability to intervene in national affairs that required spending. The 16th Amendment (1913) gave the federal government the power to levy an income tax and its spending rose accordingly. In 1929 federal government spending accounted for approximately 25 per cent of government spending. Today federal government spending accounts for 67 per cent of all government spending.

A considerable amount of federal government spending takes the form of transfers to state and local governments. Such transfers account for approximately 25 per cent of state and local government income. The traditional method of transfer is the **grants-in-aid programme.** Grant programmes began in the nineteenth century when the federal government gave land to the states to establish state universities (also known as land-grant colleges) and, in 1862, granted land by the side of the tracks to the railway companies. However the system really took hold during the New Deal. The sixteen grants-in-aid programmes were launched by Roosevelt and were valued at $2 billion.

Categorical grants and block grants

Grants-in-aid take two forms: categorical and block.

Categorical grants are given to state and local governments for specific purposes. The federal government attaches strings to the funds. The extent of the conditions reduces the effectiveness of state governments as units of government in their own right and transforms them into means of delivery for federal funds. It also prevents programmes being designed to take local conditions into account.

Block grants allow state governments much more discretion. Although funds have to be spent on the key areas of their responsibilities the states are free to distribute the money.

During the 1960s, categorical grants accounted for 98 per cent of grants. Under Nixon's **New Federalism** this declined to 75 per cent.

Lyndon Johnson's Great Society programmes led to a further expansion of the federal budget. Grants-in-aid amounted to $19 billion in 1968, having stood at $8 billion when he took over from Kennedy.

New Federalism

Since the 1960s the Republican presidents, particularly Richard Nixon (1969–74) and Ronald Reagan (1981–88), reacted against the system of grants-in-aid. Richard Nixon complained about the extent of federal government spending and the bureaucratic nature of grants-in-aid. In addition he claimed that federal government programmes encouraged state governments to accept funding for programmes they did not really need or want. Therefore grants-in-aid were making state and local governments dependent on central government. As a result President Nixon attempted to redefine federalism once more. This time it became known as New Federalism and it involved greater freedom for states and local governments in deciding how to spend funds.

Revenue-sharing

The main means by which Nixon intended to allow this greater discretion was **revenue-sharing**. This involved the federal government sharing some of its revenue with state and local governments. The idea was first proposed during the Kennedy administration, when economists were concerned that the federal government was accumulating too much money through budget surpluses.

Richard Nixon proposed revenue-sharing in 1969 but found some considerable opposition to it in Congress. Many committee chairs were unwilling to give up their power to direct so much of the federal government's finance. In addition many liberal members of Congress were reluctant to give such freedom to conservative, southern states. Eventually Congress did pass the State and Local Fiscal Assistance Act, which allocated $6 billion to be shared between the lower tiers of government.

Flexible funding

When added together, revenue-sharing and block grants, collectively known as **flexible funding**, accounted for 20 per cent of federal grants.

Despite the expansion of revenue-sharing, Nixon failed to achieve his basic objectives and the level of categorical grants has continued to rise. This can be attributed to the strength of bureaucratic power in the federal funding system. Federal government bureaucrats build cliental relationships not only with interest groups but also with state and local governments. The size of their budgets and their degree of control over them are important parts of their power base, which they are reluctant to give up.

'Picket-fence' federalism

Terry Sandford, former governor of North Carolina, has also referred to **'picket-fence' federalism** (*Storm over the States*, 1967). This is a reference to the control exercised by bureaucrats in the federal financing system. They work together closely, share the same training and belong to the same professional organizations. As a result they are likely to co-operate with each other, and wield a great deal of control over intergovernmental programmes.

Topocracy

Furthermore, state and local governments have gained greater *representation* in Washington since the 1960s. The National League of Cities and the US Conference of Mayors are just two examples of groups that lobby central government on behalf of the state and local government. American political scientist Samuel Beer has gone so far as to invent the term 'topocracy', which refers to rule by intergovernmental officials.

Reagan

President Reagan came to office in 1981 determined to reduce the size of the federal government. He adopted the New Federalism label that Nixon had used and began by proposing a greater use of block grants by combining 83 categorical grants into six major categories of block grant (health, preventive health, local education, state education, social services, and energy and emergency assistance). Despite some opposition Congress did approve some of these consolidations and some of the cuts in federal spending that Reagan also proposed.

'Swaps'

In 1982 Reagan took his plans for a New Federalism further by suggesting that the federal government would take full responsibility for Medicaid programmes if the state governments would take responsibility for food stamps and welfare. He also proposed that after a five-year period of grace the state governments would take responsibility for many more grants-in-aid programmes. Again the programme was met with hostility from Congress and the **'swaps'** and devolution of programmes to the states were abandoned.

The efforts of Nixon and, in particular, Reagan represent the most recent attempts to return to a system of federalism that relies less on the finance of the federal government. In effect it was an unsuccessful attempt to return to dual federalism.

'Marble-cake' federalism

In fact some political scientists have argued that dual federalism in the strictest sense never existed. Morton Grodzins (1917–1964) argued in *The American System* (1966) that the 'layer-cake' conception should be replaced by that of **'marble-cake' federalism.** This doctrine illustrates the fact that the responsibilities and powers of the federal and state governments are intertwined to such an extent that a strict separation is impossible.

Questions

Short questions

1 How are American cities governed? (ULEAC, June 1991)

2 What are the main sources of income of a State of the Union? (ULEAC, January 1993)

3 Distinguish between (a) dual and (b) co-operative federalism. (ULEAC, June 1993)

4 What was New Federalism? (ULEAC, January 1994)

5 What limits does the constitution impose on the action of individual states? (ULEAC, June 1994)

US questions

1 **a** What do you understand by 'dual federalism'?
b Why is it no longer possible?
(ULEAC, January 1995)

2 Is a federal system of government still appropriate for the United States? (ULEAC, June 1994)

3 **a** What are the main constitutional powers of the states?
b What are the major limitations on the exercise of these powers?
(ULEAC, June 1993)

4 Assess the changing relationship between the federal government and the states. (UCLES, June 1994)

5 Are the rights of individual states effectively protected in the USA? (UODLE, June 1992)

4 Elections

Questions to be answered in this chapter

- How are presidential candidates chosen?
- Why are American election campaigns so expensive?
- How does the electoral college affect the result of presidential elections?

Terms to know

- Advisory primaries
- Binding primary
- Brokered conventions
- Caucuses
- Closed primaries
- Counties
- Delegates
- Democracy
- Democratic Party
- Districts
- 'Dream ticket'
- Electoral college
- Fixed term
- 'Fratricidal strife'
- Incumbent
- Independent voters
- Mandatory primaries
- Marginal states
- 'Mercantilist' campaigns
- 'Militarist' campaigns
- National conventions
- Negative campaigning
- Nomination
- Open primaries
- Party bosses
- Policy platform
- Political action committees
- Precincts
- Primaries
- Primary season
- Proportional representation primaries
- Regional primaries
- Republican Party
- 'Soft money'
- 'Sound bites'
- 'Spin doctors'
- Super Tuesday
- Vice-president
- Voter loyalty
- Wards
- Winner-take-all primaries

The number of elections

Democratic principle

The separation of powers between federal and state governments and within federal government has ensured that the United States is a country of elections. The election of the president dominates the schedule of elections but the democratic principle penetrates down through 50 states and into 78,000 units of local government. Within these tiers of government elected officials include mayors, judges and even members of education committees. Altogether there are 700,000 elected offices in the United States.

The proliferation of elected offices gives meaning to the Americans' love of **democracy** but ironically at the higher levels of elected office the democratic credentials of the United States has been questioned due to the nature and immense cost of campaigns and, in the case of presidential elections, the undemocratic nature of the **electoral college.**

Presidential elections

In the United States all office holders do so for a **fixed term:** senators for six years, the president for four and congressmen for two. Therefore elections are held on regular cycle and, since 1914, have all been held in November. As a result the build-up to an American election begins early – usually more than a year in advance.

Comparison

In Britain general elections are called by the prime minister, via the monarch, whenever he or she wishes provided that the length of a parliament is no longer than five years. The campaign that follows the announcement of an election is three weeks in duration.

Presidential elections can be divided into three parts:
- the nomination process
- the election campaign itself
- the electoral college

January	July/August	November	January
Nomination Process	National Conventions	Election Day	Electoral College

The **nomination** process begins in January of election year and is designed to help the two major parties, who dominate elections, choose their presidential candidates. Therefore throughout this seven-month period Democratic candidates compete against other Democratic candidates and likewise on the Republican side. In effect it accomplishes the same aim as the heats or semi-final before the final itself, in which the Democratic candidate will run against the Republican candidate. Nomination

The primary season

The first stage of the nomination process is also known as the **primary season,** after the principal method of choosing between candidates (primaries).

During the primary season each party holds a 'competition' in every state to decide which of the selection of candidates they would like to represent the party in the 'final', the election proper. The candidates criss-cross the country competing for states.

Comparison

Parties in Britain put forward candidates for election to national and local levels of government. The main unit of party organization away from the centre is the constituency party and in both the Conservative and Labour parties this unit carries the prime responsibility for the selection of parliamentary candidates. Therefore only party members take part in the selection process – Conservative and Labour Party voters do not have a voice.

Winning delegates

The prizes in each of these contests are **delegates** to the national party conferences which are held in July/August. Each state has a value in terms of delegates. The worth of a state is determined both by the size of its population and the strength of the party in that state. If the party is strong in a particular state it might be given 'bonus' delegates for the convention. The candidate who accumulates a simple majority of the total delegates available across the country is adopted as that party's presidential candidate.

The competitions in each state can take one of two forms: a caucus or a primary.

Caucuses

A **caucus** is not one contest but a series of party meetings at every level of party organization within a state: **wards, precincts, districts** and **counties**. At each level, party members vote for delegates who will take their opinions on the choice of candidate forward to the next level. Ultimately the state conventions choose the delegates to the national convention.

Caucuses tend to be dominated by party activists who are sufficiently committed to the party's cause to take part in each stage. Proponents of the caucus method believe that consideration of candidates by party members allows the party to choose the best organized candidate who will be able to run a strong election campaign. The caucus continues to be used in a number of states, for example Iowa, but the majority of states use primaries.

Primaries

Primaries differ from caucuses mainly in their degree of participation. Whilst caucuses are dominated by party members, primaries allow broader participation by voters.

Closed primaries

Closed primaries offer greater participation than caucuses in that voting is not confined to party members. Those voters who have declared an affiliation to a party are allowed to participate in that party's primary. States holding closed primaries include New Hampshire and California.

Open primaries

Open primaries allow the widest participation of all. The voters of a state, regardless of their party affiliation, can participate in either the Democratic or the Republican primary, but not both. The advantage of open primaries is that the candidate chosen by a party will be the one with the greatest appeal across party lines. In the election proper this is an enviable characteristic. A disadvantage of open primaries is that they encourage voters to cross party lines and vote for the opposing party's worst candidate. Of the 50 states, 29 hold open primaries.

WTA and PR

Primaries also vary in terms of the allocation of delegates to the candidates. In

winner-take-all primaries the candidate who wins the most votes takes all of the delegates. The alternative, the **proportional representation primary**, allocates delegates in proportion to the votes cast in the primary. The latter system has been employed by the **Democratic Party** since the McGovern–Fraser Commission (1969) recommended such a change in an effort to increase the voice of minority groups in the party and to broaden the appeal of its candidates. However, more recently the party has allowed exceptional,'loophole' primaries to be held on a winner-take-all basis. Some states, particularly the larger ones, favour such a system as it increases their weight in the nomination process.

Advisory and mandatory

Finally, primaries will be either advisory or mandatory. In **advisory primaries** voters show their preferences for a presidential candidate but also vote, separately, for delegates to go to the national convention. In this case the vote for the presidential candidate is merely advisory and the delegates are free to state their own preferences. In a **mandatory primary**, or **binding primary**, voters cast their ballot for the presidential candidate only and delegates, selected by the party, cast their votes at the national convention accordingly. It is worth noting however that the Supreme Court, in *Democratic Party* v. *LaFollette* (1982), declared that a state could not force a delegate to a national party convention to support the winner of that state's presidential primary.

Primary dominance

Traditionally the caucus method predominated in the nomination process. Although the direct primary was first introduced in 1904 it did not significantly affect the process until the 1970s. In 1968 only 17 states held primaries to select candidates to the National Democratic Convention. By 1976 this number had risen to 31 and after a slide back to 24 in 1984 it returned to 31 in 1988. In the **Republican Party** a similar increase has occurred from 16 states in 1968 to 34 in 1988.

The structure of the primary season

Under the caucus system votes at the national convention could be controlled by the state and national party leaders, or **party bosses**. Therefore the favoured candidate had little need to worry about the primary season. However, with 77 per cent of all votes cast by delegates to the Republican Party Convention in 1988 determined by primaries, no candidate can afford to ignore the primary season.

New Hampshire

Since 1952 the New Hampshire primary has been the first and most important primary. It is the first major test of opinion for the candidates, and a good showing is vital if a candidate is to have any chance of winning the nomination. This is partly due to its traditional, even mythical, significance but also because a candidate's performance here will affect their financial position and their ability to rally party support. The political importance given to New Hampshire has been jealously guarded by its leaders, while the date of the primary has been pushed earlier and earlier as other small states have attempted to steal the limelight. The state legislature has acted to secure its position, declaring that the New Hampshire primary must be one week earlier than any other primary, by law. In 1992 it was held in February.

Super Tuesday

In 1988, 21 states, most of them in the south, decided to hold their primary on the same day, 8 March, which has become known as **Super Tuesday**. The aim was to counteract the importance of the New Hampshire primary, which many observers feel distorts the primary process because, being a small state in the North East, it is in no way representative of national opinion. Super Tuesday also elevates the standing of the southern states because candidates can be made or broken on one day, and it most benefits candidates who are from the south. In 1988 Senator Albert Gore (Tennessee) received a boost, though not enough to take him to the nomination and in 1992 Bill Clinton (Arkansas) virtually swept the board on Super Tuesday.

Outsiders

Party support, however, comes only when a candidate has proved their ability to attract support from all over the country and appears to be a viable candidate. Jimmy Carter's emergence in 1976 illustrates this very well. The ex-governor from Georgia was relatively unknown and despite early successes was regarded by many as an outsider who was basically a Southern candidate. Only when he proved his mettle in the North Eastern, industrial state of Pennsylvania did he appear to be a realistic candidate.

Midwest and California primaries

In 1996 the midwestern states of Illinois, Michigan and Ohio plan to hold their primaries on the third Tuesday in March, which should increase the voice of the midwest in the choice of candidates. A week later California will hold its primary. Traditionally California's primary, the largest primary of all, responsible for sending 20 per cent of both parties' delegates to the **national conventions**, is held in June, by which time the nominations are often sewn up. The new date puts it before New York and Pennsylvania and will reinforce its magnitude.

Campaign pressure

These changes mean that the primary season will shape up like this: New Hampshire (February); Super Tuesday (2nd Tuesday of March); New York (2nd week of March); Midwest (3rd Tuesday of March); California (4th Tuesday of March); and Pennsylvania (April). Therefore very early in the campaign candidates will need to be ready to launch intensive media campaigns in three major areas of the country. There will be little time for the candidates to raise money as their momentum builds up and the more well-known candidates will have a distinct advantage. And financial support has become even more important in the 1996 primary season because of the development of these **regional primaries** (see above).

Finance

Campaigning expenses

The primary season is extremely expensive and funded, in part, by donations. Only a candidate performing well in the early primaries will attract the necessary funding to allow their campaign to keep moving into June. Criss-crossing the entire country with a campaign organization in tow is extremely expensive and the development of campaigning via television has sent the bill spiralling ever upwards.

Spending limits

However, there are limits on spending in primary campaigns. In 1992 candidates were allowed to spend a maximum of $27 million. The nominal amount was set by the Federal Election Campaign Act (1974) at $10 million but this is adjusted in 'real' terms to meet today's prices. Candidates are then allowed to spend a further $4–5 million on fundraising and an unlimited amount on accounting and legal expenses.

Raising funds

There are also rules about how the money can be raised. Candidates can spend as much of their own money as they wish but can only take donations of $1,000 from individuals or $5,000 from **Political Action Committees**. If a candidate raises $5,000 in donations of no more than $250 from at least 20 states they are entitled to government funding or 'matching funds'. Under this system the government will match each donation, dollar for dollar, up to $250 per donor. However, the government will not contribute more than a maximum of $5 million to each candidate. Each of the main parties also receives funding for the organization of their national conventions. In 1988 this amounted to $2 million each.

Incumbent candidates

Re-election uncertainties

Often, the **incumbent** president will be competing for one of the parties as he seeks re-election. One might imagine that the incumbent would have an easy ride through the primaries but this is not always so. Lyndon Johnson's experiences as an incumbent illustrate the varying fortunes of presidents. In 1964 Johnson won the support of 100 per cent of the delegates at the Democratic Party's national convention and he went on to win the election, against Barry Goldwater, with a huge majority. In 1968 the Vietnam War took its toll and Johnson won just over 50 per cent of the vote in the New Hampshire primary, compared to the 42 per cent of anti-war candidate Eugene McCarthy. Prior to the contest the media had predicted that McCarthy would win no more than 20 per cent of the Democratic vote. His showing was enough for him to claim a 'victory' over Johnson. Shortly afterwards Robert Kennedy announced his intention to enter the race and President Johnson decided not to seek the Democratic Party's nomination.

Johnson's decision was probably correct in that incumbent presidents who have faced a significant challenge in the primaries have, in recent years, always lost the election itself. Gerald Ford (challenged by Ronald Reagan in 1976), Jimmy Carter (challenged by Edward Kennedy in 1980) and even George Bush (challenged by Pat Buchanan in 1992) all won their parties' nominations but went on to lose the election.

The national conventions

The primary season ends with both parties holding national conventions in July or August. Ostensibly the functions of the conventions are to select a presidential candidate and to adopt the party's **policy platform** prior to the presidential election campaign. In reality the conventions do adopt manifestos but they are not binding on candidates or state parties and the choice of candidate is usually sealed by the end of the primaries with one candidate arriving at the convention having the required number of delegates already on their side.

Choosing a presidential candidate

The nomination of candidates was not always a foregone conclusion. As recently as the 1960s the conventions were real choosing bodies. Adlai Stevenson, the Democratic candidate in 1952 and 1956, never ran in primaries, he awaited the party's call. Even John Kennedy did not have a majority of the delegates under his control when he arrived in 1960. Nevertheless the need for a second ballot is rare.

'Brokered conventions'

The proposed changes in the timing of key primaries in the midwest and California could have serious implications for future national conventions. The evolution of regional primaries invites competition between regional candidates. If no single candidate is able to break clear of the crowd the national convention will, once again, be asked to choose rather than anoint the winning candidate. The convention is, as Byron E Shafer, the American political scientist, has suggested: 'a nominator of last resort'. Conventions in which decisions are reached by protracted bargaining between party leaders are known as **brokered conventions**, and the manoeuvring in 'smoke-filled rooms' can be highly controversial.

1968 The most divisive and damaging of all recent conventions was the Democratic Party national convention of 1968. Noting the beneficial effects for Republican Richard Nixon's fortunes, Nixon's biographer Stephen Ambrose describes how the Democratic Party tore itself apart: 'Inside the convention hall the delegates, tightly controlled by Lyndon Johnson, nominated Hubert Humphrey, who had not won a single primary; outside the hall the Chicago police ... went on a rampage against the youthful demonstrators of the New Left, who for their part were engaged in provoking the cops in every imaginable way ... It was a shameful disgrace for all concerned ... The only winner was Richard Nixon.' (Nixon: *The Triumph of a Politician, 1962-72*, 1989).

1972 Four years later Nixon benefited from yet another Democratic Party national convention that became a shambles – not, on this occasion, because there was any doubt about the choice of candidate, but simply due to shoddy organization and complete lack of discipline. As Stephen Ambrose states: 'The Democrats gave an appearance of being anti-religion and pro-drugs, anti-profit and pro-welfare, anti-family and pro-abortion, anti-farmer and pro-migrant worker, anti-Saigon and pro-Hanoi, anti-armed forces and pro-draft dodgers.'

The high point of any convention should be the candidate's acceptance of the party's nomination and the candidate's choice of running mate. In 1972 the undisciplined demonstrations of the delegates prevented George McGovern accepting the nomination until 2.30 a.m. As McGovern himself has reflected, that was television's prime-time in Guam and a key publicity opportunity was lost. The Democrats were in disarray and Richard Nixon went on to a landslide victory in the election.

Media events

Modern conventions

Conventions were described by the author Norman Mailer as: 'a fiesta, a carnival, a pig-rooting, horse-snorting, band-playing, voice screaming medieval get-together of greed, practical lust, compromised idealism, career-advancement, meeting, feud, vendetta, conciliation of rabble-rousers, fist fights (as it used to be), embraces, drunks (again as it used to be) and collective rivers of animal sweat.' (*Some Honourable Men*, 1976). Today the chair of the Democratic or Republican national committees would be horrified if their conventions lived up to Mailer's description. Their aim is to run a highly stage-managed party jamboree that will portray the party in the best possible light. For it is publicity and communication that dictates the nature of the modern convention.

Choreography

The Republican Party national conventions under Nixon and Reagan were highly organized and choreographed. Floor managers ensured that everything ran like clockwork and that the convention would act as a week-long advertisement for the party and the candidate. The aim was that their candidate would emerge from the conventions with a lead in the opinion polls.

Uniting the party

A national convention is also the time to bring the party together. As intra-party conflict primaries are necessarily divisive, a tendency sometimes referred to as **'fratricidal strife'**, the convention can rally the party behind the candidate and send delegates back to their states ready to work on the election campaign.

Occasionally conventions have failed to do this, however, and usually with disastrous 1964
results. The divisions in the Democratic Party in 1968 have already been mentioned, but such divisions have not been confined to the Democrats. In 1964 the nomination of right-winger Barry Goldwater split the Republican Party down the middle when with his acceptance speech he cast aside half of the party: 'Those who do not care for our cause we do not expect to enter our ranks in any case.' He went on to remind delegates that: 'Extremism in the defence of liberty is no vice! Moderation in the pursuit of justice is no virtue.'

The deep divisions within the Republican Party resurfaced in 1992 when George Bush, 1992
always sensitive to criticism as a moderate, allowed the right to take over the convention. As a result the Republicans did not address the key issues of the economy and unemployment; instead they concentrated on patriotism, family values, opposition to abortion, and Christianity.

Choosing a vice-presidential candidate

The final task of a national convention is to select a vice-presidential candidate, or

Choosing the vice-president

The **vice-president** is elected by the electorate on a joint ticket with the president. This means, as they cannot split their vote between president and vice-president, the electorate has no say in the choice of vice-president. They choose a president and get a vice-president thrown in.

Therefore the important choices regarding the vice-president are those made at the party conventions when the presidential candidates choose a running-mate.

If, however, the office of vice-president becomes vacant in mid-term, the 25th Amendment (1967) lays down the procedure for their replacement. The president nominates a new vice-president who must then be confirmed by a majority vote in both houses of Congress.

The first vice-president to be appointed according to that procedure was Gerald Ford who succeeded Spiro Agnew in 1973. One year later Ford became president following Richard Nixon's resignation and so became the only president in American history not to be elected to the office.

running-mate, for the election campaign. Under normal circumstances the presidential candidate's choice of running-mate is accepted with little controversy. Although in 1972 George McGovern's nomination of Senator Thomas Eagleton as his vice-presidential candidate was followed by 39 additional nominations from the floor; they included the name of Mao Tse-tung, leader of the People's Republic of China.

'Dream ticket'

The choice of running-mate is an important part of the build-up to the election campaign and attention focuses on the contribution the vice-presidential candidate will make to the campaign rather than to the administration. Therefore the candidate chosen usually complements the presidential candidate in order to broaden the appeal of the 'ticket'. The so-called **'dream ticket'** of 1960 brought John Kennedy and Lyndon Johnson together and their partnership is the clearest illustration of this strategy in practice. Kennedy was young, relatively inexperienced, a Catholic and a liberal from the East. Johnson was older and considerably more experienced, a Protestant and assumed to be more conservative because he was from Texas.

Quayle

Since then successive presidential tickets have been built in the same way. Walter Mondale chose Geraldine Ferraro, a congresswoman from New York, in 1984, George Bush chose the younger and more right-wing Dan Quayle in 1988 and Michael Dukakis, who had been governor of Massachusetts, chose the vastly experienced Lloyd Bentsen from Texas.

Gore

Bill Clinton's choice of running-mate, Albert Gore, was a slight departure from this pattern. Gore is almost the same age as Clinton and is, like the president, a relatively conservative Democrat from the South. However, Gore does have more Washington experience than Clinton and is particularly strong on foreign affairs. The thinking behind Clinton's choice was to garner as many votes as possible from the southern states, and to put forward an all-southern ticket seemed the best way to do this.

The election campaign

The national conventions are usually followed by a brief rest before the candidates get back on to the campaign trail. This time the contest is between the Republican Party ticket and the Democratic Party ticket, with occasional competition from a third party. And, unlike the primaries, candidates must appeal to the general public rather than party supporters.

Electoral college

Candidates spend two months travelling around the country, meeting as many people as possible, attempting to get their message across. However, the presidential election is not a nationwide opinion poll. As in the primary stage, each state is a self-contained unit carrying a particular value in the electoral college. The value is determined by the number of senators a state has plus the number of congressmen representing the state. Although each state has two senators the number of congressmen varies with the size of the population in the state. Therefore certain states are more important for victory than others. In fact it is possible to gain the required number of delegates to the electoral college by winning the 14 biggest states.

Comparison

British parliamentary election campaigns are dominated by national party campaigns. Although local candidates and activists play some role in fundraising and ensuring that party supporters actually vote most media attention is focused on the party leaders. In recent general elections party political broadcasts, television and radio interviews, stage-managed media events, 'photo opportunities' and **'sound bites'** have been predominant.

The geography of the campaign

Candidates organize their campaigns in the light of their support in particular states. Relatively little time will be spent in the states that a candidate seems certain to lose or, indeed, to win. Most resources will be allocated to the **marginal states**, those that will swing the election one way or the other.

Shaping the message

Regional variations

It is not only the itinerary that is shaped according to geography; it is also true of a candidate's message. The attitudes of voters and the issues which are at the top of the agenda vary across the country and candidates must be sensitive to these variations. In the Midwest, agricultural issues, such as subsidies, are likely to predominate whilst in the East, unemployment and law and order are likely to be important. Therefore a candidate will identify regional differences and adjust their speeches accordingly.

Broad messages

Given the likelihood that a detailed policy on every issue is sure to alienate someone, leading candidates tend to opt for a relatively vague set of messages rather than detailed policies. Patriotism, family values and law and order are priorities with which most people agree and they offend or alienate few people. Therefore candidates often concentrate on these issues, attempting to be better Americans than their opponents.

Simple ideas

A candidate's campaign is often defined by simple ideas and phrases. In 1984 the theme of Ronald Reagan's re-election bid was defined by an advertisement used in the campaign, known as 'Morning in America'. In 1988 George Bush promised a 'kinder, gentler America', 'no new taxes' and little else.

Negative campaigning

In recent years the candidates' tendency to say little about themselves has been accompanied by a desire to say a great deal about their opponent. This is known as **negative campaigning**. George Bush was criticized for running a negative campaign against Governor Dukakis. For much of the campaign Bush attacked his opponent as a 'liberal', not normally a pejorative term, but in Bush's hands it became the 'L-word'. Ronald Reagan had linked 'liberal' to high-spending and high-taxing governments; Bush went further and linked it to permissiveness, which carried connotations of the chaos of the 1960s.

Negative advertising

Dukakis was also subjected to negative advertisements. The most famous of these was about the prison furlough programme in Massachusetts, which Dukakis had overseen as state governor. Willie Horton had been allowed out of prison on a weekend furlough programme and, whilst out, had raped a woman and stabbed her boyfriend. The Bush campaign blamed Dukakis. They ran advertisements showing prisons with revolving doors, allowing prisoners to come and go as they pleased. In Illinois there was even a leaflet which said: 'All the murderers and rapists and drug pushers and child molesters in Massachusetts vote for Michael Dukakis.'

'Daisy Girl' advertisement

Negative campaigning in the United States is by no means new. Perhaps the most famous negative advertisement of all is 'The Daisy Girl' from the 1964 campaign. Johnson sought to portray his right-wing opponent, Barry Goldwater, as a warmonger who could not be trusted with nuclear weapons. The advertisement showed a little girl plucking the petals off a daisy whilst the countdown to a nuclear explosion sounded in the background.

Comparison

In the UK political parties are not allowed to buy advertising space on television. Television promotion is limited to party political broadcasts allocated to all of the main parties according to their representation in the House of Commons.

This may be partly responsible for the relative lack of negative campaigning in British politics. Although political parties and their leaders are subjected to scathing criticism during a campaign – recent general election campaigns have included 'Labour isn't working' (1979) and 'Labour's tax bomb'(1992) – a relatively small proportion is dedicated to personal scandal and gossip.

Limits of negative campaigning

The 1992 campaign seemed to suggest that the effect of negative campaigning is limited. George Bush again attempted to smear his opponent with accusations of marital infidelity, liberalism and lack of patriotism. On this occasion they worked against President Bush who seemed to be ignoring the key issues of law and order and the economy.

The style of the campaign

Independent voters

The development of negative campaigning and the shaping of messages to suit the audience is linked to the changing behaviour of the American electorate. In 1940 only 20 per cent of the electorate considered themselves 'independent'; that is, they did not identify themselves with one party or the other. By 1986 this figure had risen to 32 per cent. With this increase in the number of **independent voters**, the politicians have to work much harder to win votes.

'Militarist' campaign

In the nineteenth century the level of **voter loyalty** was very high. Voting patterns were predictable and the main aim of any candidate was to ensure that all of their supporters actually turned out to vote. This type of campaign has been called a **'militarist' campaign** (Richard Jensen, 1968) because it involves marshalling the troops who are already committed to one side or another. The rise of the independent voter has forced politicians to run **'mercantilist' campaigns** (Jensen, 1968), designed to persuade them to vote Democrat or Republican.

The need for persuasive campaigns has resulted in candidates turning to advertising techniques for their campaign tactics. Since the 1960s candidates have been packaged like any other product by advisers like Robert Ailes (adviser to Bush, 1988–92) and James Carville (Bill Clinton's campaign manager, 1992). The ideal medium for such selling techniques is television; on television, as the author Joe McGinniss has said: 'Style becomes substance. The medium is the massage and the masseur gets the votes.' (*The Selling of the President, 1968*, 1969). Candidates have used television in three ways: for the official debates, advertising and news coverage.

'Mercantilist' campaign

The presidential campaign of 1960 between John Kennedy and Richard Nixon heralded the beginning of the new era of television politics. The election debate of that year has gone down in the annals of election campaigns as an illustration of the potentially powerful alliance between television and politician. Vice-President Nixon, an accomplished debater with a well-known track record in politics, agreed to debate with the relatively unknown Senator Kennedy. Nixon arrived at the studio having been ill, wearing a light grey suit that simply blended into the studio background and he refused to wear make-up. Kennedy was young, good-looking, sun-tanned and clearly defined in his dark grey suit. Those who listened to the debate on the radio believed Nixon had won; those who watched on television believed Kennedy had been the victor. The importance of image in debates has persisted. The journalist Meg Greenfield wrote in *The Washington Post* in 1984 that: 'without exception, all those candidates who are generally thought to have lost their debates ... have believed themselves to have won "on the facts" and lost on some intangibles and presence and performance.'

TV debate of 1960

Comparison

British political parties have increasingly turned to sophisticated advertising techniques. Party political broadcasts in particular have given parties the opportunities to sell themselves.

A highlight of recent campaigns has included Labour leader Neil Kinnock's broadcast of 1987. Directed by Hugh Hudson, who was responsible for the film *Chariots of Fire*, the broadcast, very presidential in style, concentrated on Neil Kinnock's background and beliefs and ended by inviting the audience to 'vote Kinnock'.

Since 1960 the debates have become a regular part of most presidential campaigns and have been surrounded by a great deal of 'hype'. Occasionally a line or image from a debate has helped to clarify the choices of the campaign. Ronald Reagan, at the conclusion of the 1980 debate with Jimmy Carter, asked the viewers to consider if they were better off than four years earlier. That question concentrated the minds of the voters and consolidated opposition to Carter.

1980 debate

Other debates have had relatively little effect on campaigns. In 1984 President Reagan performed poorly in the debate with Walter Mondale, largely due to a strategy,

1984 debate

The 1992 presidential election

The 1992 presidential election result can be analysed from two broad perspectives: why George Bush lost or why Bill Clinton won.

In 1991 President Bush appeared to be unassailable regarding the election in 1992 His apparent successes in bringing an end to the Cold War and the fall of the Berlin Wall and the liberation of Kuwait in the Gulf War had elevated Bush's approval ratings to unprecedented levels – 89 per cent in a Gallup Poll of March 1991. Nevertheless one year later he had lost the election, polling a smaller percentage of votes (37.5) than any presidential incumbent since 1912.

Explanations of Bush's gradual decline in opinion polls to ultimate election defeat concentrate on the economic recession in America. Although the recession was by no means deep, it was prolonged. The trade deficit, the budget deficit and slow economic growth led to pessimism about the Bush presidency. Furthermore Bush's campaign strategy seemed to do little to tackle the mood of the country. He concentrated on the themes of patriotism and trust whilst attacking Governor Clinton about alleged extra-marital affairs and dodging the draft into the US armed forces during the Vietnam War. As a result Bush appeared to be disengaged from American domestic politics and unable to grasp the mood of the American people.

Bill Clinton's strategy for winning the 1992 presidential election was based on the decline of the traditional Democratic coalition of support – both geographically and socially. The New Deal coalition of unionized labour, southern democrats, ethnic minorities, poor whites and the liberal intellectuals has been disintegrating for many years. The decline of trade unions, the advance of the service sectors and technology-based industry, the migration to the suburbs and the disillusionment of white southern democrats with the Democratic Party have all contributed to shrinking support for the party. Clinton therefore attempted to put together a ticket and a policy platform that would appeal to the middle classes and to voters in areas of recent Democratic Party weakness – particularly the south.

Clinton's ticket was all southern for the first time since 1888 and policies such as a better health care system, investment in economic infrastructure and economic growth were designed to appeal to the insecurities of the middle-class whites; and Clinton's campaign stressed the need to change to a new era led by a new generation. Clinton and Gore styled themselves as New Democrats, in contrast with the 'tax-and-spend' liberals so criticized by Bush.

The success of Clinton's strategy is by no means clear. His proportion of the vote was lower (43 per cent) than that of Michael Dukakis four years earlier. There is no evidence to suggest that he made any inroads into the Republican social base. However, the geographical gains in the south, west and the north-east were crucial to Clinton's win. In the south the 'southern ticket' helped; in California concern about crime and recession may have tipped the balance; whilst in the north-east the fear of unemployment gave Clinton his largest lead over Bush.

It is not clear if Ross Perot's candidacy took more votes from Bush than Clinton and contributed to the former's defeat but his candidacy certainly complicated electoral politics.

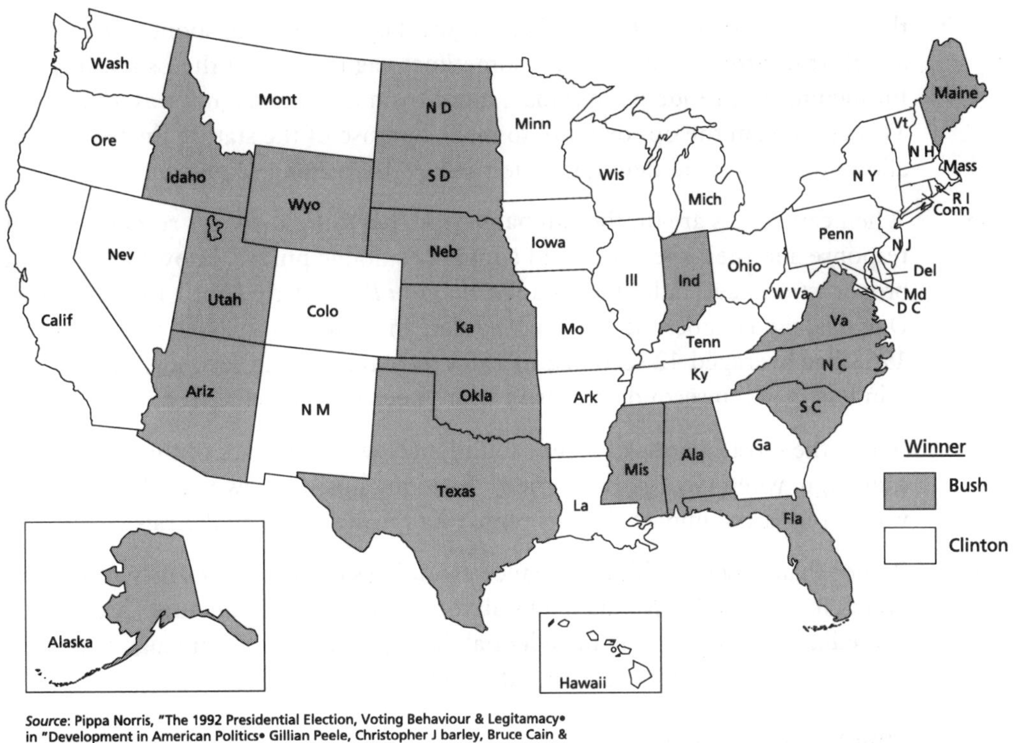

Source: Pippa Norris, "The 1992 Presidential Election, Voting Behaviour & Legitamacy• in "Development in American Politics• Gillian Peele, Christopher J barley, Bruce Cain & B. Guy Peters (eds). Macmillan 1994.

Figure 4.1 Electoral college 1992 US election

mapped out by political consultant Pat Cadell, to throw Reagan on to the defensive. Nevertheless the effect on Reagan's opinion poll rating and the final election result was minimal.

Buying an image

The idea of the candidate being promoted like soap powder is taken literally in America, where candidates are free to buy advertising slots on television channels. The advertisements are used to get a candidate's message across about a particular issue, or to portray a positive image of the candidate or a negative image of an opponent. Like the debates, the impact that candidates' advertisements have on voters is unclear, although they probably do have the effect of reinforcing the public's preconceived perceptions. Ray Price, who advised Richard Nixon on his television strategy in 1968, summed up the importance of perception in a memo of 1967: '*the response is to the image, not to the man* ... It's not what's *there* that counts, it's what's projected and ... it's not what *he* projects but rather what the voter receives. It's not the man we have to change, but rather the *received impression*.'

Daily news

Finally candidates will gain television exposure as part of daily news coverage. Even here nothing is left to chance as candidates and their advisers strive to manipulate coverage to advance their cause. The campaign managers will ensure that their candidates' schedules contain the best photo-opportunities and that seemingly spontaneous situations are highly stage-managed. The degree of control is more important for some candidates than for others. In 1972 Richard Nixon chose not to appear in public very often, preferring to remain 'presidential' and slightly distant from the campaign. In 1984 Ronald Reagan was kept away from spontaneous situations in an effort to protect him from his sometimes vague grasp of the issues. It is not unusual for incumbent presidents to remain aloof from the campaign for as long as possible. This gives them the opportunity to make best use of the stature their office bestows and allows them to avoid defending their record for as long as possible.

'Sound bites'

When candidates are on the campaign trail they should always receive an enthusiastic response and their speech should contain a suitable phrase, known as a 'sound bite', for broadcast on news bulletins. In a *Washington Post* article (April 1990) Michael Dukakis, the Democratic Party's candidate in 1988, complained that sound bites in 1968 had averaged 42 seconds; in 1988 they average 9.8 seconds: 'If you couldn't say it in less than ten seconds, it wasn't heard because it wasn't aired.'

In fact the most famous of recent sound bites was a product of the 1988 election campaign, when George Bush cried: 'Read my lips: no new taxes.' Two years later he was to regret the impact that his phrase had made when he did raise taxes.

'Spin doctors'

Rather than leave anything to chance candidates employ staff solely to interpret news events for the media. Media manipulators, so-called **'spin doctors'**, are most active immediately following the presidential debates when both campaign teams try to convince the press that their candidate won.

Finance of campaigns

Modern 'mercantilist' campaigns are extremely expensive. In 1992 the independent candidate, Ross Perot, reportedly spent $60 million of his own money on his election campaign. The candidates from the two main parties spent a total of $110.4 million. This was government funding and it is given in addition to the funds allocated for use in the primaries.

FECA

The quid pro quo of a candidate accepting federal funding is that they must also accept spending limits. This arrangement was laid down in the 1974 Federal Election Campaign Act (FECA). According to this act a candidate is not allowed to raise or spend money in excess of $20 million. This is raised in line with inflation for each campaign. In 1992 it had reached $55.2 million per candidate. In addition the parties were allowed to spend an additional $10.3 million directly on their candidate's campaign.

'Soft money'

The Republican and Democratic parties also raise **'soft money'**, which is money collected outside the limits of FECA. It cannot be spent directly on a campaign for this would violate FECA and so parties use the money to invest in equipment, develop their accommodation, and to finance party-orientated advertisements and efforts to 'get out the vote', i.e. to make sure that supporters actually turn out to vote.

Contribution rules

The rules regarding contributions are the same as those for the primaries because primaries and the election proper count as two elections. Individuals can contribute $1,000 with a maximum of $25,000 to election campaigns in any one year. Political Action Committees (PACs) can contribute a maximum of $5,000 to a candidate's campaign but there are no limits on PAC spending on behalf of a candidate, so long as it is independent of the candidate's campaign structure.

Comparison

In Britain most election campaigns are financed by money raised at national party level and most of that money is also spent on the national campaign. British election campaign law encourages this pattern as there are limits on spending by constituency candidates but not on national party organizations.

The electoral college

Indirect voting

As stated above, a presidential election is not a national opinion poll. The Founding Fathers decided that the people should only indirectly choose their president. When voters cast their vote in the presidential election, therefore, they are actually voting for a group of delegates who will cast their votes on behalf of the state in the electoral college.

Delegates

How many delegates each state has depends on its representation in the Senate and House of Representatives. Every state has two senators but the number of congressmen depends on the population of the state. According to this calculation in 1988 California had 47 delegates (2 + 45), New York 36 (2 + 34) and Alaska had 3 (2 + 1). Although not a state, Washington DC also sends three delegates to the electoral college.

The votes are counted on a winner-take-all basis, and the leading candidate in a state takes all of the electoral college delegates from that state. Candidates are elected president when they gain an overall majority of the total electoral college delegates. If no candidate is able to gain an overall majority the decision is referred to the House of Representatives, where congressmen will vote in state blocks, each block having one vote.

Comparison

British elections are conducted on a first-past-the-post, or winner-take-all, basis. This means that parties win constituencies so long as their candidate has more votes than their nearest rival, rather than needing an overall majority. As a result there is often a discrepancy between the proportion of votes a party receives and the percentage of seats gained in the House of Commons.

'Faithless voter'

The delegates themselves are either selected by voters when they are casting their vote for president or are chosen at meetings of the winning party in that state. The electors meet in their state capital (the whole electoral college no longer meets) to cast their votes, usually in January. Conventionally they cast their votes according to the popular vote in their state. However, they are not bound to do so and occasionally someone will refuse. They are referred to as 'faithless voters'. In 1988 a delegate in West Virginia cast her presidential vote for Lloyd Bentsen (vice-presidential candidate) and her vice-presidential vote for Michael Dukakis (the presidential candidate).

Winners can lose

The electoral college has been criticized because its winner-take-all basis can distort the

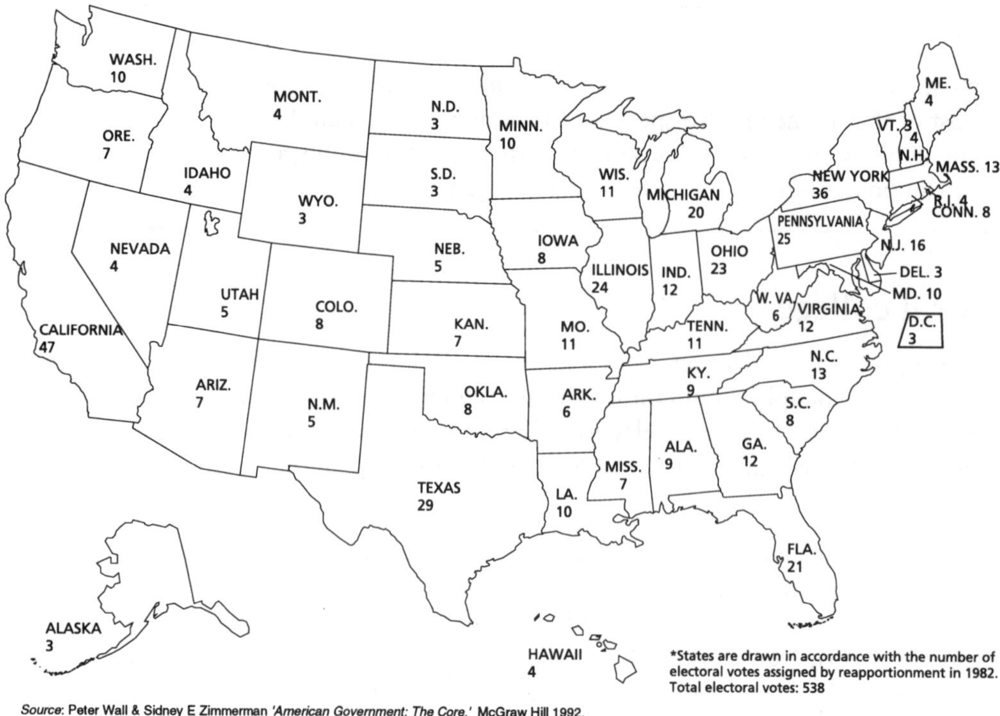

Figure 4.2 The electoral college: apportionment of electoral votes

election result. Three times in history – 1824, 1876 and 1888 – the candidate who won the popular vote did not become president. In 1888 Grover Cleveland gained 100,000 votes more than Benjamin Harrison but was defeated in the electoral college by 233 votes to 168.

However, under normal circumstances the electoral college is merely a formality and the identity of the next president is known on election night in November.

Congressional elections

Congress is divided into two houses:

- the Senate
- the House of Representatives

Senators represent entire states, with two senators coming from each state, regardless of the population. Members of the House, or congressmen, represent districts within states, each with a population of approximately 450,000.

Congressional elections occur every two years. Members of the House of Representatives serve a two-year term and so the whole house comes up for re-election every two years. Members of the Senate serve a six-year term on a staggered system with a third of senators coming up for re-election every two years.

Mid-term elections

Mid-term elections are congressional and local elections that occur every four years in the middle of a president's term of office. In other words they occur in non-presidential election years.

At the federal level the whole of the House and one third of the Senate come up for re-election mid-term. Therefore they are very significant elections, which can change the balance of power in Washington DC. This was clearly illustrated in 1994 when Republican victories in the House and Senate gave control of Congress to the Republican Party for the first time in 40 years.

Such a swing from one party to another has serious implications for a president. Since 1994 President Clinton's outlook has changed dramatically. When he won the presidency in 1992 he faced a Congress controlled by his own party, the Democrats. Today Capitol Hill is controlled by the Republicans, and the President has moved from an uneasy relationship with a Democratic Congress to an almost impossible relationship with his Republican opponents. Conflict between the White House and Congress reached such a pitch in November 1995 that a budget could not be agreed and the federal government was almost brought to a standstill.

Mid-term elections can also have an impact on a president's standing with his own party. Here again President Clinton's position illustrates this problem with many Democrats blaming the President for their poor performance in the polls.

Mid-term elections can therefore have serious implications for the impending presidential campaign, with the fortunes of an incumbent president and potential challengers changing considerably. Usually it is the president's party that fares badly as the voters make the president aware of their 'mid-term blues'.

Primaries

Congressional campaigns

Like presidential candidates the majority of candidates for congressional office are nominated through a system of primaries. Since the 1960s the system has spread across the country so that most candidates are selected by the voters rather than the party. As a result congressional campaigns have been affected in the same way as presidential campaigns. Political parties have been weakened, so candidates organize and finance their own campaigns, owing their election to their constituents more than their party.

Finance

The advent of the primary in congressional elections has meant that, like presidential candidates, candidates for Congress campaign as individuals as much as members of a party. They have their own campaign teams, they sell themselves on television just like any other product and, in order to make this possible, they raise a great deal of money to pay for their campaigns.

FECA

Traditionally a candidate's endorsement by a party or group would be enough to secure sufficient funds to pay for a campaign. However, in the wake of Watergate, the Federal Election Campaign Act (FECA) of 1974 imposed limits on the funds that can be accepted from political parties, groups and wealthy individuals. National, congressional and state parties are limited to contributions of up to $5,000 each to House candidates and a total of $22,500 to candidates for the Senate. In addition the parties at all three of these levels are permitted to make 'co-ordinated expenditures' on behalf of candidates. This money can be spent on advertising, posters, etc. in co-operation with the candidates' own spending. In 1992 the parties at each level (national, congressional and state) were allowed to spend $27,620 for House candidates and for Senate candidates a sum that varies with the population of the state. In 1992 for the smallest states this was set at $55,250 and in California $1,227,322.

PACs

Interest groups also contribute to congressional election campaigns through their Political Action Committees (PACs). Once again FECA places limits on these contributions – $5,000 per candidate. However PACs can contribute to party funds or to 'soft money' accounts (see page 60). In 1992 the Republican Party National

Congressional elections 1994

The Democratic Party might have expected the mid-term elections of 1994 to be bad – for an incumbent party they often are. However, they could never have predicted the extent of the defeat they experienced.

In 1992 the Democrats had a majority of 56:44 in the Senate and it was here that their control of the legislature looked vulnerable. The Republicans needed to win only 7 seats to take control of the Senate. Of the 35 being contested the Democrats held 22 of which six were 'open', in that the incumbent was retiring (Arizona, Maine, Michigan, Ohio, Oklahoma and Tennessee). In the event, the Republicans held all of their own seats, took all of the open seats and won a further two seats by defeating incumbents in Pennsylvania and Tennessee. This gave the Republicans a majority of 52:48.

Despite the fact that all House seats were up for grabs Democrats felt secure; their dominance had been unbroken since 1952. Even during periods of unpopularity, such as 1978 when Jimmy Carter had been in office for two years, the Democrats had lost only a few seats in the House – 15 in 1978. However, the Democratic Party faced some serious difficulties: re-apportionment of some congressional districts to favour black candidates left the surrounding districts white-dominated and susceptible to Republican attack; a higher than normal level of incumbents was retiring; the Republicans in the House were campaigning on a national platform – 'The Contract With America'; and right-wing groups in the south, such as the National Rifle Association and the Christian Coalition, were enthusiastic in their mobilization of support against the unpopular Bill Clinton.

As a result the standings in the House were transformed from a Democrat majority of 78 to a Republican lead of 28.

Committee raised $51 million in 'soft money'; whilst the Democratic Party national congressional and senatorial campaign committees raised $36 million.

Republican advantage

In addition to contributions and donations the candidates also rely on their own funds. As a result the Republican Party and its candidates have been able to raise considerably more money than their Democratic counterparts. Their personal wealth and their access to big business allowed the Republican Party to collect $275 million in 1992, almost $100 million more than the Democratic party and its candidates.

Democratic Party success

Since 1946 the Democratic Party has dominated congressional elections. Until the 1994 mid-term elections Democrats had failed to win control of the House for only four years (1946–48 and 1950–52). Their control over the Senate had been equally impressive until 1980, when the Republicans gained a majority, on the coat-tails of Ronald Reagan, that endured for six years.

The reason for Democrat dominance seems to be the fact that the coalition of supporters forged for the party in 1932 by Franklin Roosevelt has been in the majority for much of the post-war period. This base of support consisted of immigrant families in the northern cities, unionized labour, poor working-class whites, southern Democrats, the elderly and African-Americans.

In the mid-term elections of 1994 this dominance came to a dramatic end.

Incumbency

Advantages

A major feature of congressional elections since 1945 has been the success of incumbent candidates. Between 1945 and 1992, 92 per cent of all incumbent congressmen and 75 per cent of incumbent senators running for re-election have been successful. This has resulted in many seats remaining uncontested. On average 50–70 House seats remain uncontested. Reasons for the incumbents' domination of elections include their control of the resources used to promote themselves and their ability to attract funds from interest groups. Incumbents are able to attract media attention by making speeches, they have access to free mailing to their constituents and have staff to look after constituency interests. They are also easy targets for funds from interest groups who see them as better investments than the challengers. From an interest group's point of view it makes sense to support the candidate with whom they already have a relationship. As a result of their links with pressure groups incumbent candidates can spend 200–400 per cent more than the challengers.

The advantages of incumbency have raised fears that Capitol Hill could be populated by a political elite, safe from challenges and accountability. However, 1992 was considered an anti-incumbent year. Anti-Washington sentiment led many challengers to come forward and only 17 House seats remained uncontested. Nevertheless 70 per cent of members of Congress taking up office in 1993 were incumbents.

Mid-term 1994

The mid-term elections of 1994 did bring some major surprises as some well-known incumbents were toppled from power. Speaker of the House, Tom Foley, was defeated (the first time a Speaker has been defeated at the polls since 1860), as was Jack Brooks, chair of the House Judiciary Committee. However, once again most incumbents survived, including Edward Kennedy in Massachusetts, Charles Robb in Virginia and Dianne Feinstein in California.

Questions

Short questions

1 a What were the main features of the 1974 Federal Campaign Reform Act?
  b Assess its impact on presidential elections.
  (ULEAC, June 1991)

2 a What are open primaries?
  b Are they more democratic than caucuses?
  (ULEAC, January 1992)

3 a How is the vice-president chosen?
  b What are the major considerations which affect the choice?
  (ULEAC, June 1992)

4 Account for Clinton's victory in the 1992 presidential election. (ULEAC, June 1993)

5 What criticisms can be made of the caucus process? (ULEAC, January 1994)

US questions

1 Explain Clinton's 1992 presidential election victory. (ULEAC, June 1994)

2 'The frequency, complexity and expense of elections do little to promote democracy.' Discuss. (ULEAC, January 1995)

3 What criticisms would you make of the process by which Americans nominate and elect their presidents? (UCLES, June 1994)

4 What is the contemporary significance of national party conventions in the presidential nomination process? (UODLE, June 1993)

5 What factors will a presidential candidate have in mind in selecting his vice-presidential running mate? (AEB, June 1991)

6 'Despite the many criticisms of primaries, they remain the fairest way yet devised to select presidential candidates.' Discuss. (UODLE, June 1992)

7 Does television educate the electorate or trivialize the issues in presidential elections? (UODLE, June 1994)

8 Presidential election results 1960–1988

Year	*% popular vote*		*Electoral college votes*		
	Democratic	*Republican*	*Democratic*	*Republican*	*Other*
1960	49.7	49.5	303	219	15
1964	61.1	38.5	486	52	0
1968	42.7	43.4	191	301	46
1972	37.5	60.7	17	520	1
1976	50.1	48.0	297	240	1
1980	41.0	50.7	49	489	0
1984	40.6	58.8	13	525	0
1988	45.5	54.5	112	426	0

(Taken from *The 1988 American Elections: Long, Medium and Short Term Explanations* by Dr Pippa Norris in the April 1989 edition of *The Political Quarterly*.)

Why are there such significant variations between the popular vote and the electoral college vote? Examine the effect of the electoral college system on the campaign strategies of candidates and consider how campaigns might differ if the president were elected instead by popular vote. (AEB, June 1991)

Comparative essays

1 It has been claimed that for all their apparent differences, US party conventions and UK party conferences are in fact identical in their ultimate purpose of legitimating decisions taken elsewhere.

Assess the accuracy of this statement and consider whether party conventions and party conferences are equally important in the two countries. (AEB, June 1993)

2 Compare and contrast the functions of elections in different countries. (Illustrate your answer with reference to at least two countries.) (ULEAC, January 1991)

5 Political parties

Questions to be answered in this chapter

- What is the nature of the American party system?
- How powerful are American parties in the American political system?
- How successful are third parties in American politics?

Terms to know

- Candidate-orientated
- 'Catch-all' parties
- Coalition
- Conservatives
- Counties
- Dixiecrats
- Electoral role
- 'Factions'
- Federalists
- Governing role
- Liberals
- 'Machine politics'
- Mass party
- National committees
- New Democrats
- Party bosses
- Party chair
- Precincts
- Seniority rule
- 'Solid south'
- State parties
- 'Superdelegates'
- Third parties
- Transient parties
- Two-party system
- Wards

Introduction

Factions

The Founding Fathers placed political parties and pressure groups in the same bracket and referred to both, in derogatory fashion, as **'factions'**. James Madison, in *The Federalist* No. 10, proudly proclaimed that: 'Among the numerous advantages promised by a well constructed union, none deserves to be more accurately developed than its tendency to break and control the violence of faction.'

Madison wrote these words as part of a series of articles, with Alexander Hamilton and John Jay, under the pseudonym the Federalist, in support of the constitution agreed at Philadelphia. The series was necessary because only 39 of 55 delegates to the convention agreed to sign the constitution. 'Factions' had developed before the states had even ratified the constitution.

A definition of political parties

A political party is a group of like-minded people organized as a single unit in order to gain the power necessary to govern the country. The group considers a wide range of issues and seeks to implement its solutions when in government. In a democracy parties seek power by proposing candidates for election.

The party system

Federalists

The basic division between the factions concerned the power of the central government. The Federalists believed in a strong central government that would intervene in the economy to encourage industrial growth. The Democratic-Republicans, who were based in the south and represented the interests of plantation owners and farmers, wanted to limit the power of the central government in favour of the states.

Ever since those early days America has been a **two-party system**, although occasionally the second party has merely been an observer in national politics.

Democratic-Republicans

The Democratic-Republicans were dominant between 1800 and 1856 under the leadership of Madison and, later, presidents Andrew Jackson and Martin Van Buren. Under Jackson and Van Buren the control of the political system by aristocrats was ended as the party developed into a national, **mass party,** which put the emphasis on the views of ordinary people. It was renamed the Democratic Party in 1828. The Federalists fell into extinction in 1816 and were replaced by a weak **coalition** known as the Whigs.

Republicans

The Republican name was resurrected in 1854 when a coalition of anti-slavery Whigs and Jacksonian Democrats formed a new party which took Abraham Lincoln to the presidency in 1860. During the civil war it was the pro-Union party. It continued to dominate national politics until the election of Franklin Roosevelt to the presidency in 1932.

Party systems

A party system is a way of describing not only the number of political parties in a country but also the relative power of the parties and the issues around which they are formed.

Political systems that are dominated by only two parties are referred to as *two-party systems*. These tend to occur in countries using a first-past-the-post, or winner-take-all, electoral system.

When a political system boasts a range of political parties, many of which have an opportunity to participate in government, to a greater or lesser extent, it is known as a *multi-party system.*

'Solid south'

Although the Democratic Party had developed as the party of the people it was unable to live up to its ideals so long as it stood for slavery. During the Civil War the party became firmly linked to the south and was largely a 'whites-only' party. It was at this time that the term **'solid south'** was born. Southern states were largely a white preserve because black Americans were discouraged from voting through poll taxes and intimidation. Those blacks that did vote tended to support the Republicans – the party that, under the leadership of Abraham Lincoln, freed the slaves.

New Deal coalition

Franklin Roosevelt's victory in the presidential election of 1932 was a major turning point in the fortunes of the Democratic Party. Roosevelt forged a coalition of southerners, urban poor, ethnic groups, liberal intellectuals and unionized labour, which has been the basis of Democratic support ever since. This coalition gave the party control of the White House between 1932 and 1968 for all but eight years, and control of Congress from 1932 to 1994, with the exception of four years (1947–48 and 1952–54) and a further six years (1981–87) in which the Senate was controlled by the Republicans.

Democratic divisions

However, the coalition has not been without cracks, particularly over civil rights. The divisions first became apparent in 1948 when the party adopted a civil rights platform for the first time. At the Democratic Party convention that year Hubert Humphrey exhorted the party to move to a more liberal position: 'The time has arrived for the Democratic Party to get out of the shadow of states' rights and walk forthrightly into the bright sunshine of human rights.' Only part of the party wanted to take that step and the party split in the 1948 presidential election. Whilst Harry Truman represented the Democratic ticket, Strom Thurmond ran for the **Dixiecrats**, or States' Rights Party, and won five southern states.

'Southern Strategy'

The division within the Democratic Party over civil rights has persisted and has opened the door for the Republican Party to win five of the last seven presidential elections. Richard Nixon launched his 'Southern Strategy' in 1968 in order to win traditional, conservative, white Democratic voters over to the Republican cause. He gained considerable success and, with the exception of Jimmy Carter's victory in 1976, the Republican Party began to consider the south solidly behind them, at least in presidential contests.

Clinton

Bill Clinton made some ground toward regaining the south for the Democratic Party in the 1992 election. Both he and his running mate, Albert Gore, are southerners and their relatively conservative platform played well in southern states. However, the incredible Republican victories in the 1994 Congressional elections suggest that the Clinton gains may be short-lived.

Throughout its history, therefore, the United States has been to a greater or lesser extent a two-party system. However, the nature of the system has moved through a number of phases with the dominant party changing. Each period of change has been associated with the rise of a third party.

Third parties

Although the American political system has always been dominated by one or two parties, **third parties** have surfaced at various times in American history.

Populist Party

In the nineteenth century the Populist Party gained some degree of popularity by advocating that the role of government should be to defend the 'little man' against the powerful and wealthy. In the presidential election of 1892 the party polled 8.5 per cent of the vote and won 22 electoral college votes.

Progressive Party

The beginning of the twentieth century saw the largest third-party showing in a presidential election to date. Theodore Roosevelt, having won the 1904 election as a Republican, stood on behalf of the Progressive Party, also known as the Bull-Moose Republicans, in 1912. He gained 4,118,571 votes (27.4 per cent), won 88 electoral college votes and beat the incumbent, President Taft, into third place.

More recently third-party candidates have included George Wallace, former governor of Alabama, who stood as an American Independent in 1968 on a segregationist platform. He gained 13.5 per cent of the vote and 46 electoral college delegates. John Anderson stood in 1980 as a National Unity candidate but failed to win any electoral college votes.

Perot

In 1992 Ross Perot became the most successful third-party candidate, in terms of the popular vote, since Theodore Roosevelt in 1912. After a stop-start campaign, with Perot leaving the race in July only to re-enter in October, he eventually polled 19 per cent of the vote but failed to carry any states in the electoral college. Following the presidential election he launched an organization called United We Stand to monitor the work of the Clinton administration, and more recently he has launched the Independence Party, which may provide the support for another tilt at the presidency.

The popular votes accumulated by Roosevelt, Wallace and Perot prove that it is possible for third-party candidates to capture the imagination of the electorate. However their appeal is very much candidate based. Third parties tend to fare less well when their charismatic candidate disappears. Despite his success at the polls George Wallace left the Independent American Party (AIP) and subsequently returned to the Democratic Party. The AIP continues to put up candidates in presidential elections but they have fared badly

Transient parties

Most third parties are **transient parties**, in that they will be active in one election campaign and will never be heard from again. Usually they are parties of protest, either against one of the major parties or against a particular set of policies. Despite winning the primaries in 1912, Theodore Roosevelt lost the Republican Party's nomination to the incumbent, President William Taft. Roosevelt's Bull-Moose Republicans were a protest against Taft and his conservative policies.

'Catch-all' parties

In 1968 George Wallace was campaigning against both of the main parties, arguing that there was no real difference between them. His campaign slogan summed up the mood of protest in the south and border states: 'Send Them a Message'. Wallace's argument that there is little difference between the two main parties is not quite accurate but it does contain within it the seeds of third-party defeat. The Republican

The Independence Party

On 26 September 1995 Ross Perot appeared on CNN's 'Larry King Live' to announce the launch of the Independence Party. Perot's aim is to establish a third force in American politics to challenge Republican and Democratic Party dominance of presidential and congressional elections. According to opinion polls this move should satisfy 62 per cent of Americans, who have declared their support, in principal, to a third party.

Perot's initial aim is to support a candidate for the presidency in 1996 – possibly himself. Much of the support will be financial. Perot's intention is to be able to provide a candidate with sufficient financial backing to release them from the pressures of interest groups, which are the usual sources of finance. Of course, Ross Perot will provide the funds and may be seen as a vested interest himself. In congressional elections his party will endorse candidates, either Democrat or Republican, who satisfy his criteria.

Newt Gingrich has dismissed the new party as 'a fantasy of delusion'. Given Perot's performance in the 1992 presidential election when he withdrew only to re-enter a few weeks later Gingrich might be forgiven for believing this. However, Perot believes that the American people are so disillusioned with politicians that the Independence Party will eclipse one of the two main parties.

and Democratic parties are **'catch-all' parties**. They are loose coalitions encompassing a broad range of opinion, so almost anyone can find a home in one or other of the parties. This leaves little room for alternative policies or ideologies.

Finance

Transient parties are unlikely to be backed by a professional, national organization and so their ability to make an impact on the two main parties is limited. Many lack the funds necessary to build such an organization and to gain the media exposure required to break through into national politics. Ross Perot is actually an exception to this rule because he was able to use his personal wealth to make a considerable splash on the national stage. Perot reportedly spent $60 million of his own money on his campaign.

WTA

Furthermore the electoral system is based on the winner-take-all (WTA) principle. Unless a candidate is able to win states he will not gain any representation in the electoral college. Therefore Ross Perot's 19 per cent of the popular vote counted for nothing in the electoral college.

Third-party influence

Although third-party candidates are unlikely to break the mould of Republican–Democrat victories they can play an important part in the determination of an election result. Most main-party candidates fear them because, although they cannot win, they may gain sufficient votes to open the door for the leading opposition candidate. Wallace's candidacy in 1968 brought severe complications to the race between Richard Nixon and Hubert Humphrey. It was unclear during the campaign whether Wallace would damage Nixon or Humphrey more. His supporters were traditionally Democrats, or Dixiecrats, but they were right wingers and therefore potentially Nixon voters. In the end Nixon gained 43.4 per cent of the vote compared to Humphrey's 42.7 per cent.

Party competition

Single ideology

American political divisions are not ideological. There is broad agreement on the fact that the United States is a liberal-democratic country with a capitalist economy. Within this framework people are bound together by a strong belief in individual liberties and the 'American Dream' (the idea that all individuals can improve spiritually and economically in America). Under these circumstances alternative ideologies, such as socialism, have made little impact.

Comparison

In Britain competition between the two main parties is based on ideology. The Labour Party is a party of the left and espouses socialism with its emphasis on change toward greater economic equality. Traditionally it has been viewed as the party of the working class. The Conservative Party is a party of the right and favours slow change. It has tended to be seen as the party of the middle and upper classes.

Government role

However, the parties are divided over the role the government should play in society. The Democratic Party became the party of government intervention in the economy with the policies of the New Deal. In the 1960s Kennedy and Johnson made it the party of civil rights and social welfare. The Republican Party on the other hand has always been more reluctant to interfere in economic and social affairs. This has never been clearer than in the Reagan years.

Reagan

More right wing than many of his predecessors Ronald Reagan advocated rolling back the state to give the American people more freedom from restriction. His years in office were marked by a commitment to free-market economics and conservatism on issues like welfare, abortion and civil rights.

Class

To an extent the Republican and Democratic parties are class-based parties. The New Deal coalition made the Democrats the party of the lower classes, whilst the Republican Party tends to be the home of the more affluent. However, voting behaviour in the United States is by no means solely determined by class factors. A complex web of historical, ethnic and geographical factors shapes the voting habits of the electorate. The Democratic coalition includes the minorities and an awkward combination of Northern **liberals** and Southern **conservatives**. The Republicans draw their support from the suburbs, small-town America and rural areas.

New Democrats

Ronald Reagan appealed directly to the better-off sections of society and aroused resentment against the less fortunate. By doing so he captured a considerable amount of traditional Democratic support. In an effort to cope with the shift of the political agenda to the right many Democrats have taken up more right wing positions. Jimmy Carter won the 1976 election by being slightly more right wing than the traditional Northern Democrat. In 1992 Bill Clinton and Al Gore adopted a right wing Democratic platform and became known as **New Democrats.** They believe in the free market and free trade; welfare reform and the *earning* of benefits; they are tough on crime and advocate individual responsibility. They want the Democratic Party to speak for all America not merely the 'desperate, damned, disinherited, disrespected and despised' – so called by former candidate for the party's presidential nomination and leading civil rights activist, Jesse Jackson.

Suburban voters

They must also be aware that in the 1992 census in America 50 per cent of the population considered themselves to be suburban. The New Democrats have fashioned a philosophy that will attract those Americans looking for a 'kinder, gentler America', without alienating them with talk of tax increases, special programmes for special interests and 'big government'.

The Democrats' move to the right is not without its critics. Many traditional Democrats have been alienated by President Clinton's policies. His stand over the North American Free Trade Agreement was extremely controversial and did not win the approval of the unions or civil rights groups.

Party structures

Of course the idea that the American party system is a two-party system is far too simplistic. It does consist of two party labels but in many ways America could be said to have 100 parties – a different Democratic and Republican party in each state. As we have seen, American political parties have a relatively limited ideological mission and so their aim has been to win as many elected offices as possible. They are structured to achieve that aim.

Local government

The federal structure of the United States means that most elected offices are elected at state level or below. Each state has its own unit of government consisting of a Governor and a state legislature.

Within each state there are further units of local government, amounting to a total of 80,000 units across the country. Even federal offices are elected at state levels. Senators represent states and each state is divided into congressional districts to select congressmen. Only the president is elected on a national basis and the composition of the Senate and the House has no effect on the make-up of the executive branch of government.

Comparison

In Britain too elections take place on a local scale. In local government each ward elects a councillor. At national level each constituency elects a member of Parliament. However, in the case of national government, these constituency elections decide the composition of the House of Commons, which in turn determines the composition of the executive branch of government. In the United States this is not true.

Party units

The main units of party organization are:
- precincts
- wards
- counties
- states
- national committees

Precincts are the smallest unit of organization. Usually they are sub-divisions of cities and counties. There are approximately 178,000 precinct committees across the country; each elects a chair, known as a 'captain,' and is responsible for fundraising and getting out the vote at election time.

Wards are groupings of precincts, usually headed by a ward chair. They often coincide with the electoral districts for local government elections.

'Machine politics'

In the era of **'machine politics'** at the end of the nineteenth and beginning of the twentieth centuries it was the precinct captains and ward chairs who would be responsible for the tight organization of the party's voters. They knew everyone in their area and were able to have a firm control over the nomination of candidates and election results themselves. They became known as **party bosses**. In New York the stronghold of the Democratic party bosses was Tammany Hall, which has since become synonymous with the corruption of the 'boss' system.

Counties are perhaps the most important unit of party organization within a state because they coincide with many of the constituencies for elected offices at state level and they co-ordinate the lower units of organization. County committees are made up of representatives from the lower levels and are headed by a county chair who is likely to be a key figure in county and state politics. At this level there may be a further unit of organization to coincide with congressional districts.

State parties co-ordinate the selection of candidates for state-wide offices. Their committees are often made up of representatives from county levels or are elected through a system of primaries. Each year the state will hold conventions which have the power to adopt party platforms, and candidates for party or state offices will be endorsed. They will also determine who their representatives will be at national level.

National committees are made up of two representatives from each state plus any additional members, such as state **party chair** or senior national figures, and are formally chosen at the national convention. This makes national committees too large and cumbersome to be very active in the affairs of the party. They are responsible for organizing the national convention.

Party reform

Each national committee is headed by the party chair, who is formally selected by the national committee but in practice is the choice of the presidential candidate. In recent years the national party chairs have been much more active in the affairs of state parties. In particular the Democratic Party's National Committee (DNC) has established its authority by enforcing a series of party reforms, including the McGovern-Fraser (1969), Mikulski (1972–74), Winograd (1975–78) and Hunt (1981–82) reforms.

Some state parties have resented the intervention of the DNC in their affairs. However when tested in the Supreme Court the national party's ability to do so was confirmed in *Cousins* v. *Wigoda* (1975).

Nevertheless the basic structure of American political parties is federal to match the organization of the political system. As a result individual units have a relatively high degree of freedom to tailor their approach and their platform to suit local needs.

Functions of political parties

In most political systems political parties have two basic roles:
- an electoral role
- a governing role

The former relates to the key functions national parties play in elections and the second to the role they play in organizing the government and allocating government offices.

The electoral role

The **electoral role** can be divided into five functions:
- nomination of candidates
- organization of campaigns
- finance of campaigns
- provision of policy
- organization of the voter

Comparison

In Britain national political parties control all of the electoral functions. The national importance of elections to the House of Commons means that parties nominate candidates. The main thrust of election campaigns is organized at national level and funds are received at national level. Most candidates for the major parties will fight their campaigns on the basis of national policy and the electorate will make their decision on the basis of national policy and the appeal of national leaders.

In the United States national parties play a relatively limited role in electoral politics because over recent years election campaigns have become **candidate-orientated** rather than party-orientated as they are in Britain.

In the nineteenth century and the first half of the twentieth century political parties controlled elections. Candidates were nominated by the party through the 'boss' system. Voter loyalty was high and parties concentrated on getting their vote out.

Nomination and voter loyalty

Independent voters

In the second half of the century the level of voter loyalty diminished. In 1940 only

20 per cent of voters considered themselves independent but by 1986 this figure had increased to 32 per cent. Furthermore the turnout in elections has been declining consistently. In 1900 the turnout in the presidential election was 73.2 per cent; in 1988 it was 50.1 per cent. Both of these factors have been taken to indicate dissatisfaction with the two main parties.

Primaries

In response greater use of primaries was made, so that grassroots support of the party could play a greater role in the choice of candidates. The intention was to enhance the candidates' appeal to the voter. In fact it meant that the national parties lost control of the nomination process.

Democratic reforms

The Democratic Party went further by implementing the McGovern-Fraser, Mikulski and Winograd reforms. The main aim of these reforms was to increase participation in the choice of candidates and in party affairs in general. They advocated the use of proportional representation primaries and broader representation of women, youth and minority groups at the national convention. The result was to strengthen the role of grassroots party activists in party affairs and to diminish the power of the national party.

'Superdelegates'

Since then the Democrats have further reformed their organization by adopting the suggestion of the Hunt Commission that **'superdelegates'** be allowed to take part in the national convention. These delegates are party professionals and senior figures in the party. This is an attempt to balance the influence of the grassroots and to allow the national party to regain some control of the nomination process.

Organization and finance of campaigns

The parties' loss of control of the nomination process has led to a deterioration in their other electoral functions.

Personal staff

Campaigns are no longer organized by the political parties but by the candidates themselves. This stems from the public's dissatisfaction with the two main parties - candidates know that the party label counts for less and their own appeal counts for more. They therefore develop their *own* organizations to manage their campaigns; their staff is responsible for policy development, their itinerary and the promotion of their image. Advisers like Robert Ailes (Ronald Reagan and George Bush), James Carvill (Bill Clinton) and Pat Caddell (Walter Mondale) may be associated with a particular party but they work for individual candidates.

Primaries

The extension of the use of primaries has also emphasized the importance of candidate organizations. Throughout the nomination process campaigns cannot be organized by the parties because they are intra-party battles. Therefore each candidate must have their own organization. This is true not only for presidential campaigns but also in Congress. The Democrat Senator Jesse Helms, for example, has a number of 'think tanks' working specifically for him; they include the Centre for a Free Society and the Institute of American Relations.

CREEP

Perhaps the most famous candidate-based organization was Richard Nixon's Committee to Re-elect the President (CREEP). This was not only responsible for the organization of Nixon's 1972 campaign but also the fundraising for the campaign.

FECA

In the area of finance, campaigns have also become candidate-orientated, with most money being channelled directly to candidates rather than to parties. The Federal Election Campaign Finance Act (1972) and its subsequent amendments institutionalized the financing of candidates rather than parties.

Provision of policy

Candidate-led policy

Although the national party conventions do adopt party platforms, their role in determining party policy is virtually non-existent. At the presidential level, once a candidate has been adopted as the party's candidate they have the freedom to determine their own policies and, at least for the duration of the campaign, the party should step in behind those policies. Having said this, presidential candidates must be aware of the divisions within their own party. Jimmy Carter was aware that he was more right wing than many traditional Democrats and George Bush was conscious of his poor standing with the Reaganite wing of his party in 1992.

'Catch-all' parties

At every other level of party organization the federal structure allows politicians to determine their own policies. It is for this reason that American political parties consist of such a wide range of political opinion. This can be seen most clearly in the Democratic Party, in which right wingers such as Jesse Helms and George Wallace can rub shoulders with left wingers Richard Dellums, a member of the Socialist Democratic Alliance, and Jesse Jackson.

The governing role

The **governing role** can be divided into three functions:

- provision of policy
- organization of the legislature
- allocation of government offices

In Britain the electoral role reinforces the governing role; in the United States the weak electoral role weakens their governing role.

Provision of policy

The federal structure of the parties means that it is extremely difficult for the parties to lay down a national party policy. At state levels the parties will pursue the policies most appropriate to local electoral politics. This concern for local politics persists in federal government. Congressional leaders will attempt to set policy but, under most circumstances, their ability to enforce a party line is extremely limited.

The organization of the legislature

Party discipline

Even if it were possible for the national parties to lay down a strong party line their control of the legislature is insufficiently strong to enable them to enforce the line. Given the candidate-based electoral campaigns, members of Congress are aware that they owe their positions to their own organizations, local parties and their constituents.

Comparison

In Britain, parties carry out all the elements of the governing role. Their strong electoral role gives them the foundation from which they can control the government. MPs know that they owe their positions in the House of Commons to the electoral role of the party. They also know that any promotion opportunities also depend on the party. Being a parliamentary system of government the leader of the party in government has the ability to promote MPs to or dismiss them from the executive. Both of these factors encourage MPs to fall in behind the policy line set by the party.

It is to these three bodies that they will give their loyalty, and party loyalty in Congress is weak. Candidate-orientated election campaigns lead to candidate-orientated government.

The allocation of government offices

The presidential system and the separation of powers reduces the parties' control of promotions. The chief executive in the United States is elected in his or her own right and has the power to appoint their own senior staff and the highest layers of the bureaucracy. Many of these personnel may be taken from the ranks of the party but they are more likely to come from the president's own supporters. President Clinton plucked Lloyd Bentsen (former Treasury Secretary) and Leon Panetta (Chief of Staff) from Congress but most of his other staff are from outside the congressional party.

Pendleton Act

In the nineteenth century, party control over government offices was much stronger. All positions in the bureaucracy were allocated on a patronage basis by the president and his party. This was known as 'the spoils system'. However the Pendleton Act of 1883 created a permanent civil service that is recruited on merit.

Party fightback

RNC fundraising

In recent years the parties have tried to improve their co-ordination of government. In the Republican Party the emphasis has been on fundraising and the co-ordination of election campaigns. Ray Bliss, Bill Brock and Lee Atwater were all involved in fundraising at the national level whilst holding the office of party chairman. Between 1976 and 1984 the income of the Republican Party's National Committee increased by $75 million. In 1981–82 alone Brock raised $58 million for House elections. Republican Party fundraising reached a peak in 1984 when it collected almost $300 million, $200 million more than the Democratic Party. However the Democratic Party has begun to improve its own fundraising, reaching $175 million in 1992.

Capitol Compact

During the Reagan administration there was a greater effort to co-ordinate the activities of the Republican Party at all levels. The Capitol Compact was the high point of party unity as the party in the Senate and the House agreed to support the five major points of Reagan's platform.

Seniority rule

Within Congress the parties have moved to increase their control over key promotions. For most members of Congress the greatest opportunities for advancement arise through the committee system. Most members will aspire to become chairs of Senate or House committees. Until the 1970s promotion was not a matter for the parties to consider. The **seniority rule** meant that the longest-serving member of the majority party on the committee automatically became its chair. This rule lapsed in the 1970s when the majority party caucus in both the House and Senate took control of the appointment of chairs. As a result the parties have strengthened their hands and can use the position of chair to reward loyal party members.

Contract with America'

Perhaps the most striking illustration of party fightback has occurred in the last two years. The Republican Party, under the inspirational leadership of Newt Gingrich,

The Contract with America

The 'Contract' was the right-wing manifesto adopted by most members of the Republican Party in Congress for the 1992 mid-term elections. It was the brainchild of Newt Gingrich and was an effort to wrest both houses of Congress away from the Democratic Party for the first time since 1948. Not only would this give the Republicans the power in Congress that many had failed to even dream of, it would also leave the Democrat Bill Clinton isolated in the White House.

The 'Contract' was made up of ten measures that Gingrich hoped to make the centre-piece of a resurgence in the legislative power of Congress. Since Franklin Roosevelt's New Deal of 1933 the White House had been the focus of legislative programmes leaving Congress as an assembly *reacting* to presidential initiatives. Many on the right believed that these legislative programmes had been too liberal – despite the fact that the Republican Party had controlled the White House for almost half of the postwar era. Gingrich intended to redress the balance between Congress and president whilst implementing his radical, right-wing agenda.

The ten measures of the 'Contract' included limits on the number of terms that members of Congress could serve; a constitutional amendment to ensure that the federal government lived within its means (*The Balanced Budget Amendment*); the introduction of a line-item veto, to allow presidents to reject selected parts of a bill without vetoing the whole package; an anti-crime package that would put more police on the streets, increase prison places and strengthen death-penalty legislation; far-reaching welfare reform that threatened food stamps and prohibited welfare for teenage mothers.

All but one of these measures (term limits) were passed by the House but the Contract encountered considerable opposition in the Senate, even before reaching the White House, where President Clinton has threatened to veto some of the measures.

fought the 1992 mid-term elections on a manifesto known as *The Contract With America*.

However, *The Contract with America* was not merely an election manifesto. Gingrich, as the new Speaker of the House, used it as the basis for the legislative programme in 1995. In fact all but one of the proposals (the introduction of term limits on members of Congress) were passed in the House after only 92 days of business. Therefore it seems that Newt Gingrich has been able to create an agenda for the Republican Party in the House along with the party discipline necessary to have measures passed.

Republican agenda

Republican Party unity has been less apparent in the Senate. The power of Bob Dole, the Majority Leader, is less than that of the Speaker of the House and the rules of the Senate allow for longer debates, more amendments and generally a more relaxed attitude to the business of legislation. By August 1995 only four parts of *The Contract with America* had successfully moved through the Senate.

Senate block

Conclusion

It would not be true to say that the role of American political parties is non-existent because we have seen that candidates not carrying the Republican or Democratic banner rarely make an impact on national or state politics. However, when compared to their British counterparts one must conclude that they are weak. This is largely due to the fall in voter loyalty and the subsequent rise of the direct primary.

Direct primaries have strengthened the grassroots of the parties at the expense of the centre. They have also encouraged the development of candidate-orientated elections which in turn have helped to undermine party loyalty in Congress.

In 1980 both the Democrats and the Republicans organized something of a fightback both in elections and in government but the full impact of these remains to be seen.

Questions

Short questions

1 a What do you understand by 'party identification'?
  b Why has it declined?
  (ULEAC, June 1991)

2 Account for the failure of third parties in American politics. (ULEAC, June 1992)

3 What are the main weaknesses of the American party system? (ULEAC, June 1994)

4 Why did Ross Perot gain so much support in the 1992 presidential election? (ULEAC, January 1995)

US questions

1 Account for the decline in the importance of parties in American politics. (UCLES, June 1993)

2 To what extent do parties still have a role in relation to (a) elections and (b) congressional politics? (ULEAC, January 1994)

3 Given the decentralization of American politics, why is there basically a two-party system? (ULEAC, June 1992)

Comparative question

1 **a** What are the key functions that political parties perform?
b To what extent are parties declining in importance? (Illustrate your answer with reference to at least two countries.)
(ULEAC, June 1994)

6 The presidency

Questions to be answered in this chapter

- What are the constitutional constraints on the president?
- How effectively are presidents able to work within these constraints?
- What is the 'imperial presidency'?
- Have presidents been more restricted since 1974?

Terms to know

- 'Backlash' effect
- Bureaucracy
- Candidate-orientated
- Charisma
- Chief diplomat
- Chief executive
- Chief legislator
- 'Coat-tails' effect
- Commander-in-chief
- 'Executive privilege'
- 'Frontlash' effect
- Head of state
- 'Imperial presidency'
- 'Imperilled presidency'
- 'Impotent presidency'
- Iran-Contra Affair
- Lobbyists
- Log-rolling
- 'Overshoot and collapse'
- Pocket veto
- Prerogative powers
- 'Resurgent Congress'
- Separation of powers
- Split-ticket voting
- State of the Union
- 'Toe the party line'
- Veto
- 'War power'
- Watergate

Perceptions of the president

We are all familiar with the awesome power possessed by the American president on the world stage. The United States has been considered a world superpower since its decisive entry into World War I. Its status was further confirmed by a similar intervention in the war against Japan and Adolf Hitler's Germany. Perhaps the president became inextricably linked with this power when Harry Truman took the decision to drop atomic bombs on the Japanese cities Hiroshima and Nagasaki. The carnage caused by nuclear weapons has identified the president, in the popular imagination, as 'the man with his finger on the button'.

Economic power

The root of the United States' dominance of international politics is economic. Economic wealth has made military growth possible; it has also made much of the developed world dependent on its markets and much of the third world dependent on its aid. Most impressively it gave its leaders the confidence to believe that the superiority of the capitalist way is so vast as to guarantee the demise of its greatest ever adversary, communism.

Although its predominance may be challenged by Japan and Germany the continued importance of the United States has been illustrated by the recently ratified North American Free Trade Agreement (NAFTA) proposal, which has created the largest trading bloc in the world, with a GNP of $7 trillion, of which Canada and Mexico contribute only 15 per cent. And, so far, Germany and Japan lack the political clout, and perhaps ambition, necessary to displace the United States from its position as the only remaining world superpower.

Media attention

Naturally the leader of the most powerful country on earth carries with him the stature which economic and military power bestows. Since 1945 the eminence of the American president has reached levels which would have been beyond the imagination of Jefferson, Lincoln and Wilson. In fact, in the era of summit meetings, shuttle diplomacy and surgical strikes, all covered by the insatiable international media, the president has been elevated to the level of celebrity once reserved for movie stars. Nixon in China, Reagan in Reykjavik and Bush in the Gulf were all turning points in international affairs but at the same time were international media events.

JFK

Perhaps it was John F Kennedy who was responsible, more than anyone else, for the image of president as superstar. Who but a Hollywood scriptwriter would have put a young, gifted and good-looking senator into the White House, to address the issues of welfare and civil rights at home and the most dangerous crisis of the postwar world on America's doorstep? And where, but in Hollywood, would it have ended so tragically?

Presidents Roosevelt, Kennedy, Johnson, Nixon and Reagan are all 'stars' of the twentieth century. All are men who have shaped international events and whose images are familiar all over the world. But it would be all too easy to confuse the predominance of the country and international recognition with the power of the office. All of us are guilty, at some time or other, of believing the American president to be the most powerful man in the world and, as a result, assuming that he must be the most powerful man in America.

The Founding Fathers and the presidency

The perception of the president holding ultimate power is by no means an entirely modern phenomenon. During the debate over the ratification of the constitution in 1787–88 there was considerable disagreement about the nature of the governmental system being created. Some of the Founding Fathers, such as Alexander Hamilton, favoured a strong executive branch. Hamilton said in *The Federalist* No. 70, 'a feeble executive implies a feeble ... government [which] must in practice be a bad government'. He had a strong ally in George Washington who in a letter to Hamilton stated that, 'the men who oppose a strong and energetic government are, in my opinion, narrow minded politicians'.

Checks and balances

One of those men was James Madison, who believed, with Thomas Jefferson, in the strong **separation of powers** backed up by a system of checks and balances, which would limit every institution. Madison stated in *The Federalist* No. 47, 'the accumulation of all powers, legislative, executive and judiciary, in the same hands, whether of one, a few, or many, and whether hereditary, self-appointed, or elective, may justly be pronounced the very definition of tyranny'. Whilst Hamilton and Washington advocated a strong presidency, Madison and Jefferson were equally convinced that the legislative branch of government should be dominant.

Of the four men it was Madison and Jefferson who won out. Hamilton's proposal for a president holding office for life was rejected for fear that it would create an aristocratic or even monarchical government. Nevertheless the adoption of a president elected for a fixed term of four years was not enough to satisfy everyone that the executive was adequately constrained. Patrick Henry, a leading Antifederalist, argued that, 'there is to be a great and mighty president, with very extensive powers – the powers of a king'.

In fact for the greater part of the United States' history the success of Madison and Jefferson has been clear. Presidents have been constrained by both the Congress and the Supreme Court and have rarely come close to the monarchical powers Patrick Henry predicted.

The realities of the restrictions of the constitution have done little to dispel the notion of the president as the most potent force in the politics of the United States. America's people, media and politicians have fallen under the spell of the presidency. They too look to him as the omnipotent leader, capable of solving any and every problem. Every issue becomes a presidential issue, viewed through a White House prism. As a result presidents are under a great deal of pressure to meet public expectations. Those, such as Lincoln, Wilson and Roosevelt, who have to a greater or lesser extent succeeded, have only made the demands on their successors the more testing.

Constitutional powers

The role and powers of the **chief executive** are enumerated in Article II of the constitution, 'The executive power shall be vested in a President of the United States of America'. Section 1 deals almost entirely with procedures for his election, inauguration, compensation and replacement in the case of disability. Sections 2 and 3 deal with most of his powers and, as importantly, with the congressional constraints on those powers. However, the fact that most of the Founding Fathers expected power to reside with the legislature is clearly illustrated by the lack of time devoted to the enumeration of the president's powers. Article I, relating to the power of Congress, runs to ten sections; those concerning the president to a mere four. Article II is brief and lacks detail. As a result presidents have often taken the opportunity to interpret their powers more liberally than the Founding Fathers might have wished.

Chief executive

Bureaucracy

As chief executive the president is responsible for the implementation of laws and policy. As Section 3 states, 'he shall take care that the laws be faithfully executed'. The president is therefore responsible for the **bureaucracy** through which the laws will be carried out. At the turn of the eighteenth century the federal bureaucracy amounted to approximately 3000 civilians. Almost 200 years later this figure has grown to 3.9

million. Washington's three departments – State, Treasury and War – have become fourteen. Added to these are independent executive agencies, independent regulatory commissions and, to help co-ordinate the rest of the bureaucracy, the executive office of the president.

Comparison

Chief executives are responsible for the control and co-ordination of the executive branch of government. In Britain this function is carried out largely by the prime minister, who is responsible for appointing Cabinet and junior ministers. Increasingly prime ministers are identified with all government policy, particularly given the media attention that the leader receives. This perception has a been a contributing factor to the view that prime ministers have become more presidential. However, the prime minister is only one member of Cabinet and decision-making is collective.

Appointment

To enable the president to better control the civil service the constitution gives him the power to appoint 'public ministers' and to 'require the opinion, in writing, of the principal officers in each of the Executive Departments, upon any subject relating to the duties of these respective offices'. It is this power which gives the president the ability to fill government offices. The top four layers of departments, from Cabinet level downwards, the officials of the executive office of the president, the heads of independent executive agencies and independent regulatory commissions are all appointed by the president.

Checks

The executive powers of the president are checked, in so far as the president should implement only laws and policies approved by Congress and the president's nominations for official positions need Senate ratification. Furthermore the power of Congress to scrutinize the executive means that the legislature has the right to question members of the bureaucracy.

Although not a constitutional constraint, the president is also checked by the bureaucracy itself. Given that the civil service, with power and aims of its own, can be difficult to manage, it is a constraining influence.

Chief legislator

Presidential veto

Despite Madison's concern for a clear separation of powers the chief executive is also the **chief legislator**. Article I of the constitution lays down the president's **veto** power: 'Every bill ... shall, before it becomes a law, be presented to the President of the United States; if he approves he shall sign it, but if not he shall return it, with his objections, to that house from which it shall have originated.' Even this power is checked. Congress has the power to override the president's veto with a two-thirds majority in both houses.

State of the Union address

The constitution also states that the president 'shall from time to time give to the Congress information of the **state of the Union**, and recommend to their consideration such measures as he shall judge necessary and expedient'. In the twentieth century presidents have used this provision to expand the legislative role of the presidency.

The president's veto

The president has the power to veto legislation presented to him for signature by Congress. He returns the bill to Congress with his reasons for vetoing it. The veto can be overridden by a two-thirds majority in both houses of Congress.

Presidents will usually use it sparingly. To use it profusely may reduce its effectiveness as a statement of the president's views. In addition overuse of the veto would illustrate a poor relationship with Congress and might exacerbate the problem still further. In the wake of **Watergate**, Gerald Ford used the veto 48 times and was overridden 12 times.

Presidents may also use the **pocket veto**. When Congress is in session if a president does not sign a bill within ten days it automatically becomes law but if there are fewer than ten days to a congressional adjournment the president can hold on to the bill and in so doing, kill it. President Eisenhower used the pocket veto 108 times in his eight years in office.

Many state governors have an 'item' or 'line' veto which enables them to veto separate points of a bill. The president does not, despite President Reagan's attempts to have Congress grant him that power.

Modern era

Most political scientists identify the beginning of the 'modern presidency' with Woodrow Wilson or Franklin Roosevelt. They do so not only because they can both be considered 'great' presidents but also because they mark the beginning of an era in which presidents have tended to take responsibility for setting the legislative agenda for the federal government. Subsequent presidents have often aspired to follow their example and almost every one since Harry Truman in 1948 has laid a legislative programme before Congress.

Eisenhower's restraint

Although some conservative presidents like Eisenhower were reluctant to adopt this modern role, believing that the executive was usurping the role of Congress, most have recognized the fact that the American system is now so complex and the degree of government intervention in society so great that the legislature would find it difficult to cope with its workload if it was not led by the president. Even in America, home of the free market, Keynesian economics has taken hold and demands a degree of government intervention in the economy. In addition social welfare provisions, such as Medicaid, have increased the workload of government.

Budget

A president's legislative proposals have implications not only for Congress's legislative timetable but also for the federal budget. The president has taken on the responsibility of putting his budgetary proposals before Congress every year. It is prepared by the Office of Management and Budget, part of the Executive Office of the President. In 1994 the budget of the federal government was approximately $1.5 trillion.

Checks

Of course the president's power to achieve his legislative and budgetary ambitions is checked. Laws, and the budget, can only be passed by both houses of Congress.

In Britain we are accustomed to 'strong' and 'responsible' governments which are able to do the 'right thing' because they have a majority in the House of Commons, which they can control 99 per cent of the time. American presidents can only dream about such a state of affairs.

Chief diplomat

The president is the **head of state** and as such is the **chief diplomat** – the main spokesperson for the United States on foreign affairs. The original intention of the Founding Fathers had been to keep America out of foreign affairs. As he departed the presidency Washington clearly articulated this view: 'Why quit our own to stand upon foreign ground? Why by interweaving our destiny with that of any part of Europe, entangle our peace and prosperity in the toils of European ambition, rivalship, interest, humor or caprice?'

Of course, it was not possible to stay apart from the rest of the world, although the policy of isolationism did dominate foreign policy for most of the nineteenth century.

World role

In the twentieth century President Wilson took the most dramatic steps away from the isolationist tradition when he decided that the United States would intervene in the World War I in 1917 to make the world 'safe for democracy'. Immediately after the war Wilson, having been fully converted to internationalism, was the main mover behind the creation of the League of Nations. Unfortunately the American Congress and people were not ready to move so far, so fast. As the historian Hugh Brogan has written, 'Americans were still isolationists at heart; the unpleasant experiment of 1917 had never been intended to be a prelude to permanent involvement in the affairs of the world, and its results changed few minds on this point'.

WWII

The outbreak of World War II gave President Roosevelt the opportunity to begin the repeal of the Neutrality Acts, which prevented any administration giving aid to a belligerent nation. This process and America's entry into the war in Europe and Asia put America back in the forefront of international affairs and the Cold War has allowed it to remain there ever since. The scale of this transformation is illustrated by Stephen Ambrose in *Rise to Globalism*. In 1939 the United States had an army of 185,000 men, with an annual budget of $500 million. It had no military alliances and no troops stationed abroad. Only thirty years later the army totalled 1.5 million soldiers, the Defence Department budget was $500 billion and the United States had alliances with 48 nations with troops stationed in no fewer than 119 countries. The postwar years have seen the United States explode on to the world scene. At the same time the president has become 'leader of the western world' and the arbiter of national security interests.

Checks

The constitution gives the president the power to appoint ambassadors and make treaties, both needing Senate ratification, but in reality the president's dominance in this field has expanded far beyond such limited visions.

Commander-in-chief

The constitution states that: 'The President shall be Commander-in-Chief of the Army and Navy of the United States, and of the militia of the several States, when called into the actual service of the United States'. This **'war power'** gives the president the authority to command America's armed forces. The last president to do so on the field of battle was James Madison in 1814 against Britain at the battle of Bladensburg. Subsequent presidents have foregone the opportunity to command in battle but have made extravagant use of their position at the top of the military hierarchy.

Checks

The 'war power', like all the president's other powers, is checked. Only Congress has the power to declare war and Congress controls the appropriation of finance for the armed forces.

Judicial power

The constitution gives the president a limited, although significant, power regarding the judicial branch of government. He has the power to appoint judges to all federal courts, for example the Supreme Court.

Checks

The president's freedom to make appointments is restricted by the need for Senate ratification and by the fact that judges hold their offices for life, during good behaviour.

Long-term influence

Nevertheless this is a significant power. The Supreme Court is able to review the work of the other branches of government and in so doing becomes the interpreter of the constitution. A president who can influence the composition of the court can leave his mark on judicial decisions long after he has left office. The Senate's power of ratification can limit the president's ability to this. For example the Senate rejected Ronald Reagan's nomination of Robert Bork (former Solicitor-General) as a blatant attempt to shift the political complexion of the Court to the right. However, a president's nominees are usually accepted and during the Reagan–Bush years the Supreme Court certainly moved to the right (see pages 142–3).

Operating within constitutional constraints

The constitution, then, matches the president's powers with considerable constraints. Constitutions are, however, made up only of broad rules and principles and sometimes they reveal only part of the political reality. A president who can operate within the constitutional constraints can build up considerable power within the American system. In the era of the modern presidency Franklin Roosevelt, Lyndon Johnson and Ronald Reagan have all proved this. Whether or not the president is able to do so depends on a variety of political, economic and social factors, not all of which are within his control.

Foreign or domestic policy?

We have seen that the constitution gives the president specific powers in foreign policy. Although Congress also has foreign policy powers and has interfered in international affairs, the role of international representative lies mainly with the president. In *The United States* v. *Curtiss-Wright Export Corporation* (1936) the Supreme Court affirmed that 'the president alone has the power to speak or listen as a representative of the nation,' and that he must be given a 'freedom from statutory discretion which would not be admissible were domestic affairs alone involved'.

Figurehead

As the main spokesperson for the United States the president can usually expect the support of the other branches of government and of the people by appealing to patriotism. When the United States is acting in the international arena the country is likely to unite behind the president. Most presidents are aware of this and have a tendency to 'wrap themselves in the flag'. This means that presidential appeals to patriotism are usually heeded and the president is secure in the knowledge that he is relatively safe from domestic attack.

Comparison

Like most world leaders the British prime minister benefits from periods of international activity. Both Margaret Thatcher (Falklands War, 1982) and John Major (Gulf War, 1991) saw their popularity ratings soar during international conflicts. The country tends to unite behind the leader for patriotic reasons and public attention is diverted from domestic problems.

Domestic focus

The president's safety when on international duty is also due to the fact that members of Congress do not usually win or lose elections on issues of foreign policy. They know that their futures depend on domestic politics and so they tend to confine the greater part of their activity to home affairs.

Advice

As the head of the executive branch of government, the president is in a strong position with regard to foreign policy. The State and Defence Departments, the National Security Council and intelligence agencies such as the CIA and the National Security Agency are all under the president's control. This gives the president access to the most up-to-date intelligence on foreign affairs and the ability to centre foreign policy-making in the White House.

Media spotlight

It is also the case that foreign policy lends itself to control by individuals or small groups. All 535 members of Congress cannot negotiate a treaty and cannot rapidly respond to international crises. The media have recognized this and provided presidents with a stage on which to perform, with Congress relegated to a supporting role.

Presidents have occasionally discovered that the support of the media and the public can be fickle, even in the sphere of foreign affairs. John Kennedy, following the disatrous 'Bay of Pigs' invasion of Cuba in 1961, and Lyndon Johnson, during the Vietnam War, suffered a considerable loss of popularity when foreign policy adventures went wrong.

Electoral success

An obvious link between Roosevelt, Johnson and Reagan are the overwhelming electoral victories they achieved in taking possession of the White House. They were

US Election results, 1932–1992

Year	Candidate	Vote
1932	**FD Roosevelt (D)**	57%
	H Hoover	40%
1936	**FD Roosevelt (D)**	61%
	A Landon	37%
1940	**FD Roosevelt (D)**	55%
	WL Willkie	45%
1944	**FD Roosevelt (D)**	54%
	TE Dewey	46%
1948	**HS Truman (D)**	50%
	TE Dewey	45%
1952	**DD Eisenhower (R)**	55%
	AE Stevenson	44%
1956	**DD Eisenhower (R)**	58%
	AE Stevenson	42%
1960	**JF Kennedy (D)**	50%
	RM Nixon	50%
1964	**LB Johnson (D)**	61%
	BM Goldwater	39%
1968	**RM Nixon (R)**	43%
	HH Humphrey	43%
1972	**RM Nixon (R)**	61%
	G McGovern	38%
1976	**J Carter (D)**	51%
	GR Ford	48%
1980	**R Reagan (R)**	51%
	J Carter	42%
1984	**R Reagan (R)**	59%
	WF Mondale	41%
1988	**GHW Bush (R)**	53%
	MS Dukakis	46%
1992	**W Clinton**	43%
	GHW Bush	38%

all victors by large margins. As a result they could be said to represent sea changes in American politics giving their legislative programmes a mandate from the people. Such a national mandate does encourage members of Congress to co-operate with a president, either for reasons of constitutional propriety or for electoral self-interest. Ronald Reagan, in particular, used his massive electoral victories to boost his authority with Congress.

Control of Congress

In the United States, where the executive and legislature are elected separately, there is no guarantee that the president's party will be in a majority in either house of Congress. Nor is it guaranteed that a president will have any control over their party in the legislature.

> **Comparison**
>
> In a parliamentary democracy, like Britain, the executive is drawn from Parliament and therefore the party forming the government is guaranteed the support of the House of Commons, at least initially. If a government loses the support of the House it can be brought down by a vote of no confidence. In many cases the first-past-the-post electoral system means that the governing party is likely to have a large overall majority and so is safe from the fear of defeat.

Split-ticket voting

The separation of powers and the rise of **split-ticket voting**, when people vote for different parties in different types of election, have helped to divorce the electoral interests of the president and members of Congress. A landslide electoral victory in a presidential election in no way guarantees a similar swing in either the House or the Senate. Ronald Reagan's immense popularity did produce something of a **'coat-tails' effect** and the Republicans dominated the Senate between 1980 and 1986. However, recently such effects have been weak.

Republican difficulties

Harry Truman, Richard Nixon, Gerald Ford, Ronald Reagan and George Bush have all been confronted by a Congress dominated wholly or in part by the opposing party. In recent years Democratic dominance of the House and to a lesser extent the Senate has meant that Republican presidents have suffered most, although the Republican victories in the 1994 mid-term elections may give a future Republican president a more favourable relationship with Congress. Even those presidents who do face a Congress controlled by their own party know that parties 'control' Congress in name only. Party discipline is built on the role parties play in elections.

> **Comparison**
>
> In Britain political parties control the nomination of candidates, organize and finance the campaigns, provide the manifestos for the campaign and command quite a high level of voter loyalty. British MPs know that they owe their jobs in the House of Commons to their party and, more often than not, they will **'toe the party line'**.

In the United States election campaigns are **candidate-orientated** rather than focused on a party. The development of direct primaries has reduced the power of the party leadership in favour of the grass-roots supporters. Members of Congress know that it is to these grass-roots voters that they owe their jobs in Congress so they tend to vote as their constituents, rather than their party, would wish. As Thomas Mann, the American political scientist, has said: 'Senators and Representatives are in business for themselves. They are likely to view themselves first and foremost as individuals, not as a member of a party or as part of a President's team.' (*Elections and Change in Congress*, 1981).

Candidate-orientated campaign

For a president whose party does not control Congress weak party discipline is a distinct advantage. If it were not the case their legislative proposals would face certain defeat. However, for presidents such as Kennedy, Carter and Clinton, who all faced supposedly friendly Congresses, it can be frustrating. Between 1953 and 1984 Democrat presidents faced defections from their own party by an average of 31 per cent in the House and 39 per cent in the Senate. A lack of party discipline on this scale makes a president's life extremely difficult.

Weak party discipline

Despite the difficulties, a president normally benefits when his own party controls Congress. The achievements of Roosevelt and Johnson were undoubtedly made possible by their Democratic majorities in the Senate and in the House.

Personality and experience

How effectively presidents cope with the constitutional and political constraints placed upon them depends, at least partly, on their personality and experience. This does not necessarily mean that a president must have **charisma**. Franklin Roosevelt was charismatic and Ronald Reagan became known as 'The Great Communicator' but Lyndon Johnson was not the charismatic, good-looking, eloquent leader that his predecessor, John Kennedy, had been. Johnson succeeded because he was a shrewd and experienced political operator.

Comparison

In Britain many comparisons have been made between Margaret Thatcher and her successor, John Major. The former was considered to be a strong and dominant prime minister who had a clear programme of policies to be implemented during each parliamentary term and would tolerate little or no opposition.

John Major appears to be a more conciliatory leader who prefers to govern through consensus and agreement rather than by confrontation. However, personality can be over-estimated as a determinant of political success. British prime minister Clement Attlee governed effectively though his style was quiet and undramatic. In addition, personality is sometimes used to explain differences in governing performance when changing political circumstances might also be responsible.

Persuasion

Richard Neustadt's suggestion that 'the greatest power of the President is the power to persuade' (*Presidential Power*, 1960) is well known and remains relevant, particularly because it is a vague statement open to a variety of interpretations by presidents with many different styles. Regardless of the style, if a president is to be successful they must persuade the bureaucracy and, in particular, Congress to work with them.

LBJ

President Johnson is widely regarded as the president who was able to work with Congress to the greatest effect. He built on his Senate experience to manufacture coalitions around the legislative proposals to create his Great Society.

According to Johnson's biographer Doris Kearns: 'If it's really going to work, the relationship between the President and the Congress has got to be almost incestuous. He's got to know them even better than they know themselves. And then, on the basis of this knowledge, he's got to build a system that stretches from the cradle to the grave, from the moment a bill is introduced to the moment it is officially enrolled as a law of the land.'

Although Johnson had a distinct programme he wished to put in place he always consulted with congressional leaders when formulating legislation, and organized a full briefing session for members prior to a bill's introduction. Furthermore a bill was never introduced until the right moment, to minimize opposition and maximize support. Finally, when a crucial vote was due to take place, Johnson would intensively lobby key members of Congress who could influence the votes of others.

Lobbying

The intensive lobbying employed by any president will include **log-rolling**, by which the president may implicitly trade favours for support. In some cases lobbying may even become arm-twisting. Johnson was adept at the use of embarrassment, threats and reprisals to achieve his ends. Johnson's intimate knowledge of Congress is well illustrated by his biographer Eric Goldman: 'He knew where every wire of power ran, whose influence was waxing or waning, the rules and habits of the committees, what each had done three years before and wanted to do next year, the skeletons and hopes in scores of closets.' (*The Tragedy of Lyndon Johnson*, 1968).

Clinton

President Clinton has also proved adept at congressional coalition-building. The successful passage of the North American Free Trade Agreement (NAFTA) in 1993 was due largely to his willingness to 'deal' with Congress. As David Bonior, the Democrat Chief Whip in the House, opposed to the White House on NAFTA, has said: 'they [the administration] did a deal for sugar, they did a deal for citrus, they did a deal for vegetables, they did a deal for a lot of other commodities, and this is supposed to be a free trade agreement?'

Failure

Presidents Kennedy and Carter harboured legislative ambitions but achieved only limited success. Kennedy understood the need to work with Congress but lacked the experience of Johnson, the ex-Senate leader who would succeed him. Only 39 per cent of Kennedy's proposals were passed by Congress. Jimmy Carter's experience was limited to the governor's mansion in Georgia and he seemed unwilling to work with Congress on its own terms. His style was aloof, distant and perhaps a little self-righteous. Even though the Democrats controlled the House and the Senate Carter's success rate in Congress was very low.

Of course not every president aspires to emulate Franklin Roosevelt by being an activist president. President Eisenhower had relatively limited ambitions for the presidency because he believed that the activism of previous holders of the office had usurped the legislative power of Congress. Therefore one must remember to assess the effectiveness of presidents on their own terms rather than by the yardstick of the 'New Deal' or the 'Great Society'.

Eisenhower

Staff

Obviously a president does not work alone with Congress. In 1939 the Executive Office of the President (EXOP) was set up to give support to the chief executive. The branches of EXOP contain the president's closest advisers, speech writers, 'spin doctors', etc. The most successful presidencies have rested on excellent staff members.

In Ronald Reagan's first term of office his chief of staff, James Baker, is generally thought to be responsible for a great deal of the president's success with Congress. Some believe that the remarkable political skills of the Texan made him the best chief of staff in history. Certainly the performance of the Reagan White House deteriorated significantly when Baker was replaced by Donald Regan in 1984.

Chief of staff

Comparison

The civil service in the UK is permanent and so gives prime ministers little opportunity to influence staff appointments. Although Mrs Thatcher's alleged interference in the civil service appointments has given rise to some doubt about this.

British prime ministers are however responsible for the appointments of Cabinet and junior ministers. These are often a prime minister's closest colleagues and will make an enormous difference to a government's performance.

In 1993 Howard Paster was President Clinton's chief congressional liaison and played a significant role in the administration's achievements in the first year. To accomplish their NAFTA success the Clinton White House became a 'war room' for 56 days, during which time William Daley, a Chicago businessman, was brought in to organize the presidential programme of 18 public events, meetings with over 150 congressmen and phoning marathons to sway undecided members.

Clinton administration

In fact during times of intense presidential activity the White House staff become the president's **lobbyists**. They handle Congress, manage the press and orchestrate public opinion. It is no surprise, then, that at the beginning of 1994 President Clinton replaced Howard Paster with Pat Griffin who, in the past, has worked as a lobbyist.

Lobbyists

Media relations

Given the expectations the American people have of them it is vital for every president to make the best use of the media. The media will shape the electorate's perception of the president which in turn could affect the president's relationship with other branches of government. A president who is popular in the country is more likely to achieve his legislative ambitions in Congress, for example. This is by no means a hard-and-fast rule, as the presidencies of Kennedy and Bush prove, but a direct appeal to the nation through the media can put more pressure on a recalcitrant legislature.

FDR

Since the 1960s the president's relationship with the media has become a great deal more complicated. Cosy relationships with journalists and 'fireside chats', as employed by Franklin Roosevelt, are now rare as the relationship has become more cynical and confrontational.

LBJ and Nixon

The Vietnam War and Watergate were turning points in the relationship between the president and the media. Successive presidents misled the American people and the media about the tide of the war in South-east Asia until questions began to be raised about Johnson's 'credibility gap'. The lies and deceit of the Nixon White House was the final nail in the coffin of cosy relations.

'Spin doctors'

Therefore the president and the 'spin doctors' must manage the media effectively in order to put the best 'spin' on every news item that concerns the White House. Failure to do this, no matter how difficult, can mean a disastrous time for the president. This is well illustrated by the trials and tribulations of Jimmy Carter in 1979–81 as the media counted the days of internment suffered by the American personnel held hostage in Tehran by the Ayatollah Khomeini's regime and Carter lost the 1980 presidential election.

Political, social and economic circumstances

Presidents, like prime ministers, do not operate in a political vacuum. Their popularity, political strength and success all depend on the circumstances facing them at any one time.

Depression

Perhaps the clearest illustration of this point is the early days of the administration of Franklin Roosevelt. In 1933 America was suffering badly in the Depression. Unemployment had reached 13 million (25 per cent of the labour force), national income had halved since 1929 and the production of manufactured goods had fallen by 77 per cent. Roosevelt had been elected in 1932 promising a 'New Deal' for the American people. Roosevelt himself summed up his situation in his inaugural address: 'I am prepared under my constitutional duty to recommend the measures that a stricken nation in the midst of a stricken world may require.'

The American historian Arthur Schlesinger Jr has outlined the circumstances more vividly: 'It was not just a matter of staving off hunger. It was a matter of seeing whether a representative democracy could conquer economic collapse. It was a matter of staving off violence, even (at least some thought) revolution' (*The Cycles of American History*, 1974).

'100 days'

The circumstances were so dire that he was able to take the opportunity to put together the most far-reaching legislative programme ever seen in the United States. During the legendary first '100 days' no fewer than 15 major pieces of legislation were enacted.

He was to repeat this success on a lesser scale in 1935 during what has become known as 'the second 100 days'.

'Resurgent Congress'

For many presidents the circumstances under which they take office offer fewer opportunities. President Ford was Richard Nixon's successor and faced a **'resurgent Congress'** seeking to reassert itself over the presidency after the disgrace of the Watergate scandal (see page 136). The fact that President Ford used his veto power 66 times (including 18 'pocket vetoes') and that they were overridden 12 times is indicative of his relationship with Congress.

Congressional reform

President Carter faced similar problems in the late 1970s. Not only was Congress still in its 'resurgent' phase it was also going through a period of renewal. It had reformed itself to create a whole host of sub-committees to add to its already extensive committee system and many of its personnel were inexperienced. In the 96th Congress (1979–80) half of the senators were 'freshmen', having served less than one term. Both of these facts made Congress very susceptible to the influence of interest groups and many of Carter's legislative proposals died or were emasculated in committee. Perhaps his Energy Bill is the most well-known example of Congress's willingness to destroy Carter's proposals. When first introduced in 1977 the bill was so seriously dismembered that the administration allowed it to die. The follow-up proposal was eventually passed in October 1978 minus the key taxes on oil and petrol.

Cycles

Propitious circumstances seem to occur for presidents only rarely. Arthur Schlesinger Jr has argued in *The Cycles of American History* that the American political pendulum swings between the 'public purpose' of liberalism and the 'private purpose' of conservatism on a thirty-year cycle. Theodore Roosevelt in 1901, Franklin Roosevelt in 1933 and Lyndon Johnson in 1965 were all liberal, activist presidents and all were followed by a tide of conservatism – in the 1920s Harding, Coolidge and Hoover; in the 1950s Eisenhower; and in the 1970s and 1980s Nixon, Carter (a conservative Democrat), Reagan and Bush.

This cycle of liberal activism generally coincides with high points of presidential legislative leadership. The exception is Ronald Reagan. Although a conservative when placed on the political spectrum; when examined in terms of legislative leadership he is a radical.

According to Schlesinger's cycle a new phase of liberal activism was due to begin in the 1990s, a prophecy which has surely not been lost on President Clinton. He should also be aware that if there is a confluence of advantageous circumstances it tends to be short-lived. After only a few years Roosevelt, Johnson and Reagan had all lost their touch with Congress. In 1965 President Johnson's success rate in Congress was as high as 93 per cent but by 1968 it had fallen to 75 per cent. Similarly, President Reagan experienced a rating as high as 82.4 per cent in 1981 but by 1987 it was as low as 43.5 per cent. Lyndon Johnson himself said: 'I have watched the Congress from either the inside or the outside, man and boy, for more than forty years and I have never seen a Congress that didn't eventually take the measure of the president it was dealing with.'

Operating outside constitutional constraints

The conflict between the president's predominance in the system and the lack of political clout to achieve their aims has caused presidents to be frustrated. As a result many have attempted to achieve their ends by going around the constitutional constraints.

Prerogative powers

The United States constitution has survived the test of time because it is relatively vague. It is particularly vague on elements of presidential power. Many presidents have realized that this presents an opportunity for them to widen their authority by adopting **prerogative powers**. These are powers not specifically given to the president in the constitution but which successive presidents have felt able to adopt as their own.

'War powers'

The tendency to use prerogative powers has been particularly prevalent in the realm of foreign affairs and is by no means new. Incidents of the use of the 'war powers' without congressional authority go back to George Washington who, in 1794, called out troops to quash the so-called Whiskey Rebellion. Many presidents have followed his example; they include: James K Polk, who, in 1846, ordered an invasion of territory claimed by Mexico, thus provoking the Mexican–American War; Abraham Lincoln in 1861, who ordered southern ports to be blockaded during the Civil War; William Howard Taft in 1912, who ordered troops into Nicaragua; Harry Truman, who sent troops to Korea in 1950; John F Kennedy, who ordered the Bay of Pigs invasion of Cuba in 1962; and George Bush who ordered troops into Panama to capture General Noriega.

Congressional authority

In many cases congressional support for an action has been requested, and given, in retrospect. For example, in 1983 Congress authorized US troops to remain on their peace-keeping mission to the Lebanon for 18 months. In other cases congressional authorization has been gained through deceit or has not been sought at all. Lyndon Johnson sought authority from Congress to respond to a supposedly unprovoked attack on American ships by North Vietnamese forces in the Gulf of Tonkin. In 1964 Congress gave him *carte blanche* to respond as he saw fit by passing the Gulf of Tonkin Resolution. In doing so Congress was giving Johnson the power to fight an undeclared war in Vietnam. The resolution was the legal basis for all of the actions of Johnson and Nixon in Vietnam. Whether the initial unprovoked attack ever took place has never been proved.

War Powers Act

However, this and the actions subsequently taken by the Nixon administration (see pages 99–101) persuaded Congress to pass the War Powers Act in 1973. It states that a president may commit United States' troops into 'hostilities' or 'imminent hostilities' only if Congress has declared war or has passed enabling legislation or if the United States has been attacked. Once troops have been committed the president must submit a report to Congress, within 48 hours, explaining the circumstances, justification and intentions. The submission of the report begins a countdown of 60 days within which time troops should be withdrawn unless Congress gives its approval for the operation. If such approval is withheld the president has a further 30 days to withdraw the troops.

All presidents have sought to comply with the Act whilst appearing not to do so. For example presidential reports always state that the president is acting 'consistent with' rather 'in compliance with' the resolution.

Legislative veto

The first part of the resolution relies on the use of a 'congressional veto' or 'legislative veto' (see page 118). The constitution does not give the Congress a veto power and so it was declared unconstitutional by the Supreme Court in 1983. This further weakened the War Powers Act.

The 'countdown' provision of the Resolution remains although it has never been used to force the withdrawal of troops.

'Frontlash'

Given that the president tends to dominate foreign affairs, most have successfully extended their power through the use of prerogatives and have been stronger as a result. Richard Pious, an American political scientist, describes this as a **'frontlash' effect.** For example, in 1940 President Roosevelt agreed to give destroyers to Britain in exchange for Caribbean bases. He did not sign a treaty with Britain, for this would have required Senate ratification, but made an executive agreement, which did not. Roosevelt had avoided the isolationist Senate and had made, what turned out to be, a popular agreement.

'Backlash'

Presidents who have sought to adopt prerogative powers in domestic politics have often been less fortunate and have experienced what Pious refers to as a **'backlash' effect.** For example, in 1952 President Truman ordered the secretary of commerce to take possession of and to operate America's steel mills. At the time the mills were experiencing an industrial dispute which Truman feared would hinder the United States war effort in Korea. The Supreme Court, in *Youngstown Sheet and Tube Company* v. *Sawyer*, declared his action to be in breach of his constitutional powers.

The 'imperial presidency'

Monarchical powers

Arthur Schlesinger Jr coined the term **'imperial president'** to describe the increasingly monarchical powers being adopted by presidents. The greater world role for America had encouraged its presidents to adopt more and more prerogatives in foreign policy but similar prerogatives were gradually adopted in the domestic arena.

Centralization

Schlesinger characterized an 'imperial president' as one who centres decision-making in the White House, refuses to co-operate with Congress and avoids Congress in policy-making. These trends he described as 'revolutionary' because they involved a fundamental redistribution of power within the American political system.

Nixon

The presidency of Richard Nixon best illustrates the characteristics of the 'imperial president'. Nixon came to power in 1969 having been on the political scene since 1946. A conservative, his main aims lay in foreign rather than domestic policy and it was here that his 'imperial' tendencies first began to show. He centred foreign policy-making in the White House, working closely with his national security adviser, Henry Kissinger. Both men had an inclination toward secret diplomacy on the grand scale of Europe in the early nineteenth century. Their exploits included the secret bombing of Cambodia, the opening of diplomatic relations with China, the policy of détente with the Soviet Union, the Paris Peace Talks to negotiate the end of the Vietnam War and

Richard Nixon (1913–1994)

Richard Nixon's rollercoaster political career began in 1946 when he was elected to the House of Representatives, from California. After four years he was elected to the Senate, where he served for four years and established a reputation as a fervent anti-communist.

In 1952 the Republican Party chose him to be Eisenhower's running-mate for the presidency. During his eight years as vice-president the headlines included the 'kitchen debate' with Khrushchev, the 'Checkers speech' and being stoned in Caracas.

He lost the 1960 presidential election to John Kennedy by 118,574 votes, amidst concern over electoral fraud by the Democratic Party in Cook County, Illinois. He subsequently lost the election for governor of California in 1964 and lowered his profile for two years.

He returned to the political spotlight in 1968 as the Republican candidate for the presidency. He won and was re-elected in 1972 by a massive margin.

As president his main achievements lay in foreign policy. He gradually withdrew US forces from Vietnam, pursued the policy of détente with the Soviet Union and became the first president to visit China.

He resigned from the presidency in 1974 before he could be impeached on the charges collectively known as 'Watergate'. His successor, Gerald Ford, granted him a pardon.

After his resignation he gradually rehabilitated himself, writing books, articles and commenting on politics for the media. Republican presidents, such as Reagan and Bush, turned to him for advice and he gradually became an elder statesman of the Republican Party.

Nixon died in 1994. His funeral was attended by the five living presidents and President Clinton's eulogy concentrated on his career achievements rather than his fall from grace.

the overthrow of President Allende of Chile. The secrecy of their activity and the centralization of decision-making excluded Congress and, in the case of the secret bombing of Cambodia, they blatantly misled Congress as they extended the war in South-east Asia.

Impoundment

As his presidency went on Nixon appropriated further powers in the domestic arena. Throughout the period of his administration he refused to spend monies allocated by Congress if their use did not meet his approval. This is known as impoundment and is in breach of the constitutional provision that Congress controls the purse strings. By 1974 the Nixon administration had impounded $18 billion.

'The plumbers'

President Nixon was notoriously ill at ease with the media and the predominant attitude in the White House was defensive, if not paranoid. As a result the White

House created a secret organization known as 'the plumbers'. Their role was to plug government leaks and to bug the homes and offices of political opponents. It was this group that was eventually caught bugging the offices of the Democratic Party National Committee in the Watergate Building, an event which triggered an investigation that would culminate in President Nixon's resignation in the face of impeachment proceedings.

Executive privilege

Even during the investigations that followed, President Nixon continued to push his presidential powers further. Initially he refused to allow members of his staff to testify before the Senate Watergate Committee, claiming **'executive privilege'**. This is the convention that all communications between a president and his advisers should be confidential. He relented only to resurrect the claim to absolute 'executive privilege' when asked to hand over copies of tapes made of his conversations in the Oval Office.

'Overshoot and collapse'

President Nixon's unconstitutional activities became collectively known as Watergate. According to Pious they illustrate the **'overshoot and collapse'** of a president intent on adopting prerogative powers to the extreme. Whether such activity is exceptional is a matter for debate. President Nixon was always convinced that his actions were not particularly worse than those of any of his predecessors and that his fall was due to the Democratic Congress finally catching up with their long-time foe, Dick Nixon. The term 'imperial presidency' remains in use and, in fact, was applied to President Reagan's administration.

Iran-Contra

The **Iran-Contra Affair** arose in 1986 and involved a number of illegal acts committed by the Reagan White House. In brief, the Reagan administration sold arms to Iran, above market prices, in return for Iranian help in freeing the American hostages in Beirut. The funds were then used to fund a guerrilla group, the Contras, in Nicaragua. The sale of arms to Iran was illegal as was channelling funds to the Contras, and negotiating for the release of hostages was contrary to the president's stated policy.

It has been difficult to label Ronald Reagan an 'imperial president' because he claims not to remember the events of the Iran-Contra Affair. However, the Irangate scandal seems to fit the pattern of presidential frustration leading to unconstitutional activity.

Too much or too little power?

It should, by now, be clear that since Franklin Roosevelt most presidents have tended to see themselves as the leader in the American political system. They have taken on the responsibility of activism at home and abroad, and in doing so they have raised popular expectations. Their power to fulfil these expectations remains checked and the opportunities for a strong presidents to come to the fore are limited. The presidencies of Roosevelt, Johnson and to a lesser extent Reagan are exceptions to the normal rules of the presidential game.

Therefore many presidents and their supporters have believed that they are expected to work under impossible constraints. Complaints of an **'imperilled presidency'** or an **'impotent presidency'** were common in the Ford–Carter era as Congress reasserted its authority. On the other hand President Nixon and to a lesser extent President Reagan have shown that a president frustrated by congressional restraint can amass a great deal of power without Congress's knowledge.

Questions

Short questions

1 a What is a 'pocket veto'?
  b Under what circumstances does the president use a veto?
  (ULEAC, January 1992)

2 Why are most presidents sparing in their use of the veto power? (ULEAC, January 1993)

3 What has been the impact of the War Powers Act? (ULEAC, June 1993)

4 What are the main constraints on presidential power? (ULEAC, June 1994)

US questions

1 How powerful in practice is the office of president of the United States? (UCLES, June 1994)

2 President Truman said his only power was 'the power to persuade'. How far is this view of presidential power still valid? (UCLES, June 1993)

3 Jimmy Carter's failure to understand or accept the rudimentary facts about the policy-making process is entertainingly but vividly conveyed by a member of Congress who envisaged the following exchanges between the speaker of the House of Representatives, Tip O'Neill, and the president after the latter's famous 'energy is the moral equivalent of war' speech.

   O'Neill: A fine speech, Mr President. Now here's a list of members you should call, you know, to keep the pressure on. We need their votes.

   Carter: Tip, I outlined the problem to the people of the United States of America. It was rational, and my presentation was also rational. Now the American people are the most intelligent people in the entire world, Tip, and I am sure that when they see their Representatives think my program over, they will see that I was right.

   O'Neill: Lookit, Mr President. We need you to push this bill through. This is politics we are talking here, not physics.

   Carter: It is not politics, Tip, not to me. It's what is right and rational and necessary and practical and urgent that we do... Say, do you like my sweater?

   O'Neill (later to a congressional colleague)*:* That guy is hopeless. It's gonna be a long winter.

   Source: Jack Beatty quoted in *Roosevelt to Reagan: The Development of the Modern Presidency*, David Mervin (C. Hurst and Company)

   How far is *prior* political experience in Washington DC an essential requirement for a president to achieve his political objectives? (AEB, June 1992)

4 a What was the 'imperial presidency'?

b How successful were President Reagan's attempts to restore it?
(ULEAC, January 1993)

5 a Why has there been an extension of presidential power?
b Has the presidency become too powerful?
(ULEAC, January 1992)

Comparative questions

1 'Not all heads of government are effective political leaders.' Discuss. (Illustrate your answer with reference to at least two countries.) (ULEAC, June 1993)

2 a What factors have advanced the powers of heads of government in recent years?
b What limits exist to their exercise of power? (Illustrate your answer with reference to at least two countries.)
(ULEAC, January 1993)

7 The federal bureaucracy

Questions to be answered in this chapter

- How is the bureaucracy structured?
- Why is it so difficult to co-ordinate the bureaucracy?
- How do the president and Congress attempt to control the bureaucracy?

Terms to know

- 'Alphabet agencies'
- Bi-partisan
- 'Big government'
- Cabinet
- Clientelism
- Congressional oversight
- Congressional veto
- Departments
- EXOP
- Federal administration
- Government intervention
- IEAs
- IRCs
- 'Iron triangles'
- Keynesian economics
- Lobbyists
- Medicaid
- Medicare
- Meritocratic
- Military-industrial complex
- Neutral
- Pendleton Act
- *Primus inter pares*
- 'Revolving door'
- Senate ratification
- Senior Executive Service
- Social welfare
- 'Spoils system'
- Statutory agencies

The executive branch of government

The executive branch of government can be divided into two parts:
- the political
- the administrative

In the USA the president sits at the apex of the executive branch and is the only member of this branch to be elected. Beneath the president are his administrative officials, who are responsible for providing him with advice and carrying out his decisions. However, unlike the system in the UK, many of the members of the top layers of the administration are political, in that they are appointed by the president and have not achieved their positions through a **meritocratic** appointment system. The distinction between political and non-political members of the executive is therefore less distinct than in the UK.

Cabinet

The blurring of the distinction between political decision-makers and non-political administrators, that predominates in British constitutional theory, is clearly illustrated by the **Cabinet** in the US. The president has the power to select his cabinet secretaries from any walk of life, although they are subject to **Senate ratification**. Within the Cabinet the president is the ultimate decision-maker.

Comparison

The British executive branch of government is headed by the prime minister and Cabinet. The prime minister is the leader of the governing party in the House of Commons. He or she chooses Cabinet colleagues, all of whom must be members of either the House of Lords or the House of Commons. Most Cabinet members head civil service departments.

Constitutionally, decision-making is collective with the entire Cabinet responsible for determining government policy. Within the Cabinet the prime minister is the chair but is ***primus inter pares*** (first among equals) and can be outvoted by Cabinet as a whole. At times it has been argued that British government is becoming more prime ministerial, with the prime minister dominating the decision-making process.

Below Cabinet level the prime minister also selects junior ministers who fill secondary ranks in civil service departments. Again, they must be drawn from parliament.

Civil servants are appointed on a meritocratic basis. They are permanent and so do not change when the government changes. As a result they are expected to be neutral.

Even senior officials below the level of cabinet secretary in the United States are not permanent, and therefore need not be neutral. Unlike in the UK, the higher echelons of the departments are politically appointed and can be removed at any time, and are therefore expected to be loyal to the president's administration rather than any greater ideal of the state.

As in the UK, however, the vast majority of officials, albeit below the senior positions, are recruited on a meritocratic basis, are expected to be neutral and are just as difficult to control and co-ordinate as their British counterparts.

The origins of the US bureaucracy

In 1789 the first president of the United States, George Washington, asked Congress for authority to create three 'executive departments' to be headed by 'principal officers'. The Senate gave its approval and the **departments** of State, War and the Treasury were created. The secretary of the Treasury, Alexander Hamilton, had a staff of 39; Thomas Jefferson, the secretary of state, had five assistants; Henry Knox at the Department of War had an even smaller staff. On such a small scale was the federal bureaucracy born. Two hundred years later when Ronald Reagan left office there were 3.9 million employees in the federal government.

Expansion

The explosion of the **federal administration** could never have been foreseen by the framers of the constitution. As the twentieth century nears its end the world of government has grown beyond the imagination of the Founding Fathers. As a result the constitution makes only passing references to 'principal officers' and 'executive departments'. Whilst the president, Congress and Supreme Court are all based on the prescriptions of the constitution, the federal administration has developed without a constitutional blueprint.

As Madison and Jefferson wrestled to create an elaborate system of checks and balances in order to restrain the main branches of government, they could not know that a 'fourth branch of government' would be one of the most powerful of all forces in twentieth-century politics.

The growth of the federal administration

The growth in the federal administration has reflected the increasing workload of the central government. In the nineteenth and twentieth centuries the responsibilities of governments in all countries grew enormously. America is no exception to this trend. As society has become more complex so the number of statutes it requires swells. Much of the complexity results from technological innovation. Think of the number of rules and regulations that have followed the development of the mass-produced motor car.

New Deal and 'big government'

In all modern states the government is responsible for regulation and management of the economy. In many European states **government intervention** is considerable, with state-owned corporations and commitments to support and subsidize key industries. Even the United States, which considers itself to be the home of undiluted capitalism, did not escape the move towards **Keynesian economics,** which preached the virtues of government management of the macro economy. Franklin Roosevelt's New Deal policies marked the beginning of **'big government'** in America and required a whole host of new bureaucratic agencies to make it possible. These became known as **'alphabet agencies'**, and included the Agricultural Adjustment Administration (AAA), the Civilian Conservation Corps (CCC), the Federal Emergency Relief Administration (FERA), the National Recovery Administration (NRA) and the Tennessee Valley Authority (TVA).

Great Society

The Johnson administration continued the trend begun by the New Deal but this time took government further than ever before into the areas of **social welfare**. The creation of **Medicaid** and **Medicare** made government responsible for the social welfare of the elderly, disabled and some low-income groups. Naturally such an extension of government responsibility leads to the growth of the bureaucracy.

Budget

Perhaps the best indication of the development of 'big government' is the massive increase in the size of the federal government's budget. In 1963 President Kennedy's budget amounted to less than $100 billion. President Clinton expects the federal budget to grow to approximately $1,500 billion by 1999.

Employees

Whilst the size of the federal budget has consistently increased since World War II, the number of personnel employed has remained relatively stable, at between two and four million. However, the growth of federal governmental programmes has put a greater workload on the state governments and here the number of employees has risen from 4.25 million in 1950 to 13 million in 1983.

The structure of the federal administration

All three branches of the United States' federal government have their own administrations. The Supreme Court has its judicial network, including the inferior courts, the Administrative Office of the United States' Courts and the Federal Judicial Centre. Congress's administration includes the Congressional Budget Office and the Library of Congress. However, it is the executive branch of government that is of most interest for it is here that administrative officials make their greatest impact on the political system.

Comparison

In Britain many students of the civil service are coming to terms with the impact Mrs Thatcher's years in office have made on the administrative machine. Changes made under the Thatcher administration include the beginning of a break-up of the civil service in Whitehall in favour of executive agencies and the alleged politicization of the higher ranks of the civil service. Both of these changes could be said to be moving Britain nearer to the American model of administration.

In the United States the federal bureaucracy is divided into four different branches and each, to a greater or lesser extent, contains political appointees.

Departments

The three departments set up by George Washington have now become fourteen, with the most recent, the Department of Veterans' Affairs, being set up in 1989. Over the past 200 years departments have developed in a relatively ad hoc manner. They have emerged from agencies, been merged with others and, in some cases, abolished altogether. The Department of War was responsible for the army, whilst there was a separate Department of the Navy, until they were joined by the Air Force in the Defence Department in 1949. The Post Office was a department until 1970, when it became an executive agency. The Department of Labour and Commerce was created in 1903 but was split in 1913.

Cabinet

The departments are responsible for the greater part of the administrative load of federal government. Each is headed by a cabinet secretary, with the exception of the Department of Justice, which is headed by the attorney general. The departmental heads come together to form the president's Cabinet. The extent to which the Cabinet is involved in decision-making and policy determination is entirely up to the president. Unlike in Britain, decision-making is not necessarily collective and the president is not *primus inter pares*. President Reagan thought it important to hear the views of his Cabinet but always made the final decision himself. President Nixon called Cabinet meetings only rarely and preferred to rely on his closest advisers in the White House. In fact, Nixon held only eleven Cabinet meetings in 1972.

'Spoils system'

Until the end of the nineteenth century appointments to departments were made on the basis of what has become known as the **'spoils system'**, which was institutionalized under President Jackson. This meant that an incoming president could replace the entire staff of departments with his own appointees. For politicians this system presented an excellent opportunity to reward their political supporters but its justification was often couched in more respectable language. As the historian Richard Hofstadter has written: 'The professional politicians succeeded in persuading themselves that civil service reform ... would restrict job-holding to a hereditary, college-educated aristocracy; and that all kinds of unreasonable and esoteric questions would be asked on civil service examinations.'

Pendleton Act

This system of political patronage ended in 1883 when Congress passed the **Pendleton Act**. This introduced a permanent, meritocratic civil service to the American system. Its passage coincided with the assassination in 1881 of President Garfield by Charles Guiteau, who was disgruntled at not receiving a position in Garfield's administration despite working for his campaign in 1880. It was also associated with the rise of the Progressive Movement which believed that government could be improved if the principles of science could be brought to bear on its institutions. Taking the civil service out of the hands of the politicians and putting into place a system based on merit was one of the movement's major achievements.

Comparison

The British civil service was set up in its present form by the Northcote-Trevelyan Report in 1854. Since then it has been permanent (not changing as governments change), neutral (in order to serve different governments equally) and anonymous (not taking responsibility for decisions – which should be taken by ministers).

As it is permanent its members should be recruited on a meritocratic basis – through examinations and interviews – rather than according to political attitudes.

Initially, approximately 10 per cent of civil servants were appointed via examinations and interviews, administered by the Civil Service Commission, but gradually the balance between career civil servants and appointees has been reversed. Now 90 per cent of the staff of departments are career civil servants.

Neutrality

In the United States, career civil servants, like their counterparts in Britain, are permanent and should therefore be **neutral**. The Hatch Acts of 1939 and 1940 prevent civil servants taking part in political campaigns. Civil servants are also discouraged from becoming too politically active by a prohibition against strike action which, for a civil servant, is a federal offence.

Career Service Reform Act

The career civil service system was further reformed by the Carter administration's Career Service Reform Act (1978). Carter described the federal administration as a

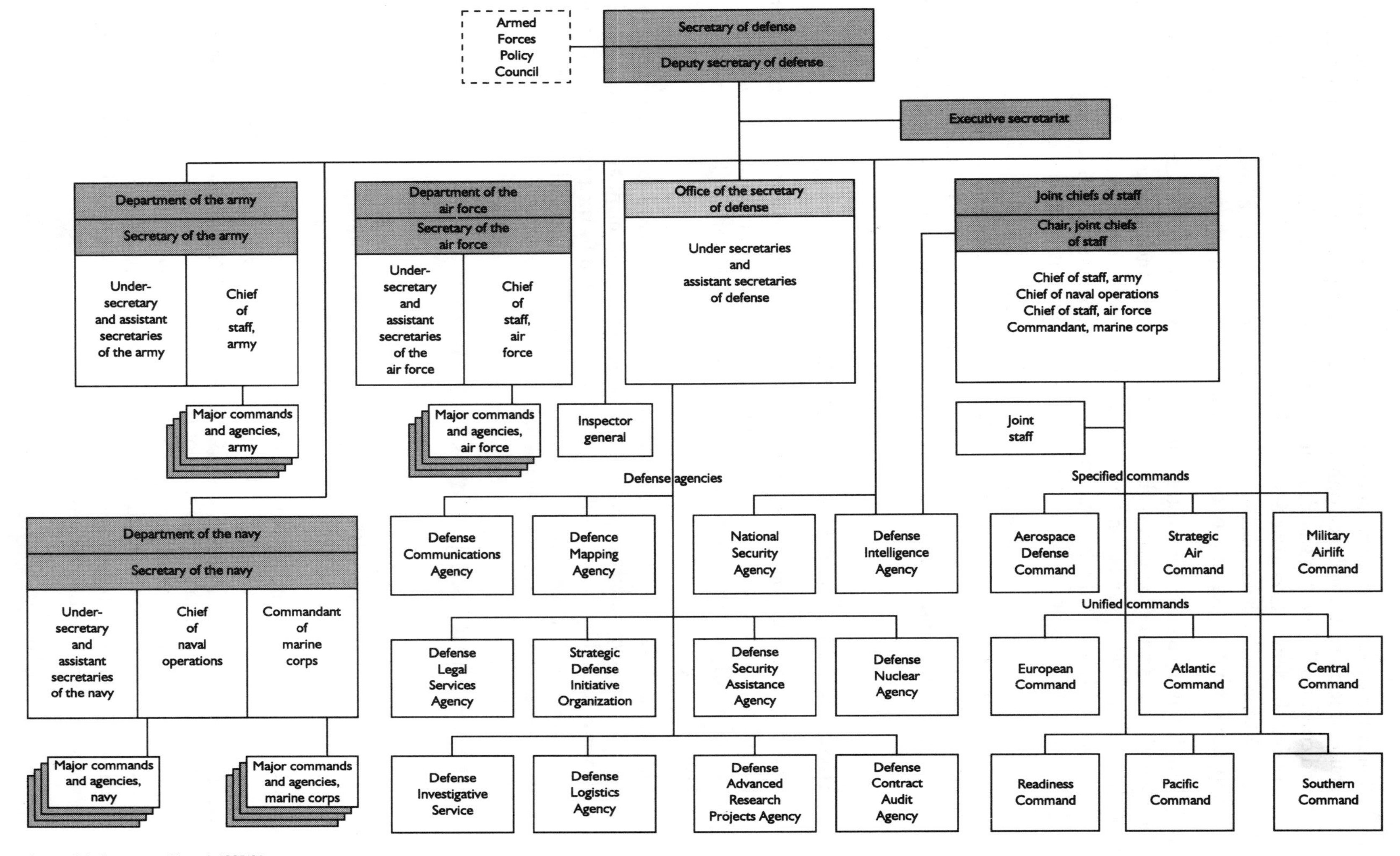

Source: U.S. Government Manual, 1985/86.

Figure 7.1 The organization of the Department of Defense

'bureaucratic maze which neglects merit, tolerates poor performance, and permits abuse of legitimate employee rights and mires every personnel action in red tape, delay and confusion'. The Act was designed to make the civil service more efficient. It created the **Senior Executive Service** which consists of an elite corps of approximately 11,000 top civil service managers, 10 per cent of whom are allowed to be political appointees but 33 per cent of positions are reserved for career servants only.

The Act also gave the administration greater powers to reward career civil servants with bonuses and promotions via the Office of Personnel Management. However, this system was open to abuse and has led to the increasing politicization of the career civil service. In 1982–83 the Reagan administration reassigned 2,326 senior executives in an attempt to strengthen their control over the administrative machine.

Political appointees

The highest levels of departments are still filled on a patronage basis. A president has the opportunity to make approximately 1,500 appointments when he arrives in office – all need Senate ratification. The levels of political appointees include cabinet secretaries, under-secretaries, deputy under-secretaries, assistant secretaries and office directors.

Independent Executive Agencies

Outside the jurisdiction of departments there are approximately 40 executive agencies **(IEAs)**, which were set up to give greater control over a specific area of policy; examples include the Central Intelligence Agency (CIA) and the Environmental Protection Agency.

The agencies are independent from departments. They recruit their own staff and submit their own budget requests to the Office of Management and Budget. Usually they are headed by a single individual who is appointed by the president, with Senate ratification, and can be removed by the president at any time. Their independence from the chief executive is therefore limited.

Independent Regulatory Commissions

At times Congress has felt the need to improve the regulation and supervision of sectors of the private economy. To achieve this aim it created the Independent Regulatory Commissions **(IRCs)**; examples include the Interstate Commerce Commission and the Federal Reserve Board.

IRCs are 'independent' in that they do not fall under the direct jurisdiction of the president. They are headed by a board or commission, the membership of which varies between IRCs. The members of the commissions are appointed by the president, with Senate ratification, for a fixed term of office. Therefore they cannot be removed by the president. Again the exact period of office varies between commissions. They are intended to be **bi-partisan**, which means that both parties should co-operate in the choice of commission members. However, most presidents will have the opportunity to shape the composition of many of the IRCs.

The powers of the IRCs are quite extensive. For example, the first IRC, the Interstate

Federal Reserve Board

'The Fed' was set up in 1913 by the Federal Reserve Act. It is a system which includes the twelve Federal Reserve Banks, all national banks and a number of state banks. It is headed by a seven-member board all of whom are appointed by the president for a fourteen-year term of office.

Its role is that of the central bank, to manage the monetary policy of the United States. It does so through rates, buying and selling government stock and by setting reserve requirements for banks.

The fixed term gives its members considerable independence from both the president and Congress. As chair of the Fed, Paul Volcker came into conflict with Presidents Carter and Reagan who disagreed with his tight money policies.

Commerce Commission has the power to license all surface forms of transport engaging in trade between states. This includes fares and the quality of service they provide.

The Executive Office of the President

Brownlow Committee

In 1939 the Brownlow Committee, which had been asked to diagnose the staffing needs of the president, reported that major reorganization of the executive branch of government was needed. Congress was unwilling to sanction a fundamental revision but did pass the Reorganization Act, which set up the Executive Office of the President (**EXOP** or EOP).

In reality it is not a single office but a collection of offices under the umbrella of EXOP. In total there are approximately twelve elements to EXOP with a staff of around 2,000. Although intended to improve the president's control of the rest of the bureaucracy, EXOP has become a bureaucracy in its own right.

Comparison

British prime ministers have been building up power around the Cabinet Office since its formation in 1916 and, more recently, in the Number 10 offices such as the Press Office, the Policy Unit and the Efficiency Unit. In addition, prime ministers use special advisers to provide specialist advice on particular areas of policy.

Presidents are free to vary the composition of EXOP as they wish although the core offices usually remain and have become known as the **statutory agencies**. These include the White House Office, the Office of Management and Budget, the National Security Council and the Council of Economic Advisors.

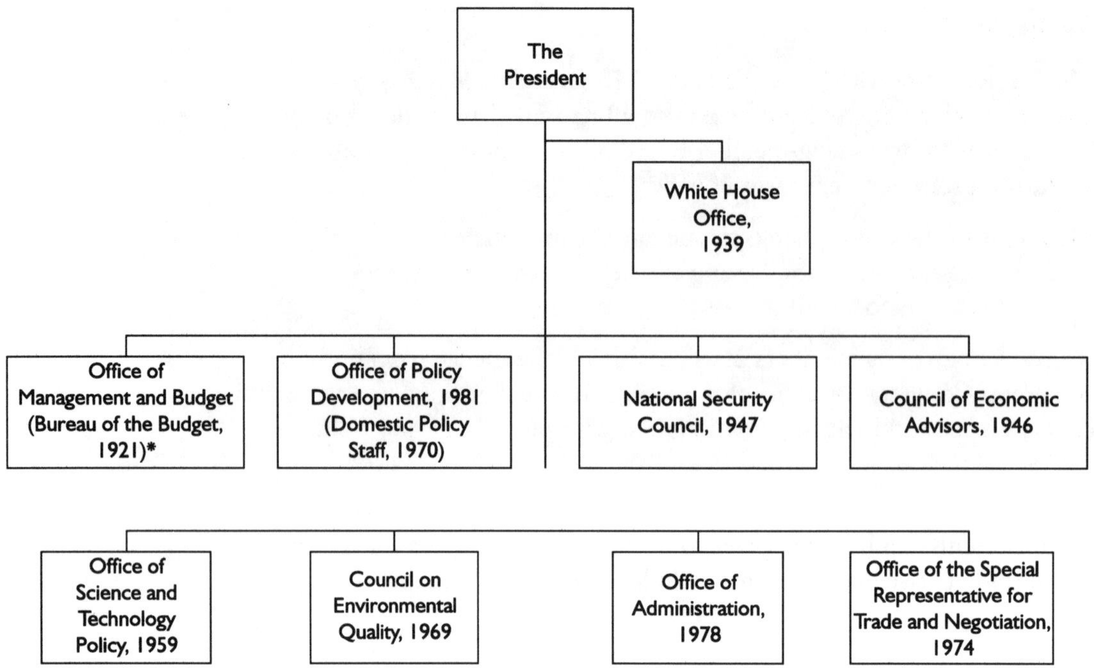

Figure 7.2 The Executive Office of the President, 1989

The White House Office (WHO)

This consists of a president's closest advisers. The staff will include special advisers on policy, speech writers, congressional liaison staff, communications staff. However, only a small number, two or three, are likely to have the 'ear' of the president on a regular basis. For that small group their authority comes from their proximity to the leader and they will work hard to protect that authority, often by restricting access to the president.

Watergate

WHO was made famous during the Watergate hearings in 1974 when it became apparent that President Nixon's closest advisers had been partly responsible for the Watergate cover-up. Chief conspirators Bob Haldeman, John Ehrlichman and John Dean were all based in the White House Office.

Reagan

During the Reagan administration power appeared to be held by a troika of James Baker, chief of staff; Edwin Meese, special counsel; and Michael Deaver, deputy chief of staff. They formed a hard core of advisors who had contact with Reagan on a daily basis and were largely responsible for the successes of his first term.

The Office of Management and Budget (OMB)

In 1970 President Nixon created the OMB out of the Bureau of the Budget, intending that it should become a major tool of policy-making. In fact it is possibly the most important element of EXOP as it has responsibility for drawing up the president's budget proposals. It is therefore the office through which the president can control all other elements of the executive branch.

It is intended to act as a management tool rather than another economic advisory unit. It assists the president in monitoring the efficiency of the bureaucracy and the way in which its parts are co-operating with the president and with each other. Due to their budgetary implications it is the office that takes responsibility for co-ordinating departmental legislative proposals.

The director of the OMB is a key member of the president's staff and probably ranks a close second to the president in terms of political power. He is one of the few members of EXOP to require Senate ratification.

The National Security Council (NSC)

The NSC was established in 1947 with a view to helping the president with matters of national security, both domestic and foreign.

NSC

The members of the NSC are the president, vice-president and the secretaries of state and defence. In addition the national security adviser directs the staff of the NSC.

Nixon and Kissinger

The NSC achieved some notoriety under the so-called 'imperial presidents', who liked to centre decision-making within the White House rather than with the rest of the bureaucracy. President Nixon preferred to make foreign policy through the NSC and his national security adviser, Henry Kissinger. As a result William Rogers, secretary of state during Nixon's first administration, was almost completely excluded from the foreign-policy-making process. During the Reagan administration it was the NSC that was at the centre of the Iran-Contra Affair.

Conflict

Even during the presidency of Jimmy Carter there was considerable conflict between the NSC, headed by Zbigniew Brzezinski, and the State Department, headed by Cyrus Vance. Brzezinski was a 'hawk' on foreign policy issues and often took a hard line on relations with the Soviet Union, Whereas Vance, a 'dove', usually took a more conciliatory stance.

The Council of Economic Advisors (CEA)

Unlike the OMB the CEA has an advisory rather than an administrative or managerial role. It is made up of senior economic staff, usually from major universities. The president will usually choose economists who share his own economic perspective.

In addition to these 'statutory agencies' the president can create whatever offices he wishes in order to reflect his policy objectives. Under George Bush additional offices included the Office of Policy Development, the Office of the United States Trade Representative, the Council on Environmental Quality, the Office of Science and Technology Policy and the Office of National Drug Control Policy.

Methods and problems of co-ordinating the executive branch

Main responsibility for the co-ordination of the executive branch of government lies with the chief executive, the president. Although there are many sources of help available it is by no means an easy task. As German sociologist Max Weber pointed out at the beginning of the twentieth century, the bureaucracy is a powerful force in modern politics.

Size

The first difficulty the president faces is the very size of the administrative machine. Obviously it is impossible to expect one person to be able to control almost four million members of the civilian administration. However, it is equally difficult to even guide the bureaucracy in the right direction. As Eisenhower prepared to take office in 1953, Harry Truman sympathized with the man accustomed to giving orders to his troops and expecting to have them obeyed: 'Poor Ike – it won't be a bit like the army. He'll find it very frustrating.'

The bureaucracy can be likened to a ship which, when set on course, will take miles to slow down or change course. Once a bureaucratic organization has built up a head of steam its momentum will carry it forward long after orders to change course have been given. As the journalist Hedrick Smith has written: 'Most bureaucrats put a high premium on continuity in policies, careful to make slow, incremental changes so as not to jar the system.' (*The Power Game*, 1988).

Bureaucracy

The German sociologist Max Weber believed that the bureaucracy would be one of the most powerful political forces in the twentieth century.

According to him, bureaucrats are professional administrators, recruited on merit rather than as political appointees. They work inside a hierarchical structure, following strict rules of procedure and decision-making and recording all decisions for future reference.

The advantages of bureaucracy are that it is efficient, consistent and gives advice on an objective basis, free from political bias. It also brings continuity to the system of government.

Bureaucrats are criticized for excessive red tape and form-filling and the danger that they might use their knowledge and expertise to subvert the governing role of their political masters.

It should be clear from these points that the technical description 'bureaucrat' can be strictly applied only to the permanent members of the US bureaucracy and not the senior levels of political appointees.

Advice and implementation

Persuasion

Of course the privileged position that bureaucrats hold gives them a great deal of influence over the ship's course. Max Weber's analysis of bureaucracy is based, in part, on the opportunities bureaucrats have to shape the advice that policy-makers receive and to obstruct the implementation of policies. The president and his senior advisers are dependent on the co-operation of the civil service and the epigram that 'the greatest power of the President is the power to persuade' (Richard Neustadt, *Presidential Power*) is as important in the context of executive co-ordination as it is with regard to president–Congress relations.

Divisions and conflict

Perhaps even the analogy with a ship is too simple. An oil tanker will, at least, move as one unit and does not have a mind of its own. The bureaucracy is divided into many different units, each of which could have its own methods of operation and its own goals. Even of Jefferson's administration, the historian James Sterling Young has written that 'departmental segmentation locks conflict into the system of executive government' (*The Washington Community 1800–1828*: Columbia University Press, *1966*).

Bureaux

Conflicts between departments and agencies or EXOP are only one manifestation of the divisions. Each department is sub-divided into bureaux, or offices, which can build up a considerable degree of independence from the rest of the department. The most well-known bureau is the Federal Bureau of Investigation (FBI), which forms part of the Department of Justice. From 1924 to 1972 it was headed by J Edgar Hoover who built it up to be an independent force in American politics.

The Executive Office of the President

To help the president there is the EXOP. The OMB in particular has become the president's main tool for managing the federal bureaucracy, its control of finance allowing them to use finance to persuade bureaucrats to 'toe the line'. The offer of funding for a 'pet' project or the threat to withdraw funding may encourage civil servants to co-operate with the White House.

Mini-bureaucracy

However, EXOP in turn has become a mini-bureaucracy. Watergate and the Iran-Contra Affair illustrate very well the difficulties involved in controlling and co-ordinating the office, which should be there to help the president.

Reorganization

Presidents do have the option of reorganizing the bureaucracy, with congressional approval, in an effort to reinforce their own priorities. Jimmy Carter created two new departments, Energy in 1977 and Education in 1979. When Bill Clinton came to office he elevated the United States' ambassador to the United Nations to Cabinet level as an indication of his commitment to the UN.

The National Performance Review

In September 1993 President Clinton launched the Reinventing Government Initiative, also known as the National Performance Review, under the aegis of Vice-President Al Gore.

The Review intends to improve government performance and reduce costs by giving the president the power to cut wasteful spending; releasing bureaucrats from many rules and regulations, enabling them to make more decisions for themselves; and encouraging the bureaucracy as a whole to put customers first.

These proposals are in tune with New Democrat thinking, which emphasizes cost-conscious liberalism rather than the traditional 'tax-and-spend' image of the 1960s Democrat. However, they cannot be implemented without congressional approval and to many members of Congress, 'cuts in wasteful spending' means cuts in 'pork-barrel' projects that have guaranteed money to their constituencies (see page 130).

Comparison

Since the publication of 'The Next Steps' Report in 1987 the British civil service has been subject to a great deal of reorganization. It has been moving towards greater use of executive agencies. By 1994, 64 per cent of British civil servants were employed in agencies, such as the Employment Service and the Inland Revenue.

Political appointees

The political appointees of the departments and executive agencies should give presidents the opportunity to infiltrate deeper into the layers of the permanent, career civil service, thus giving them more control. It is sometimes assumed that political appointees will be loyal to a leader whilst the permanent civil service will not. However, the American example shows that this is not always the case. Political appointees are as likely to have their own agenda as the permanent staff. This may be because they come under the influence of the permanent staff and so adopt 'departmental views'. John Ehrlichman, former adviser to President Nixon, summed up the feelings of the Nixon administration on this subject, saying: 'We only see them [the political appointees] at the annual White House Christmas Party: they go off and marry the natives.'

Revolving door

Political appointees may also be concerned about their careers outside the bureaucracy. Many will stay in office for one or two years before leaving for more lucrative careers in law or as political **lobbyists**. In 1978 Congress passed the Ethics in Government Act which was designed to prevent ex-members of the bureaucracy from lobbying their former colleagues. However, the **'revolving door'** between the public and private sectors continues to be a problem. As recently as November 1993 two of Bill Clinton's key aides, Howard Paster (liaison with Congress) and Roy M Neel (deputy chief of staff) both left the White House to work as lobbyists.

Comparison

It has been argued that the British civil service was politicized under the premiership of Margaret Thatcher. She was accused of seeking to appoint and advance civil servants who shared her attitudes rather than those who were simply the best people for the job.

Margaret Thatcher might defend herself by claiming that the civil service had been politicized long before her arrival in Number 10 because they were collectively opposed to her radical right-wing policies. Similar arguments have been made by politicians from the left of the political spectrum during their terms of office.

Outside links

Links with the private sector are important, not only because of future opportunities, but also for the day-to-day brawls of bureaucratic politics. Particularly useful are the links forged with powerful pressure groups. Interest groups offer information and co-operation to the bureaucracy. Furthermore they can help to apply pressure to other parts of the administration and, more importantly, to congressional committees. The symbiotic nature of these relationships is sometimes referred to as **clientelism.**

Military-industrial complex

The most widely publicized clientelistic relationship is that between the Department of Defense (the Pentagon) and the defence industries. This is commonly known as the **military-industrial complex**. President Eisenhower warned as he left office in 1961 that 'in the councils of government we must guard against the acquisition of unwarranted influence, whether sought or unsought, by the military-industrial complex. The potential for the disastrous rise of misplaced power exists and will persist'.

Comparison

British civil servants make links within departments, between departments and with pressure groups. All of these links can make government more efficient by increasing communication within the administration but might also be used to enhance the influence of the civil servants themselves. Strong links with Treasury can augment the power of a spending department in competition for funds with another department. A department's voice can also be amplified by a relationship with a prominent and respected pressure group.

The symbiotic relationship between the Pentagon and the defence contractors has prospered since 1961. The military in the Defence Department are anxious to acquire ever more sophisticated weapons; whilst the defence industry is keen to attract as much business as possible. Sam Nunn, chair of the Senate Armed Services Committee, has said: 'Everybody scratches everybody else's back. I'd say it's very similar to the congressional system of pork-barrel projects.'

The closeness of the relationship is illustrated by the stream of staff who leave the Pentagon every year in order to work with defence contractors. A congressional enquiry of the 1960s found that the 100 largest defence contractors employed 1400 ex-military personnel as executives. In 1983 13,682 Pentagon employees left to take up jobs in the defence industries. The flow continues despite congressional measures to prevent federal employees taking up jobs within two years, with firms with which they have had dealings in the bureaucracy.

Congressional oversight

The president's ability to co-ordinate the bureaucracy is made no easier by the fact that this responsibility, as are most others, is covered by the separation of powers. Congress has a significant voice in controlling the administration. The president's nominations for the bureaucracy must receive Senate ratification – except most EXOP appointments. It is relatively rare for a president's choice to be refused Senate approval. However, George Bush's candidate for defence secretary, John Tower, was turned down and President Clinton has experienced a number of problems, including Lani Gunier, whose nomination as Assistant Attorney General with responsibility for the Civil Rights Division of the Justice Department was withdrawn in the face of right-wing opposition, and Bobby Ray Inman, who withdrew from the nomination as Defense Secretary.

Finance

Although the president has the power to threaten the bureaucracy with financial sanctions if they refuse to co-operate with him, he must always be aware that, ultimately, Congress controls the 'purse strings'. This aspect of congressional control can cause enormous problems for a president, particularly if bureaucrats are able to create strong links with Congressional Committees and interest groups. In the 1960s, analysis by Cater and Freeman (*Power in Washington*, 1964) suggested that these three groups were becoming the most influential in American politics. They became known as **'iron triangles'**. Examples of such relationships might include the Department of Agriculture, the farm lobby and the House and Senate Agriculture Committees.

The legislative veto

The legislative veto is a device used by Congress to give its approval or disapproval to presidential proposals. It was first used in 1932 when Congress gave President Hoover authority to reorganize the bureaucracy subject to congressional approval within 60 days of the reorganization.

It has mainly been used in cases of reorganization of the bureaucracy but in 1973 was included as part of the War Powers Act which stated that Congress should give is approval or disapproval on a president's use of troops abroad within 60 days of the action being taken.

In 1983, *Immigration and Naturalization Service* v. *Chadha*, the Supreme Court declared the legislative veto unconstitutional as it was not laid down in the constitution and could not be viewed as equivalent to Congress passing or rejecting a law because the president was bypassed with no opportunity to use his veto, as would be the case with a normal law.

Legislative veto

Congress also has the power to scrutinize the activities of the executive branch of government, mainly via the review of departmental and agency budget requirements. **Congressional oversight** has been particularly important as Congress has delegated some of its authority to make rules to the bureaucracy. However it retained the right to disapprove of, i.e. veto, those rules if it so wished. In *Immigration and Naturalization Service v. Chadha* (1983) the Supreme Court declared the legislative veto unconstitutional. However, according to Louis Fisher of the Congressional Research Service, Congress has continued to use this device and did so approximately 140 times between 1983 and 1989.

The ability of both the president and Congress to control the administration are limited given the strength of bureaucratic power. The main responsibility however falls to the president whose task is made considerably more difficult by the dual system of control.

Questions

Short questions

1 a What are Independent Regulatory Commissions?
b Why are there now so many?
(ULEAC, January 1991)

2 Outline the respective functions of *two* important Independent Regulatory Commissions. (ULEAC, June 1992)

3 What are the functions of the Executive Office of the President? (ULEAC, June)

4 What are the functions of (a) the Office of Management and Budget and (b) the Office of Economic Advisors? (ULEAC, January 1994)

5 a How is the Cabinet appointed?
b What role does it perform?
(ULEAC, June 1994)

6 a What is the role of the secretary of state?
b Why does the holder of this post often come into conflict with the national security adviser?
(ULEAC, June 1992)

US questions

1 Assess the effectiveness of the Executive Office in co-ordinating the work of the presidency. (UODLE, June 1993)

2 How important is the president's Cabinet? (UODLE, June 1994)

3 Examine the part played by the federal bureaucracy in government and in policy-making in the United States. (UCLES, June 1993)

4 a Describe the administrative machinery of government in the United States.

b How effectively is it co-ordinated?
(ULEAC, June 1992)

5 **The politics of the bureaucracy**

'A new cabinet member in Washington often discovers that a title does not assure actual authority over his or her department. "I was like a sea captain who finds himself on the deck of a ship that he has never seen before," wrote one. "I did not know the mechanism of my ship; I did not know my officers – even by sight – and I had no acquaintance with the crew."

As the cabinet member had quickly realized, the bureaucracy has its own sources of power that enable it to resist political authority. Cabinet secretaries come and go; the civil service remains. The expert technician in charge of a bureau within a department may have carved out considerable independence over the years and may resent the efforts of a political appointee to take control of the bureau.'

(Adapted from MC Cummings and D Wise, *Democracy Under Pressure*.)

To what extent and by what means is the president able to ensure that the executive branch of government operates as he wishes? To what extent and by what means is the executive branch subjected to domestic scrutiny? (AEB, June 1994)

Comparative questions

1 Why is there now so much concern about bureaucratic power? (Illustrate your answer with reference to at least two countries.) (ULEAC, January 1994)

2 **a** What are the major functions of bureaucracies?
b How do politicians attempt to control the performance of these functions? (Illustrate your answer with reference to at least two countries.)
(London, June 1994)

3 What problems are involved in the executive co-ordination of the administration? (Illustrate your answer with reference to at least two countries.) (ULEAC, January 1995)

4 Compare and contrast the role of the federal bureaucracy in the United States with that of the Civil Service in Britain. (UCLES, June 1994)

8 Congress

Questions to be answered in this chapter

- What are the functions of Congress?
- How effectively does Congress perform its functions?
- How does the power and effectiveness of the US Congress compare to that of the UK Parliament?

Terms to know

- Bicameral
- Budget deficit
- Chief legislator
- Conference committee
- Democracy
- Filibuster
- Freedom of Information
- Impeachment
- Legislature
- Legitimation
- 'Lobby-fodder'
- 'Mark up'
- Party discipline
- Party whips
- 'Pigeon-hole'
- Pocket veto
- Pork-barrel
- 'Report'
- Representative democracy
- Resurgent Congress
- 'Rule'
- Select committee
- Seniority rule
- Separation of powers
- Speaker of the House
- Standing committee
- Sub-committee
- 'Sunshine rules'

Introduction

Although the functions of the United States' Congress are not unlike those of any **legislature** around the world, it has established itself as probably the most powerful of all democratic assemblies. It does not possess the same constitutional powers as the British Parliament, it is not the sovereign body in the American political system, but it has guarded the powers bestowed by the constitution more jealously than its British counterpart. There is no talk of 'elective dictatorship', 'talking shop' or **'lobby fodder'** when the subject is the Congress. Perhaps with the exceptions of the 'imperial presidents' its functions have not been usurped by the executive. On the contrary, recently, discussion tends to centre on the 'imperilled' or 'impotent' presidency.

Congress and the constitution

Article I of the constitution states that: 'All legislative Powers herein granted shall be vested in a Congress of the United States, which shall consist of a Senate and House of Representatives.' Sections 1 to 8 of Article I go on to enumerate the powers invested in Congress, leaving little doubt that the Founding Fathers expected the Congress to be the dominant institution of the American political system, and for most of the last 200 years so it has been.

Checks and balances

However, Congress is no exception to the Founding Fathers' objective, that all political institutions are restrained within a system of checks and balances. Within the federal government Congress is checked by both the president and the Supreme Court. The constitution outlines the chief executive's checks on the legislature whilst the Supreme Court's power to review the actions of Congress was established by the Marshall Court in *Marbury* v. *Madison* (1803) (see page 145).

Comparison

A parliamentary system of government, such as that in Britain, is made up of three elements:

- an elected assembly
- an executive branch that is drawn from the assembly
- an executive branch that is accountable to the assembly

The second of these elements means that the **separation of powers** between the legislative and executive branches of government is relatively weak because the members of the executive are also part of the legislature and their party is likely to have a majority in the assembly.

Federal government power

Congress is also constrained by the separation of powers between the federal government and state governments. It was relatively limited in the actions it could take regarding state affairs until the ground-breaking case, *National Labor Relations Board* v. *Jones & Laughlin* (1937). The Supreme Court ruled that the NLRB, a federal agency, had the power to regulate worker–management relations in Pennsylvania, and in so doing it opened the way for greater federal government intervention in state affairs.

Following their experiences with the British government, the Founding Fathers were adamant that they wanted to create a democratic system of government. However, at the same time, they were concerned that unrestrained **democracy** could be dangerous. In *The Federalist* No. 63 James Madison expressed concern that: '...there are particular moments in public affairs when the people, stimulated by some irregular passion, or some illicit advantage, or misled by the artful misrepresentations of interested men, may call for measures which they themselves will afterwards be the most ready to lament and condemn.'

Bicameral

As a solution to the problem of too much democracy the framers decided to create a **bicameral** legislature. One chamber, the House of Representatives, would represent the people whilst the other, the Senate, would be a little more distant, representing the states.

Senate prestige

Although both chambers have co-equal powers on most matters, the Senate is generally regarded as the more prestigious. This is partly due to the six-year term of office which is believed to insulate it from public opinion and certainly makes it a more attractive option for many senior politicians. It is also due to the additional responsibilities allocated to the Senate in the constitution. It has the power to ratify presidential appointments to the bureaucracy, the federal judiciary and ambassadorial positions. It also has the power to ratify treaties. The House of Representatives has the power to impeach whilst the Senate has the power to try impeachments. All bills concerning finance must begin their life in the House but, like all bills, they need the approval of both houses.

Functions of Congress

Congress can be said to have four main functions:

- representation
- legislation
- investigation and scrutiny
- financial control

Representation

A pure democracy in which everyone has the opportunity to participate in making the decisions which affect their daily lives is not possible in most modern states. The sheer size of their populations makes it impractical. Therefore most democratic states are best described as **representative democracies** within which the people choose representatives to act on their behalf. These representatives make up an assembly.

Composition of House

The House of Representatives has 435 members. The composition of the House is based on delegations from the states, the size of which depends on the population within each state. Each congressman represents a single district. Elections for the whole chamber are held every two years. As James Madison has said in *The Federalist* No. 57: 'The House of Representatives is so constituted as to support in the members an habitual recollection of their dependence on the people.' To become a member a candidate must have been a citizen for no less than six years and be at least 25 years of age.

Comparison

The British Parliament is only partially representative. Whilst the lower house, the Commons, is elected by the people, the upper house, the Lords, is not. Made up of peers who have inherited their positions or have been appointed by the monarch, on the advice of the prime minister, the House of Lords can in no way be considered to be representative or democratic.

Passing a bill

Bills can be initiated by members of Congress, interest groups or the executive branch of government. However, they may be introduced only by a member of Congress. They can begin their life in either the Senate or the House, unless they are concerned with revenue in which case they must begin in the House.

Once introduced the bill is in the hands of the **Speaker of the House** or the Majority Leader in the Senate. These officials refer the bill to the appropriate standing committee in their respective houses. If the bill falls within the jurisdiction of a number of committees the Speaker or Majority Leader has the authority to use their discretion regarding its allocation.

When it is received by a committee the chair has the power to decide if it should be considered by the full committee, referred to a **sub-committee** or **'pigeon-holed'**. In the latter case it will never be considered and dies.

Bills concerning revenue are automatically referred to the House Ways and Means Committee, which deals with all proposals concerning taxation. Although not a constitutional requirement, bills concerning spending are referred to the House Appropriations Committee.

The Committee stage is the most thorough examination of the bill. It is often carried out via public hearings, unless it deals with sensitive material. After the hearings the bill will be amended or **'marked up'** and voted on by the committee before being returned, if the report is positive, to the full chamber. In the House the bill goes to the Rules Committee, which has the power to grant the bill a **'rule'**, i.e. a time for debate, or not. In the Senate this decision is taken by the Majority Party Policy Committee. Bills which have been 'reported' by the House Ways and Means Committee bypass the Rules Committee and go straight to the full House.

The bill is then debated on the floor of the House and of the Senate. By this stage most of the detailed work on the bill has been completed and the floor is likely to follow the recommendations of the committee. In the House members are usually allowed five minutes to contribute to the debate; whereas in the Senate there is a tradition of unlimited debate which opens the way for a **filibuster**, by which a bill can be 'talked out'.

If the bill is passed by both houses but with different amendments, the differences must be reconciled before the bill is sent to the president. This is done by a **conference committee** made up of members of the original standing committees.

The finished version of the bill is returned to the full House and Senate for a vote. If approved it will be sent to the president for signature. At this point the president may decide to sign or veto the bill. If vetoing the bill the president returns it, with an explanation, to Congress. If Congress is near the end of the session the president could use the **pocket veto**.

The Senate is made up of representatives from the states. Each state has two senators, regardless of population size. Members must be at least 30 years of age and have been citizens of the United States for no less than nine years.There are currently 100 members of the Senate. Each senator has a term of office of six years but elections are held on a two-year cycle, with 33 per cent of the Senate coming up for re-election every two years.

Composition of Senate

Legislation

In most representative democracies the assembly is also the law-making body. The combination of the representative and legislative functions permits **legitimation.** Laws can be made only with the approval of the people's representatives. Therefore the people are, indirectly, giving their consent to the law that will govern them. As a result the citizens can be expected to obey those laws and public order will be maintained.

Comparison

In Britain the House of Commons dominates the legislative process. The powers of the upper chamber have been reduced to such an extent that the Lords can only delay bills, and financial measures are completely outside its jurisdiction.

In the United States both the Senate and the House are responsible for law-making.

Investigation and scrutiny

The executive branch of government has become increasingly predominant in every political system in the twentieth century. Responsibility for social welfare, foreign policy and the economy have increased the workload of all branches of government but increasingly it is the executive that is expected to initiate programmes as well as to implement them. Therefore it is important that the legislature should check and scrutinize the work of the executive branch.

In the United States congressional oversight is achieved by both houses but the Senate has a particular responsibility in this area because the constitution gives it the power to ratify presidential appointment and treaties. Like the crucial parts of the legislative process, most of Congress's investigative role is carried out through its committee system.

Comparison

In Britain the executive branch of government is drawn from Parliament. More precisely it is drawn from the House of Commons. Therefore the majority of members of the government are part of the House of Commons and it is here that most of parliamentary scrutiny takes place, through debate, questions and Commons committees.

Financial control

A traditional function of legislatures is that they should control the 'purse strings'. To some extent it is one of the legislative and investigative functions because Congress controls spending and taxation through law and monitors the way the executive uses that money.

Inter-relationships

The way in which the financial power is linked to the legislative and investigative functions illustrates very well the interdependence of Congress's functions. Representation lies at the heart of representative government but is of little significance if it is not backed up with real law-making and financial power. Similarly the investigative function is reinforced by Congress's ability to make law. For example, at the time of Watergate, Congress passed the War Powers Act (1973), the Case Act (1972) and the Budget and Impoundment Control Act (1974) to extend its investigative powers.

Congressional performance

The four functions of Congress are common to most legislatures around the world but the effectiveness with which they are performed varies enormously from state to state and from system to system. In many countries the legislature is dominated by the executive. At times in the United States' history this has also been the case. However, executive dominance has always been short-lived and has been followed by a reassertion of congressional authority.

Structure of government

The separation of powers laid down in the constitution of the United States means that Congress is secure in its own position and with its own powers. The constitution is clear about the role of Congress, so it is difficult for the executive branch of government to encroach on congressional functions.

Comparison

In Britain the parliamentary system of government means that the government is drawn from Parliament or, more accurately, from the House of Commons. Therefore it is likely that the government will have a majority in the House of Commons. The British constitutional theorist Walter Bagehot summed up the fundamental distinction between parliamentary and presidential systems as follows: 'The independence of the legislative and executive powers is the specific quality of Presidential government, just as their fusion and combination is the precise principle of Cabinet government.'

Congressional independence

The president is not a member of Congress, cannot formally introduce legislative proposals or take part in congressional debate. Furthermore, because the president, Senate and House are all elected separately the chief executive does not have a guaranteed majority in either house. Even though presidents have adopted the title of **chief legislator** it is extremely difficult for them to dominate Congress.

Impeachment

Impeachment is a process by which the president, the vice-president and federal judges can be removed from office. They may be impeached for treason, bribery and high crimes and misdemeanours, although no precise definition of what actually constitutes a 'high crime' or 'misdemeanour' exists.

The impeachment process must be brought by a majority vote in the House of Representatives. The charges must be tried in the Senate, with the chief justice of the Supreme Court presiding. Only the Senate may vote on the final judgment.

The House has brought impeachment charges against a president twice. Andrew Johnson was acquitted by the Senate in 1868. In 1974 Richard Nixon resigned and the impeachment procedure stopped.

Whilst this independence helps Congress to guard its powers and to fulfil its functions more effectively in many respects it also helps to maintain the executive's autonomy.

In Britain the parliamentary system allows Parliament the power to bring the government down, through a vote of no confidence. This is not available to Congress. The president is secure in his or her position unless they resign or are impeached.

Impeachment

One should bear in mind that impeachment and the vote of no confidence are by no means equivalent. Impeachment is a quasi-judicial procedure, initiated if the president is suspected of 'high crimes and misdemeanours' and has only been begun twice in the history of the United States. The vote of no confidence is a political tool and has been used many times.

Another of Parliament's political tools is also denied to Congress – Question Time. Although often decried as political theatre, Question Time does give members of Parliament the opportunity to cross-examine the prime minister in the House of Commons. As the president is not a part of Congress he is not questioned before Congress.

Party discipline

It is one thing for a government to have a majority in the assembly, it is quite another to be able to control it. In most democracies political parties are the means of putting some organization and coherence into the legislature.

Comparison

In Britain **party discipline** is strong. MPs rely on their party for their electoral success and for any future promotions into government positions. As a result they will tend to step into line when the party demands it. Although party loyalty in Britain is no longer as strong as it was in the 1960s it is still much stronger than in the United States.

'Catch-all' parties

One reason for weak party discipline in the United States is that it is difficult to impose a party line on members of 'catch-all' parties of the American type. The Republican and Democratic parties are decentralized to allow state and local parties to maximize their local appeal. The corollary is that national party platforms are difficult to formulate let alone enforce.

Candidate-orientated campaigns

The candidate-orientated nature of American election campaigns leaves members of Congress well aware that they owe their election not to their party but to their own organization and their constituents. Therefore the pressure that **party whips** can bring to bear on members is small.

It would not be true to say that party discipline is non-existent in Congress. Party members are likely to vote with their party if there is no conflict with the needs of their constituency. It is also the case that party loyalty appears to be rising in Congress. In 1970 Democrat members were likely to vote with their party on 57 per cent of divisions; Republicans did so on 59 per cent. By 1989 these figures had risen to 81 per cent and 73 per cent respectively.

Although these figures are only averages and mask the extent to which some members buck the party line they do indicate a rise in party loyalty. This may be attributable to the efforts the parties have made to increase their control over their members.

The Speaker of the House

'Most people think of me as the presiding officer of the House and nothing else. Yet I'm also the political leader in the House. I'm the House chief executive officer. I appoint lots of committees and commissions. I am the House's chief administrative officer. Everyone I see working in this building is working for me.' (Ex-Speaker, Carl Albert).

It is true that the office of Speaker of the House encompasses a wide variety of roles, including being referee of the House and the leader of the majority party. As referee he has the power to appoint select and conference committees; he assigns bills to committees and puts them to the vote. As party leader he is a spokesman for his party and chairs the Steering and Policy Committee.

The Speaker is allowed to take part in debate and to vote (but rarely does), and is also second in line to the presidency, behind the vice-president.

Newt Gingrich, the Speaker since 1995, has already proved to be one of the most active and powerful of recent speakers. *The Contract with America* (see page 80), virtually his personal political agenda, has recaptured the legislative initiative from the president. Whilst most recent presidents have failed to emulate Franklin Roosevelt by pushing their legislative agenda through Congress in the first 100 days of their administration, Gingrich needed only 92 days to push all but one element of *The Contract* through the House.

Seniority rule

One area which had always been outside the control of parties was the allocation of committee chairs. Since 1910 the chairs of committees have been chosen according to the **seniority rule.** This meant that the longest-serving member of the majority party on the committee automatically became its chair. As a result those members of Congress with safe seats, often in the south, made the committees their own private kingdoms. The system had long been criticized along the lines expressed by first black congresswoman Shirley Chisholm in 1970: 'The seniority system keeps a handful of old men ... in control of the Congress. These old men stand implacably across the paths that could lead us toward a better future. But worse than they, I think, are the majority of members of both houses who continue to submit to the senility system' (*Unbought and Unbossed*, 1970).

Lapse of seniority rule

In the mid 1970s a new crop of freshmen entered Congress as incumbents experienced the electoral backlash caused by Watergate. They found the seniority system extremely frustrating and in 1975 the majority party caucus removed a number of committee chairs. They included W R Poage (Agriculture), F Edward Herbert (Armed Services) and Wight Patman (Banking, Currency and Housing). Although the seniority rule continues to exist, it is not the only consideration when committee appointments are being made. The majority party has more freedom to take party loyalty into account.

Representatives or delegates?

The weakness of party discipline in Congress is both a help and a hindrance to the performance of its functions. With regards to representation it helps. Congressmen do not follow the British model of becoming party delegates nor are they constituency delegates but perhaps are closer to Burke's idea of a representative, making up their own mind whilst being responsive to their constituents.

President of the Senate

This office is held by the vice-president, who fulfils the role of referee and only votes in the event of a tie. In practice the vice-president does not attend sessions very often.

President pro tempore

This is a formal office held by a senior figure of the majority party. He chairs the Senate in the absence of the vice-president

The Senate Majority Leader

The Senate Majority Leader is elected by the majority party in the Senate and is the leader of his party in the Senate but, unlike the Speaker, does not fulfil the role of referee. His role is to guide legislation through the chamber on behalf of his party. If his party controls the White House he will work usually closely with the president. When the Republicans took control of the Senate in 1981 Senator Howard Baker proved to be an extremely effective bargainer and arm twister as he achieved an unprecedented 80 per cent level of party unity.

Quantity or quality?

The dispersed nature of power in Congress also helps Congress perform its legislative and investigative roles, in the sense that it is less likely to be dominated by the executive. In no sense could members of Congress ever be accused of being 'lobby-fodder'. However, the decentralization of Congress gives it a negative power. It is accomplished at preventing things happening. During the 92nd Congress, for example, 25,354 bills and resolutions were introduced but only 707 became law in the two-year period.

It would be easy to believe that Congress prefers quality in its legislation rather than quantity. This is not necessarily the case. In Britain commentators have expressed concern that the British Parliament is liable to have legislation forced upon it and given the dominance of the government it can do little about it. This is not true of the American Congress but it is the case that many laws are not passed unless legislators can see a particular benefit of the legislation for their own constituency. This is known as **'pork-barrel'** legislation. Mendel Rivers, chair of the House Armed Services Committee (1965–70), set an extreme example. By the time he left office the Pentagon was spending the equivalent of $1,000 per annum for each of his constituents in South Carolina.

Information and facilities

Any decision-making organization is only as good as the quality of information it receives. Congress is no exception. The standard of its legislation, its ability to scrutinize the executive branch and its ability to control finance all depend on its members and committees being well informed.

Staff

Access to information depends, to some extent, on a legislator's staff support. As the workload of legislatures has grown so it has become unfeasible to expect members to be able to fully research every issue. The executive branch of government has long understood this fact and has built up a huge civil service to cater to its demands. Nevertheless some legislatures are catching up.

British Members of Parliament are notoriously lacking in staff support, on average having one or two each. In 1972 there were a total of 9402 staff working for members of Congress. By 1983 the total staff serving Congress had risen to 25,000. Individual congressmen had an average of 17 staff working for them, whilst senators averaged a staff of 36 (the highest is 71). The total staff serving committees totalled 2000 in the House and 1200 in the Senate. In addition staff will work in the Library of Congress and the Congressional Budget Office. In 1991 the total staff in Congress had risen to over 38,000. Administrative support on this scale helps to redress the balance of staff between the executive and the legislature and improves congressional performance of its functions.

Freedom of Information Act

An additional boon for Congress is the **Freedom of Information Act.** Passed in 1966 this makes the activities of the executive agencies of government open to public scrutiny. The only records which are exempt are those that might impair national security or individual privacy if they were to be open to the public. The availability of such information contrasts sharply with the British Official Secrets Acts. The difference in nomenclature illustrates a fundamental difference between the British and American attitude toward the conduct of government. The latter in full view of the public; the former behind screens of secrecy.

The committee system

All legislatures that are fighting a losing battle against the lack of time and information eventually turn to a comprehensive system of committees. The Congress has done so to perhaps a greater extent than any other legislature and with mixed results.

The advantages of committees to any legislature are numerous. They allow bills to be examined in detail, they are able to shadow the work of particular components of the bureaucracy and they can allocate and monitor finance more effectively.

Congress has basically two types of committee:
- **standing committees**
- **select committees**

Standing committees

Standing committees combine the legislative, investigative and financial functions. There are approximately 37 permanent standing committees in Congress. They range from Foreign Affairs to Agriculture and from Veterans' Affairs to Standards of Official Conduct. Those committees that specialize in particular subject areas are known as authorization committees.

Standing committees are perhaps the most powerful organizations in Congress, with each committee building up its domain around a particular area of policy. For example all business regarding agriculture must go through the House Agriculture Committee. The members of the committee develop their knowledge of agricultural issues and soon become recognized as 'experts'. The committee 'marks up' bills concerning agriculture and its **'report'** is usually accepted by the floor of the House. As a result they are sometimes referred to as 'little legislatures'.

Conference committees

These are joint committees set up at the end of the legislative process in both houses to iron out any differences between the final version of a bill approved by each house.

The members of the committee are selected by the Speaker of the House and the vice-president of the Senate and are usually drawn from the standing committees that originally had responsibility for the bill.

Rather than ironing out differences the committees gained a reputation for completely rewriting bills before sending them back to both houses for approval. The **'sunshine rules'**, adopted in 1973 made conference committee meetings open to the public, which reduced the tendency to rewrite. In 1982 President Reagan said: 'You know, if an orange and an apple went into conference consultations, it might come out a pear.' (*New York Times*, 18 December 1982).

Comparison:

In Britain standing committees in the House of Commons are set up on an ad hoc basis to review specific pieces of legislation. Their composition reflects that of the House of Commons.

Select committees carry out the investigative function of the House. They are permanent to allow members to develop specialist knowledge. The structure of the select committee system largely mirrors that of civil service departments.

Traditionally the chairs of standing committees are also extremely powerful. They control the dates and agendas of the meetings, the use of committee staff, and often write the report on a bill, speak on the floor on behalf of a committee and take the lead on conference committees. The extent of their power led Woodrow Wilson to state: 'I know not how better to describe our form of government in a single phrase than by calling it a government by the Chairmen of the Standing Committees of Congress.' (*Congressional Government: A Study in American Politics*, first printed 1885. Published in UK by Constable 1914).

'Sunshine rules'

In 1970 the power of committee chairs was reduced by congressional reform. The 'sunshine rules', adopted by the House in 1973 and the Senate in 1975, require committee meetings to be open to the public, including the press. This has reduced the chairs' ability to shape reports in accordance with their own ambitions.

Select committees

Select committees are set up on an ad hoc basis to deal with particular issues. They cannot review legislative proposals and are mainly concerned with the investigative function.

The lapse of the seniority rule has made the chairs more accountable to the party in both houses. Since 1975 the majority party caucus in both the Senate and the House have been able to remove committee chairs and nominate their own replacements.

The Steering and Policy Committee

Created in 1973, the SPC is a committee of the Democratic Party in the House. It is made up of the Speaker, the floor leader, the whip and deputy whips and additional members elected on a regional basis.

It was set up to give greater co-ordination to the work of the Democratic Party in the House, and is responsible for the party's policy and tactics in the House.

In particular it is responsible for allocating committee assignments to House Democrats. Since the lapse of the seniority rule, and as long as the Democrats control the House, it is responsible for nominating committee chairs for approval by the party caucus.

The actors in the budgetary procedure

The *president* submits budget proposals to Congress in January/February and may update them in April. When Congress returns the proposals as a law (with their amendments) the president must sign or veto. There is likely to be protracted discussions between the White House and congressional leaders to find an acceptable compromise.

Authorization committees review the spending plans for their policy area and may propose changes. To come into force their plans must take the form of law, therefore they 'report' spending proposals in the same way as a normal law.

Appropriations committees are responsible for allocating money to each of the authorization committees' programmes. This is again done via law.

Revenue committees are responsible for any laws that may be necessary to raise additional revenue. In the House it is the role of the Ways & Means Committee; in the Senate it is carried out by the Finance Committee.

Budget committees 'report' the budget resolution as a whole. They are responsible for reviewing and setting overall spending limits.

'Sub-committee bill of rights'

Finally the House's adoption of the 'sub-committee bill of rights' in 1973 has strengthened the hand of sub-committees in relation to the chair of a full committee. The main provisions of the 'bill of rights' were that: a full committee with 20 members or more must have at least four sub-committees; the chairs, composition and jurisdiction of the sub-committees should be determined, and written down as rules, by the Democratic caucus on the committee; bills should be referred to a sub-committee within two weeks of receipt, rather than be 'pigeon-holed'; no congressman may be chair of more than one legislative sub-committee.

Whilst the 'sub-committee bill of rights' has reduced the power of the committee chairs it has institutionalized the power of sub-committees. Woodrow Wilson once wrote that 'the House has as many leaders as there are subjects of legislation'. (*Congressional Government*). Today this might be paraphrased as, 'the House has as many leaders as there are sub-committees'.

Lobbyists

Therefore the committee system in Congress is extremely powerful. It makes possible the effective review of legislation, the control of finance and the scrutiny of the executive branch of government. However, it does slow the whole system of law-making down. It is also open to the attentions of interest groups and their lobbyists who will fight for influence with a committee in order to maximize their own self-interest.

Financial powers

Congress's ability to control the purse-strings is wrapped up in all of the factors that affect its performance. However, to some degree, finance is a special area of responsibility and it has its own systems for congressional oversight.

Budget and Impoundment Control Act

As the role of the federal government has expanded so has the federal budget. Until the 1970s a president's budget proposals were scrutinized by the Senate and House Appropriations Committees. The role of these committees is to scrutinize the spending requirements of the different elements of the administration with regards to specific legislative programmes. If any of these programmes required additional revenue to be raised they would be referred to the House Ways and Means Committee and the Senate Finance Committee, which have sole responsibility for taxes. Although very powerful all of these committees were limited to looking at budgetary proposals on a piecemeal basis, with little or no perspective of the budget as a whole package. Therefore in 1974 Congress upgraded its systems of financial scrutiny with the Budget and Impoundment Control Act, which created a parallel budget procedure for Congress. It created the Senate and House Budget Committees, which review the president's budget proposals as a whole and are able to put forward their own alternative proposals. The procedure was reinforced by the creation of the Congressional Budget Office, which supports Congress with information and its perspective on the budget.

The budgetary procedure begins 15 days after Congress reconvenes in January when the president presents his budget to Congress. It is a lengthy process and will continue until October or November of that year (the new fiscal year begins on 1 October).

Although the budgetary system has been improved it has not necessarily achieved the desired results. A persistent criticism of Congress in recent years has been financial

Reaganomics

Ronald Reagan came to the White House in 1980 committed to right-wing economic theory, sometimes known as supply-side economics, with its emphasis on free-market economics. Very broadly this involves reducing the extent of government intervention in the economy by deregulating the economy, reducing government spending and cutting federal taxes. The last two elements of supply-side economics were associated with the economist Professor Arthur Laffer, who suggested that if federal tax rates were cut people would have more money to spend and would have an incentive to work harder. Their increased spending would stimulate the economy and as a result incomes would rise still further. Higher incomes would result in a higher tax revenue for the government.

During the Reagan administration this simple idea became distorted into the belief that lower tax rates would actually pay for themselves or even result in *higher* revenue. It was therefore thought that taxes could be reduced without any cuts in government spending to compensate. This was perilously close to suggesting that tax cuts and higher government spending could go hand in hand.

In fact that is exactly what happened during the early years of the Reagan administration. Taxes were cut, defence spending increased and the cuts in welfare spending required to compensate were not made. As a result the amount the federal government spent outstripped the change in tax revenue and the federal **budget deficit** grew.

profligacy, although President Reagan must take some responsibility for the growth of the deficit in the first place.

Balanced budget

In an effort to bring down the deficit Congress passed the Balanced Budget and Emergency Deficit Control Act (1985). Better known as the Gramm-Rudman-Hollings Act, after its sponsors, this sought to eradicate the deficit by 1991 using legally enforceable budget cuts. Cuts were to be designated by the Congressional Budget Office and the Office of Management and Budget and then reported to the comptroller general who would review the proposals and, in turn, report them to the president. The cuts would be carried out unless Congress passed laws to make the cuts unnecessary.

The Supreme Court ruled the role of the comptroller general in this process to be unconstitutional in *Bowsher* v. *Synar* (1986). Their judgment was based on the fact that a congressional officer was being asked to play an executive role. A second version of the Act was passed, eliminating the role of the comptroller general. However, Congress has endeavoured to avoid the constraints imposed by the Act through creative accounting. In 1990 the Omnibus Budget Reconciliation Act virtually destroyed the Gramm-Rudman-Hollings Act.

The arrival of Republican majorities in both the House and Senate after the 1994 mid-term elections has seen a renewed bout of budget cutting. In 1995 Congress passed a federal budget proposal aimed at eliminating the deficit by the year 2002. The

Sandbags against a flood

... As deficits soared in the 1980s, Congress increasingly looked to the budget process itself for a solution. Its first attempt was the Gramm-Rudman-Hollings Act of 1985, which set a series of deficit targets that went to zero in 1991. But because the act had no teeth, its success depended ultimately on how badly its signatories wanted to cut the deficit. They didn't. And when the original act failed to generate progress, Congress simply revised it to push back the timetable – with predictable results.

It was not until George Bush and Congressional Democrats agreed on the 1990 Budget Enforcement Act that any deficit cuts became possible. Unlike its feebler predecessors, this established two strict mechanisms to constrain spending. The first was a tight cap on all discretionary spending in the fiscal years from 1991 to 1995 (which has subsequently been extended to the end of 1998). If appropriations exceed the spending limits they are automatically cut to meet the caps. The second component dealt directly with the portions of the budget that have lives of their own: entitlements and revenues. It required that any legislation which increased forecast entitlement spending, or decreased forecast tax receipts, should be completely paid for with offsetting spending cuts and tax increases. Although this could not undo the effects of laws already in place, it prevented Congress from making matters worse.

The Economist, 7 January 1995.

failure of the president and congressional leaders to reach agreement led to the shut-down of the federal government for a week in November 1995. A subsequent promise saw President Clinton agree to the 2002 target, whilst Republicans accepted a formula that appears to protect welfare projects from swingeing cuts.

The Clinton White House has responded to the target of 2002 by proposing its own target of 2005. This is an attempt by President Clinton to impose his own 'New Democrat' credentials by being conservative on financial issues whilst being less radical than the Gingrich Republicans in the House.

Congressional attitude

Ultimately how well Congress performs any of its functions depends on its will to use its powers. Some commentators have argued that the 'imperial presidencies' were allowed to develop by the inactivity of Congress. The fact that Congress passed the Gulf of Tonkin Resolution (1964) illustrates very well its desire to be led by the 'strong' presidents of the 1960s. Its failure to act to bring the Vietnam War to an end illustrates its unwillingness to face up to its responsibilities to make good public policy.

'Resurgent congress'

The immediate post-Watergate period is marked by a **'resurgent Congress'**. The Budget and Impoundment Control Act (1974) and the War Powers Act (1973) symbolize Congress's determination to regain control of the policy-making reins. But neither Act is anything more than symbolic if Congress is unwilling to see its commitment through to responsible action. Congress has not used its new budgetary process to good effect and it has never forced a president to withdraw military forces in compliance with the War Powers Act.

Although Congress does not carry the mantle of sovereignty possessed by the British Parliament, it does hold considerable power. Its ability to debate legislation, scrutinize government and monitor finance is great. In fact some might argue that it is too great. Congress has a very great negative power. It is certainly capable of delaying law or halting executive action, and it replaces the lost leadership with little of its own.

Questions

Short questions

1 **a** What are the main types of Congressional committee?
 b Summarize the main functions of each.
 (ULEAC, January 1992)

2 **a** What do you understand by the budget deficit?
 b How effectively has Congress dealt with it?
 (ULEAC, June 1992)

3 **a** What are the formal offices occupied by the congressional party leaders?
 b How are these leaders selected?
 (ULEAC, January 1993)

4 a What is the role of the Speaker of the House of Representatives?
b What factors affect the relationship between Speaker and president?
(ULEAC, June 1993)

5 Why are members of the House of Representatives so sensitive to constituency interests? (ULEAC, January 1992)

US questions

1 To what extent can Congress control the exercise of presidential power? (ULEAC, June 1993)

2 Is Congress now too powerful? (ULEAC, January 1994)

3 'Ultimately it is the Senate and not the House of Representatives that wields Congressional power.' Discuss. (ULEAC, June 1994)

4 Consider the view that 'changes in the committee systems and the "seniority rule" within Congress since 1970 have had a negligible effect on either the decisions taken or the Congressional hierarchy of power'. (AEB, June 1992)

5 Examine the claim that it is in the committee rooms that the real work of Congress is done. (UODLE, June 1994)

6 In what ways has congressional power changed since President Nixon's resignation? (UCLES, June 1994)

7 What are congressional committees, how do they work and how much power and influence do they exert? (UCLES, June 1994)

8 Discuss the influence of Congress over contemporary American foreign policy. (UCLES, June 1993)

9 **The effectiveness of congressional oversight of the executive**

Ascertaining the effectiveness of congressional oversight of the executive is, in fact, very problematic. It is difficult to measure both the quantity and quality oversight. Whatever its effectiveness, though, the increased attention given to oversight, together with the great emphasis on the provision of constituency services, has led to a decline in Congress's legislative activity. Fewer measures are proposed, less time is available for their consideration, and the primacy of constituency politics means that they are more likely to encounter resistance from members concerned about their local implications.

From: Christopher J Bailey, *The US Congress* (Basil Blackwell)

Assess the *relative* importance of legislation and oversight of the executive in the work of Congress. By what means and for what reason does Congress seek to scrutinize the activities of the executive and what is the significance of the increase in 'constituency politics' mentioned above? (AEB, June 1993)

10 Discuss the main influences on how members of Congress vote. (ULEAC, January 1995)

Comparative questions

1 **a** What are the major functions of legislatures?
b How important is the law-making function of contemporary legislatures? (Illustrate your answer with reference to at least two countries.) (ULEAC, June 1994)

2 Discuss the changing role of legislatures. (Illustrate your answer with reference to at least two countries.) (ULEAC, June 1993)

3 'The main function of a legislature is scrutiny and control of the executive.' Discuss. (Illustrate your answer with reference to at least two countries.) (ULEAC, January 1994)

4 Consider the view that the House of Commons is more socially representative than either of the houses of the US Congress but that senators enjoy greater personal prestige than members of the House of Lords. (AEB, June 1991)

9 The Supreme Court

Questions to be answered in this chapter

- How are American courts structured?
- How are appointments made to the Supreme Court?
- How powerful is the Supreme Court?
- What role has the Supreme Court played in a range of political and social issues?

Terms to know

- Appellate court
- Civil liberties
- Civil rights
- Constitutionalism
- 'Court-packing'
- De facto
- De jure
- 'Gerrymandering'
- Judicial activism
- Judicial decisions
- Judicial restraint
- Judicial review
- 'Loose constructionists'
- Malapportionment
- Original intent
- Original jurisdiction
- Political decisions
- Politicization
- Rule of law
- Self-restraint
- 'Strict constructionists'
- Writ of certiorari

Introduction

Article III of the constitution states that: 'The judicial power of the United States shall be vested in one Supreme Court and in such inferior courts that the Congress may from time to time ordain and establish.' In Section 2 it goes on to state that: 'The judicial power shall extend to all Cases, in Law and Equity, arising under this Constitution, the Laws of the United States and Treaties ...' Article III states relatively little else.

From such straightforward, innocuous beginnings has sprung an institution responsible for some of the most radical and controversial decisions in American history – the Supreme Court.

Whether the Founding Fathers would have approved of the route the Court has taken in the latter half of the twentieth century is unclear. The record of debate at the Philadelphia Convention contains few references to their intentions when laying down the power of the Supreme Court.

The structure of the federal courts system

What is clear is that the Founding Fathers placed the Supreme Court at the head of the federal judicial system. Congress was given power to create inferior courts in both Article I and III of the constitution. It did so in 1789 through the Judiciary Act. This set up three circuit courts of appeals and thirteen district courts – one for each state. These are constitutional courts, set up under the authority of Article III of the constitution. Since then this court system has expanded to eleven circuit courts of appeal, plus one for the District of Columbia, and ninety-four district courts. In addition there are four legislative courts, set up under the authority of Article I of the constitution. They are those of the District of Columbia, territorial courts, tax courts and the Court of Military Appeals.

Original jurisdiction

District courts are courts of **original jurisdiction**. This means that they are the basic trial courts of the federal system. Most decisions taken here are final although they may be reviewed by the courts of appeal. The courts of appeal are organized into 'circuits' and they may hear appeals from within their own circuits only.

Appeals

The Supreme Court is the final court of appeal, hearing cases from the inferior federal courts and from state courts when a federal issue is involved. Federal cases involve crimes against the United States; disputes between citizens of different states or between United States' citizens and those of a different country; and actions arising under the constitution or federal law. Most cases reach the Court as appeal cases.

Supreme Court

There are two methods by which a case can be referred to the Supreme Court. The first is by a direct appeal from a lower court if the Supreme Court is convinced that a constitutional issue is involved. Few cases reach the Court by this method. The second route is by petitioning for a **writ of certiorari**. This means that the records of a case in a lower court are sent to the Supreme Court for review. Such a writ can only be granted with the agreement of four justices of the Supreme Court.

Appeal

The Supreme Court acts only as a court of original jurisdiction under a limited number of circumstances. Article III, Section 2 very clearly states that the only circumstances

Coming to a decision

When a case arrives at the Court lawyers for both sides present their cases – orally and in writing. The justices retire to consider their own opinions and reassemble, alone, on the Friday of the same week. No one really knows exactly what happens in this conference. However, it is believed that the chief justice restates the cases and puts forward a personal view, followed by each justice, in order of seniority, putting forward their view. Often a vote follows, taken in reverse order of seniority. Finally opinions are written down. If the chief justice is in the majority he will write the majority opinion or select an associate judge to do it. If he is in the minority the senior justice in the majority either writes it or chooses someone else. Major cases may generate a number of opinions from the minority and the majority. Draft opinions are circulated amongst all the justices and may undergo considerable revisions before a final judgment is handed down.

'are cases affecting Ambassadors, public Ministers and Consuls, and those in which a state shall be a party'.

Judicial independence

When creating the judicial system the Founding Fathers were anxious to create courts that would be independent of political pressure. This is in line with their determination to create a system based on the separation of powers and checks and balances.

Rule of law

It also accords with the concept we commonly refer to as the **rule of law**. This concept concerns the treatment of people before the law. All people are subject to the law and should be treated equally regardless of status, colour or creed; the government is also subject to the law. No one is above the law. The aim of the rule of law is to bring predictability to the application of law. Every citizen should know how he or she should be treated by the law and the treatment should be the same for every citizen. This can be summed up as 'a government of laws not of men'. Such a conception of law can be contrasted with that in dictatorships, where citizens can face treatment based on the whim of the ruler rather than any codified system of rules.

In an effort to uphold the rule of law a distinction is usually made between

- **judicial decisions** and
- **political decisions**

Judicial decisions involve the application of law to specific circumstances. They should be made in accordance with the provisions of the law made by the legislature (the rule of law) and without reference to political belief. Political decisions are policy-making decisions made by those who are elected to do so. Therefore career civil servants and judges should not make political decisions.

Judicial independence

To maintain the distinction between political and judicial decisions the judiciary should be allowed to work without political interference. Alexander Hamilton states, in *The Federalist* No. 78, that 'the complete independence of the courts of justice is peculiarly essential in a limited constitution'.

In order to achieve judicial independence the constitution clearly states, in Article III, that the judicial power lies with the Supreme Court and any inferior courts Congress might establish. Furthermore it states that: 'the judges, of both the supreme and inferior Court, shall hold their Offices during good Behaviour, and shall, at stated Times, receive for their Services, a Compensation, which shall not be diminished during their Continuance in Office.' This provision safeguards judges against dismissal or unfavourable treatment by the other branches of government. Alexander Hamilton believed, again in *The Federalist* No. 78, that 'nothing can contribute so much to [the court's] firmness and independence as PERMANENCY IN OFFICE, this quality may therefore be justly regarded as an indispensable ingredient in its constitution'.

Judicial appointees

The Supreme Court and all inferior constitutional courts created under the authority given in Article III of the constitution are protected from political interference. Judges are nominated by the president and ratified by the Senate. Once appointed they hold their positions for life and can only be removed by an impeachment process.

Composition of the Supreme Court in 1995

William Rehnquist (Chief Justice). First appointed to the Court by Nixon (1971). Appointed chief justice by Reagan in 1986 to replace Warren Burger. A solid, highly conservative vote both politically and legally.

John Paul Stevens. Appointed by Ford in 1975. A moderate, pragmatic vote.

Sandra Day O'Connor. The first woman justice and Reagan's first appointment in 1981. A moderate, pragmatic vote. Conservative in the legal sense of not wishing to act to radically overturn precedent.

Antonio Scalia. Appointed by Reagan in 1986 to fill the associate justice seat left by Rehnquist. A solid conservative vote.

Anthony Kennedy. Appointed by Reagan in 1987 after the rejection of Robert Bork and withdrawal of Douglas Ginsburg. Pragmatic moderate vote. A legal conservative.

David Souter. Appointed by Bush in 1990 to replace Brennan. A legal conservative and the dominant force on the Court.

Clarence Thomas. Bush's controversial choice to replace the Court's first black judge, Thurgood Marshall, in 1991. Conservative.

Ruth Bader Ginsburg. Clinton's first appointment in 1993. Second woman on the Court. Believed to be a moderate liberal.

Stephen Breyer. Appointed by Clinton in 1994 upon the retirement of Justice Harry Blackmun, author of *Roe* v. *Wade* (1973). An ex-federal judge from Massachusetts with an excellent reputation. Widely perceived as a 'safe' Clinton selection.

The legislative courts, created under the authority of Article II, do not benefit from the same degree of independence. Congress can remove judges, reduce their remuneration and vary the length of their terms of office.

Senate ratification

Under normal circumstances the president's nominees for vacancies in the constitutional courts are ratified by the Senate. The main responsibility for ratification lies with the Senate Judiciary Committee, whose members have usually been prepared to allow the president a relatively free hand in choosing judges. This is particularly true if the president has been elected with a large majority and so can claim to have an electoral mandate. Presidents Reagan and Bush, during their twelve years in the White House, had the opportunity to fill five vacancies on the Court. The ideological balance of the Court undoubtedly moved to the right as a result. Of 132 nominees in the history of the United States, only 27 have been rejected.

Despite the Founding Fathers' desire to protect the judiciary from political influence the nomination process has become extremely political. Many presidents have used a nomination as an opportunity to shape the political composition of the Supreme Court or to further their own political standing. Recent rejections have been associated with

politicization, as presidents have made overt attempts to shift the political balance of the Court to the right.

Nixon nominees

In 1969 the Senate twice failed to ratify Richard Nixon's nominees for the Supreme Court vacancy left by the resignation of Abe Fortas. Nixon had announced his intention to seek a conservative judge from the south for his first appointment. This was in line with his political philosophy but also was intended to be a reward to the south for their support in the 1968 election. His first nominee, Clement Haynesworth, from South Carolina, was rejected after it was revealed that he had failed to disclose a conflict of interest in some of the cases he had tried. His second nominee, Harrold Carswell, from Florida, was rejected after he was accused of racial bias in previous cases. Finally Nixon nominated Harry Blackmun, a moderate judge from Minnesota, and the Senate ratified the appointment.

Reagan nominees

In 1987 Ronald Reagan also had his attempts to fill a Supreme Court vacancy rebuffed twice. The vacancy arose with the retirement of Lewis Powell, a Nixon appointee who had been a swing vote on many issues; the significance of the vacancy was not lost on either the president or the Senate. Reagan nominated Judge Robert Bork, a right-wing former United States' solicitor general. The Senate saw this as a political challenge and rejected the nomination after a twelve-day, acrimonious hearing. Reagan proceeded to nominate a second right-wing judge, Douglas Ginsburg, but he decided to withdraw his name after it was revealed that Ginsburg had used drugs when a student. The Senate finally ratified the nomination of Anthony Kennedy who has turned out to be at least as conservative as either Bork or Ginsburg.

Social composition

When nominating a new Supreme Court justice the president will take into account not only the political balance but also the social composition of the Court. In 1981 Ronald Reagan appointed Sandra Day O'Connor to fill a vacancy left by the retirement of Potter Stewart. O'Connor was the first woman to be appointed to the Supreme Court and the choice was undoubtedly designed to improve Reagan's standing with women voters.

Clarence Thomas

George Bush was faced with the vacancy left by the retirement of Thurgood Marshall, the first black judge to be appointed to the Supreme Court. President Bush was expected to appoint another black judge in order to maintain the ethnic balance of the Court. He did so but his choice, Clarence Thomas, was very controversial. Although black, Thomas was conservative and his judicial credentials appeared thin. His hearing were further complicated when a member of his staff, Anita Hill, accused him of sexual harassment. After a prolonged debate about race and gender his nomination was eventually ratified by the full Senate, 52–48.

Size of Court

Although the constitution does outline the method by which Supreme Court justices should be appointed it does not state how many justices should sit on the Court. Originally the Court consisted of six justices who also served as appeal judges for the circuits. The number of justices reached a low of five and a high of ten but since 1869 has settled at nine. Since 1891 Supreme Court justices have not served on the circuit courts of appeal but each one does have some responsibilities with at least one appeals court.

'Court-packing'

The constitution's lack of exactness on the number of justices required led to controversy in 1937 when Franklin Roosevelt attempted to create six additional Supreme Court justices, taking the number to fifteen. Roosevelt turned to **'court-packing'** in an attempt to create a court which would be more amenable to his New Deal policies after the court of Charles Evans Hughes declared eight New Deal statutes invalid. Congress refused to approve Roosevelt's plan but soon after Roosevelt had the opportunity to remodel the composition of the Court as its members retired.

The power of the Supreme Court

Judicial review

The 'court-packing' incident reveals the extent of the Supreme Court's power. Despite Roosevelt's huge electoral majority in 1932 the Supreme Court was able to strike down eight statutes of the New Deal as invalid in a period of sixteen months. The power of a court to scrutinize the actions of other branches of government is known as **judicial review.** It is based on the court's ability to act as arbiter of the constitution.

Comparison

In Britain there is an unwritten constitution constructed from a variety of sources. The major principle of the British constitution is *parliamentary sovereignty*, which means that no institution can overrule Parliament. Therefore, in Britain the power of judicial review is extremely limited.

Membership of the European Community, now the European Union (EU), in 1973 has made the British Parliament subject to judicial review if it contravenes European law. According to the Treaty of Rome, which governs the working of the EU, European law is superior to domestic law.

British courts also have the power to declare the executive or local government to be acting beyond their powers – *ultra vires*. In the absence of a written constitution, such judgments are based on administrative law.

Interpretation

The fact that the United States' constitution is codified means that there must be a body charged with the task of interpreting what it means. With that power comes judicial review.

The Supreme Court's power to take action such as this is not laid down in the constitution. It is identified as the supreme judicial power in the United States but the document is vague as to how this role should be put into practice.

Checks and balances

Although the constitution itself is vague and the Founding Fathers seem to have been divided over the issue of judicial power, a strong constitutional court does adhere to the theme of checks and balances that runs throughout the document. In *The Federalist* No. 78, Alexander Hamilton declares that: 'The interpretation of the laws is the proper and peculiar province of the courts. A constitution is, in fact, and must be, regarded by the judges as a fundamental law. It must therefore belong to them to ascertain its meaning, as well as the meaning of any particular act proceeding from the legislative body.'

John Marshall

Neither the power to interpret the constitution nor judicial review were made explicit in the constitution itself but were developed by the Supreme Court under its third chief justice, John Marshall. A federalist and therefore in favour of a strong central government, Marshall was appointed chief justice in 1801 by John Adams and was to serve until 1835. During his term of office he developed the power and stature of the Supreme Court more than any justice before or since.

Judicial review and Congress

Marbury v. *Madision*

The most famous case of the Marshall Court was *Marbury* v. *Madison* (1803). In this case Marshall established judicial review as a power of the Supreme Court. Perhaps the most surprising aspect of this was that he did so by cunning rather than confrontation. Immediately prior to leaving office President Adams, a federalist, appointed sixteen federal judges and a series of minor local judges on the basis of the Judiciary Act of 1801, which he had pushed through Congress. His aim was to frustrate his successor, Thomas Jefferson. Hearing that the commissions had not been delivered to the judges, President Jefferson ordered his secretary of state, James Madison, to withhold a number of them. One of those judges, William Marbury, took Madison before the Supreme Court to gain his commission. By the time the case was heard Jefferson had been in office for two years and Marshall, despite being suspicious of Jefferson's views, sought to avoid a conflict with him. Therefore Marshall declared that Marbury's commission was being illegally withheld, but that Marbury's case could not be heard by the Supreme Court because it was based on the 1879 Judiciary Act which, Marshall claimed, was unconstitutional. Therefore Marbury would have to seek redress in another court.

Of the fact that Marshall had been extremely wily there can be no doubt. As law professor Archibald Cox has written: 'By asserting this power of judicial review in a case brought before it, the Supreme Court could maintain the supremacy of the Constitution, build up its own power, and at the same time avoid a disastrous

***Dred Scott* v. *Sandford* (1857)**

The second instance of the Court declaring an act of Congress unconstitutional was the Missouri Compromise, which had excluded slavery from most northern areas of the Louisiana Purchase.

Dred Scott, a slave, had been taken from a slave state into a free state. The Court was asked to decide if this made him a free man. The Court, under Roger Taney, decided that a slave was property and should be protected as such and that Congress had no right to interfere, as it had through the Missouri Compromise. In addition he argued that Dred Scott was a slave, not a citizen, and so could not bring an action before the courts. This case was widely seen as a step towards civil war.

confrontation with President Jefferson by dismissing Marbury's suit as having been brought in the wrong court.'

Marbury v. *Madison* established the Supreme Court's right to review the actions of the Congress. The Supreme Court would not do so again until *Dred Scott* v. *Sandford* (1857). Its ability to review state law had yet to be resolved.

Judicial review and state governments

Separation of powers

At the time the constitution was framed the individual states had jealously guarded their power. As a result the separation of powers operated, not only between the institutions of the central government, but also between the federal and state governments. The 10th Amendment to the constitution states that all powers not specifically given to the federal government in the constitution were reserved for the state governments; hence both the state government and the federal government would each be sovereign in its own areas of jurisdiction.

Marshall Court

John Marshall believed in a strong central government and reaffirmed the superiority of the federal government at every opportunity. He did so most fully in *Martin* v. *Hunter's Lessee* (1816). The highest court in Virginia claimed that as a state of the Union Virginia had equal status with the federal government and therefore the Supreme Court had no jurisdiction over it. The Supreme Court argued that Virginia had relinquished part of its sovereignty when it ratified the constitution and so it was subject to Supreme Court judgments.

McCulloch v. Maryland

The *Martin* v. *Hunter's Lessee* case established the supremacy of the Supreme Court over state courts. A more famous judgement was made in *McCulloch* v. *Maryland* (1819). The state of Maryland had imposed a tax on the national Bank of the United States. Payment of the tax would have put the bank out of business so the branch refused to pay the tax. In this case Marshall used the supremacy clause of the constitution to argue that the federal government must be allowed to carry out the duties given to it. The Supreme Court declared Maryland's tax to be unconstitutional and in so doing, established their power to review state governments. It is in the realm of state law that the Supreme Court has been most active in its use of judicial review.

Earl Warren

Warren was appointed chief justice of the Supreme Court by Eisenhower in 1954. Eisenhower expected him to be relatively conservative and was surprised when the appointment ushered in a period of unprecedented **judicial activism.** In 1968 Eisenhower was quoted as saying the appointment was the 'biggest damned fool mistake I ever made'.

During a period in which the executive and legislative branches were relatively inactive Warren's Court was involved in issues of **civil rights**, the rights of the accused and the apportionment of electoral districts. The Court was active in making policy and was accused of usurping the role of Congress.

Judicial review and the executive

Since the ground-breaking cases of Marshall's Court the principle of judicial review in the United States has largely gone unquestioned. Recent cases have shown the importance of the Supreme Court's ability to review the other branches of government. In *Youngstown Sheet & Tube Company* v. *Sawyer* (1952) the Court ruled that President Truman had exceeded his constitutional power in ordering the take-over of America's steel plants which were in the midst of an industrial dispute. In *The United States* v. *Richard Nixon* (1974) the Court ruled that President Nixon could not claim absolute 'executive privilege' in withholding the so-called 'Watergate tapes' from Congress. The Court held that 'neither the doctrine of separation of powers, nor the need for confidentiality of high-level communications, without more, can sustain an absolute, unqualified, presidential immunity from judicial process under all circumstances'.

The Supreme Court and affirmative action

The Civil Rights Acts of 1964 and 1968 brought **de jure** discrimination to an end but **de facto** discrimination remained and the Court was taken into a new areas of desegregation policy and affirmative action programmes. In *Swann* v. *Charlotte-Mecklenburg Board of Education* (1971) the Court upheld the constitutionality of busing, the practice of transporting children to schools outside their area in order to encourage racial integration, where the intent to discriminate could be proven.

Regents of the University of California v. *Bakke* (1978) was so controversial that it yielded six different opinions from the Court. It ruled that race could be taken into account when deciding on admission to university but it was not to be the sole consideration.

In the 1980s the Court's new conservative outlook led to a series of decisions that restricted the opportunities for the redress of minority group grievances in cases of employment discrimination. In *Memphis Fire Dept* v. *Stotts* (1984) the Court stated that racial quotas did not take precedence over length of service in redundancy cases. *Wards Cove Packing Co* v. *Antonio* (1989) the Court ruled that the burden of proof regarding discriminatory practices should lie with the plaintiff not the employer. In *City of Richmond* v. *Croson* (1989) the Court invalidated the practice, used in many cities, of keeping a quota of contracts reserved for businesses owned by members of minorities.

The trend towards the reversal of affirmative action provisions continued in *Adarand Constructors* v. *Peña* (1995). The 5–4 majority opinion stated that federal contracts could be allocated according to race only if the Court could be convinced that a small adjustment was warranted in the pursuit of government interests. Whilst not outlawing affirmative action this case certainly opens the door for further cases which may challenge the whole concept of affirmative action.

Judicial review and civil liberties

The power of judicial review has allowed the Supreme Court to protect **civil liberties** in the United States. Its involvement in civil liberties cases has ranged from racial issues through to the rights of the accused and the reapportionment of electoral districts. In *Brown* v. *The Board of Education, Topeka, Kansas* (1954) the Warren Court ruled that racial segregation in schools was a violation of the equal protection clause of the 14th

The Supreme Court and the rights of the accused

The Warren Court laid down four important judgments relating to the rights of citizens accused of a crime.

In *Mapp* v. *Ohio* (1961) the Court overturned a conviction because some evidence had been obtained without a warrant.

Gideon v. *Wainwright* (1963) expanded the right of a defendant to a lawyer for all felony cases in state courts. Previously this had only been necessary when the death penalty was involved. This judgment was based on the 'equal protection clause' of the 14th Amendment.

Escobedo v. *Illinois* (1964) established a criminal defendant's right to a lawyer if the defendant so desired. To fail to do so is an infringement of the 'assistance to counsel' provision of the 6th Amendment.

In *Miranda* v. *Arizona* (1966) the Court held that anyone being placed under arrest must be 'read their rights', i.e. their right to remain silent and their right to a lawyer. In addition it limited the admissibility of confessions unless they were gained under laid down procedures with special safeguards.

Under the Burger and Rehnquist Courts judgments have limited some of these rights. In 1971 the Court ruled that confessions gained in violation of Miranda could be used to help jurors decide if a witness was lying in court. In *New York* v. *Quarles* (1984) the Court ruled that if public safety was threatened a suspect could be questioned before being read their Miranda rights. In *Arizona* v. *Fulimante* (1991) the Court backtracked still further on Miranda rights by declaring that a confession obtained via coercion would not automatically rule it inadmissible.

In *United States* v. *Havens* (1980) the Court limited the exclusion of illegally obtained evidence (first established in 1914) if it could be used to contradict a defendant's testimony. Under the Rehnquist Court the inadmissibility of evidence was further limited when the Court held that the police could search private rubbish without a warrant.

The Rehnquist Court has also begun to reinterpret the ban on 'cruel and unusual punishments' laid down by the 8th Amendment. In *McClesky* v. *Kemp* (1987) the Court ruled that the death penalty was not a cruel punishment. In 1989 the Court made a similar declaration regarding the use of capital punishment against youths of 16 or 17 and against people who are mentally retarded.

Amendment. In *Miranda* v. *Arizona* (1966) the Supreme Court stated that a person must be informed of their right to silence and to a lawyer when they are being arrested. *Reynolds* v. *Simms* (1966) established the criterion of one person, one vote regarding the apportionment of electoral districts.

Minority groups

The Supreme Court's ability to preserve civil liberties has been particularly important for minority groups. In a democracy there is always a danger that elected representatives will identify their interests with those of the majority. Such electoral self-interest may be at the expense of minority groups. This is sometimes referred to as the 'tyranny of the majority'. The Supreme Court, being independent of electoral interests, has the ability to stand as a guardian of minority rights. Chief Justice Marshall could have been speaking directly to minority groups when he said: 'To what quarter

The Supreme Court and malapportionment of electoral districts

Malapportionment relates to the failure of states to redraw their electoral boundaries in order to keep up with demographic movements. By failing to do so rural populations can retain a grip on politics beyond their actual numbers.

On occasions constituency boundaries can be drawn in order to engineer a particular election result. This is known as '**gerrymandering**' – so called after Massachusetts Governor Elbridge Gerry (1744–1814), who created an electoral district shaped like a salamander in 1811.

In *Colegrove* v. *Green* (1946) the Supreme Court refused to become involved in this issue but under Earl Warren the Court confirmed that it was a matter for judicial review in *Baker* v. *Carr* (1962).

In *Reynolds* v. *Simms* (1964) the Court upheld one person, one vote as the principle behind the apportionment of electoral districts. It refuted the claim of some states that, like the federal government, they could have one house of their legislature apportioned on a different basis. *Wesberry* v. *Sanders* (1964) confirmed that electoral districts should be approximately equal in terms of population.

In 1983 the Court reaffirmed these principles when it rejected New Jersey's new proposals for congressional districts because the size of the largest and smallest districts differed by 3,674 electors (less than one per cent). However, it has given states greater leeway with their own legislative districts.

Miller v. *Johnson* (1995) brought together the two highly contentious issues of malapportionment and affirmative action. For the last decade some electoral districts have been manufactured in order give an electoral majority for a particular racial group. As a result the representation of these groups in legislative assemblies at both state and federal level has increased, for example, from 45 congressmen in 1990 to 69 in 1992. The Miller case ruled this practice unconstitutional because race should not be the *predominant* factor in the design of electoral districts. In effect this was the racial gerrymandering sometimes referred to as 'affirmative gerrymandering'.

will you look for protection from an infringement of the Constitution, if you will not give that power to the judiciary? There is no other body that can afford such protection.'

Brown v. *The Board of Education, Topeka, Kansas* (1954) illustrates very clearly the role of the court in relation to minority groups. President Truman had made some little progress towards greater civil rights for black Americans, but had been reticent due to the divisions within the Democratic Party. President Eisenhower had no intention of being a reforming president and so was unlikely to show a lead toward equal treatment of blacks. Congress was dominated by right-wing southern Democrats who had no intention of championing civil rights. Therefore the only institution capable of giving a lead on the civil rights issue was the Supreme Court. In 1954 it did just that by declaring racial segregation in schools to be unconstitutional. The decision of the Warren Court overturned education policy in the southern states at a stroke.

The way in which the Supreme Court has used its powers has by no means been free of controversy. This is because the Court's ability to interpret the constitution sometimes allows it to make policy. How the Court reacts to these opportunities depends on whether the justices are advocates of **judicial restraint** or judicial activism.

'Strict constructionists'

Those who espouse the narrow interpretation of the constitution, **'strict constructionists'**, believe that judges should be guided by the principle of **original intent**, i.e. the original intention of the Founding Fathers. Justice Harlan Fiske wrote in *United States* v. *Butler* (1936), that 'while unconstitutional exercise by the executive and legislative branches is subject to judicial restraint, the only check on our own exercise of power is our sense of **self-restraint**'. Strict constructionists advocate leaving policy-making to the executive and legislative branches of government, who are elected to do so.

'Loose constructionists'

Advocates of 'judicial activism',**'loose constructionists'**, favour the use of the Supreme Court's power to promote social goals which they might consider desirable. The 'strict constructionists' believe that judicial activism usurps the power of the legislature. Ronald Reagan's remarks regarding his attitude to judicial appointments sums up the conservative approach: 'The one thing that I do seek are judges who will interpret the law and not write the law.'

The major decisions of the Warren Court were constantly denounced as political and activist by the 'strict constructionists'. But perhaps the best example to illustrate the division between activism and restraint is a decision of the more conservative Burger Court in *Roe* v. *Wade* (1973).

Abortion rights

In 1972 'Jane Roe' from Texas wanted an abortion in order, she claimed, to avoid the social stigma of single parenthood and the economic hardship that it would involve. Texas had outlawed abortion. The Supreme Court originally decided to look at the case for purely technical reasons. Chief Justice Burger saw it as an opportunity to clarify the Supreme Court's jurisdiction over state law. However, once the case had been taken on it presented an opportunity for the more liberal members of the Court to push for the issue of abortion to be confronted head on. In doing so they would consider whether to strike down all the state laws banning abortion.

Justice William Douglas saw it as an opportunity to return to the issue of privacy on which he had first given opinion in *Griswold* v. *Connecticut* (1965). This case concerned a state's right to ban contraceptives. Douglas had written the Court's majority opinion stating that such a ban was an impermissible invasion of privacy. He wrote: 'The First Amendment has a penumbra where privacy is protected from governmental intrusion ... Would we allow the police to search the sacred precincts of marital bedrooms for tell-tale signs of the use of contraceptives? The very idea is repulsive to the notions of privacy surrounding the marriage relationship.'

The 'activist,' liberal members of the court, including Douglas, Brennan and Marshall, believed that there was a fundamental constitutional right to privacy under which women had the right to decide to have an abortion or not. Those justices favouring 'self-restraint', including Burger, Rehnquist and White, believed that the Court should not strike down the state laws and leave the decision to individual states.

The final decision went in favour of the 'activist' justices, 7–2. Justice Blackmun wrote in the majority opinion: 'freedom of personal choice in matters of marriage and family life is one of the liberties protracted by the due process clause of the 14th Amendment ... that right necessarily includes the right of a woman to decide whether or not to terminate her pregnancy.'

1980s conservatism

The controversy surrounding the *Roe* v. *Wade* decision did not end in 1973. Throughout the 1980s, as President Reagan moved the Supreme Court to the right, the right-to-life movement began to push for a re-examination of the abortion issue. State legislatures began to pass laws which put more and more constraints on the availability of abortions. Congress passed *The Hyde Amendment* which prohibited the use of federal government funds and Medicaid for abortions. The Supreme Court upheld the 'Hyde' restriction in *Harris v. McCrae* (1980).

By the mid-eighties, with the advantages of Reagan's appointees to the Court the Pro-life lobby believed that *Roe* v. *Wade* was ripe for revision. In *Webster* v. *Reproductive Health Services* (1989) the Supreme Court looked set to do just that, but in the end fell short of overturning *Roe* v. *Wade*. However, the opinion did encourage state governments to regulate abortion more closely and the conservative justices on the Court did indicate their readiness to overturn *Roe* v. *Wade* given another opportunity.

Since then, in *Planned Parenthood* v. *Casey* (1992), the Court has reaffirmed *Roe* v. *Wade* once more. It has stated that state restrictions are constitutional only if they do not place an 'undue burden' on a woman's right to an abortion. To make such an affirmation possible the moderate conservatives on the Court have fallen in behind the *Roe* v. *Wade* decision. The reason for this is that the Court was being subjected to increasing criticism that liberal 'activism' was being replaced by conservative 'activism'. Whilst the 1960s and 1970s had seen liberal judges actively overturning laws with which they disagreed, the 1980s was in danger of being seen as a time when the right actively overturned judicial precedents with which they disagreed. Those who prefer 'judicial restraint' have perhaps decided on a more incremental approach to change.

Limits to the Supreme Court's power

Although the potential powers of the United States' Supreme Court are great they should not be over-estimated. It is, after all, only a court and, no matter how activist the justices might choose to be, they are constrained by this fact.

Initiation

The Supreme Court does not have the power to initiate its own cases, as **appellate court** cases must be brought before it from lower courts, except in those limited areas in which it has original jurisdiction. Therefore, even the most activist justices cannot select laws or policies with which they disagree and bring them before the Court.

Enforcement

Once a decision has been made the Supreme Court has no power to enforce its decision. For enforcement the Court relies on the support of the executive and legislative branches of government. Although *Brown* v. *Board of Education, Topeka, Kansas* (1954) broke new ground for racial minorities in America it did not mean that racial segregation in schools automatically came to an end. Three years later, in Little Rock, Arkansas, President Eisenhower sent troops to enforce desegregation by escorting black children to school when Governor Faubus refused to comply with the court decision. And de jure discrimination did not come to an end until Congress passed the Civil Rights Acts of 1964 and 1968.

Respect

Given that the Court has no power of enforcement, it is important for the Court to maintain its position of respect, both with other political institutions and with the public. Therefore justices will try to avoid dramatic reversals of decisions and will try to overturn precedents gradually, as is clearly illustrated by the Court's incremental aproach to the abortion issue.

Constitutional limits

The Supreme Court's ability to interpret the constitution is limited in some areas. The federal system cannot be reinterpreted by the Court and some sections are sufficiently precise to restrict creativity; for example, the 2nd Amendment states clearly and simply that American citizens have the right to bear arms.

Constitutionalism

Perhaps the ultimate limits on the Supreme Court, or any court, are the politicians themselves. No matter how powerful a court appears to be it can only operate within the framework laid down by politicians. Therefore the power of the Supreme Court is no more nor less than politicians would wish. When Franklin Roosevelt's policies were being obstructed by the Supreme Court he considered altering the composition of the Court but he did not consider ignoring it. This was because Roosevelt believed in the constitution and the power it gives to the Court. Any court, faced by politicians lacking that sense of **constitutionalism** would be powerless. Ultimately the power of the Court, its ability to preserve civil liberties and even its policy-making power depends on the willingness of the politicians to abide by its decisions.

Questions

Short questions

1 a What is affirmative action?

b How have recent Supreme Court decisions affected such programmes?
(ULEAC, June 1991)

2 What are (a) malapportionment and (b) gerrymandering? (ULEAC, June 1992)

3 How did the Warren Court advance the cause of equal rights? (ULEAC, January 1993)

4 a What was the Bakke case?
b Assess its contemporary significance.
(ULEAC, January 1993)

5 What impact has the Rehnquist Court had on civil rights? (ULEAC, June 1994)

6 Why have many recent appointments to the Supreme Court proved controversial? (ULEAC, June 1994)

US questions

1 To what extent is the Supreme Court a 'policy-maker'? (ULEAC, January 1994)

2 'The Supreme Court has too much power for an unelected body.' Discuss. (ULEAC, January 1993)

3 'The Supreme Court depends on lower courts (federal and state) to implement its decisions and these may not always interpret or accept the Court's judgments in an unambiguous fashion. The most celebrated examples of judicial recalcitrance and obstruction involved the enforcement of civil rights in the south.'

Source: David McKay, *American Politics and Society* (Blackwell)

How far and in what ways are the decisions of the Supreme Court undermined by its lack of powers of enforcement? (AEB, June 1992)

4 To what extent can a president hope to mould and influence the Supreme Court? (UODLE, June 1994)

5 To what extent have the decisions of the Supreme court under Chief Justice Rehnquist marked a significant departure from those laid down by the Warren and Burger Courts? (UCLES, June 1994)

Comparative questions

1 a How are senior judges recruited?
b Do and should they reflect particular interests? (Illustrate your answer with reference to at least two countries.)
(ULEAC, January 1994)

2 What mechanisms exist to ensure the impartiality of the judiciary? (Illustrate your answer with reference to at least two countries.)
(ULEAC, June 1993)

3 To what extent are courts part of the political process? (Illustrate your answer with reference to at least two countries.)
(ULEAC, June 1994)

10 Pressure groups

Questions to be answered in this chapter

- What are pressure groups?
- Why are some pressure groups more powerful than others?
- What factors affect the power of pressure groups within a political system?
- Are pressure groups good or bad for democracy?

Terms to know

- 'Access points'
- Agribusiness
- Cause groups
- Christian Coalition
- 'Clientelism'
- Corporatism
- 'Incumbent politics'
- 'Insider' groups
- Interest-group liberalism
- Interest groups
- 'Iron triangles'
- 'Issue networks'
- Lobbying
- 'Outsider' groups
- Participation
- Pluralism
- Private-interest groups
- Promotional groups
- Public-interest groups
- Sectional groups
- 'Subsystems'

Introduction

'Complaints are everywhere heard from our most considerate and virtuous citizens ... that our governments are too unstable, that the public good is disregarded in the conflicts of rival parties, and that measures are too often decided, not according to the rules of justice and the rights of the minor party, but by the superior force of an interested and overbearing majority.' With these words, in *The Federalist* No. 10, James Madison expressed his fears regarding the growth of 'interests' within the new American republic. He went on to express his confidence in the strength of that republic to overcome the power of 'faction'. Today many observers of American politics would argue that, for once, Madison was mistaken.

Interest groups

An **interest group** can be defined as a collection of like-minded individuals who are organized with a view to influencing government decisions in their favour. James Madison's preferred definition of a faction was: 'a number of citizens, whether amounting to a majority or minority of the whole, who are united and actuated by some common impulse of passion, or of interest, adverse to the rights of other citizens, or to the permanent and aggregate interests of the community.' (*The Federalist* No .10).

Comparison

In Britain we are accustomed to using the term 'pressure group' to cover all such groups and then sub-dividing them into **sectional groups** and **cause groups**. The former are concerned with protecting the self-interest of a particular section of society, examples include trade unions and the British Medical Association. The latter promote a particular cause in society, not related to the well-being of their members, examples include the Campaign for Nuclear Disarmament and Greenpeace.

In the United States the terminology used to classify groups changes a little. Those pursuing self-interest are known as interest groups whilst those promoting the interests of others are known as **promotional groups.**

Types of interest group

The interest group category is the largest and contains an enormous range of different groups, from business to labour and from agriculture to professional. In this category the term 'group' is interpreted loosely, allowing it to incorporate individual firms who will lobby government for contracts or for favourable policies. These groups are sometimes referred to as **private-interest groups**, because they are pursuing a relatively narrow self-interest.

Business groups

Until the 1970s **lobbying** by business groups in Washington was fairly limited. Preceding decades had been without excessive turmoil for the American business community and national spokespeople, such as the United States Chamber of Commerce and the National Association of Manufacturers had relatively little importance. Individual companies, meanwhile, had concentrated their activity on state and local governments, where they could be very influential, and on quietly building direct links with bureaucrats.

Climate of the 1970s

However, in the 1970s the economic climate began to move against business interests. Groups lobbying on behalf of civil rights, consumer protection, the environment, along with intensifying foreign competition, posed the greatest threat to an advantageous business climate. As a result they began to mobilize and lobby more actively in Washington.

NAM

Today the National Association of Manufacturers (NAM) represents 14,000 companies and most of the large corporations, such as Rockwell, AT&T and IBM, have their own, permanent representation in Washington. In fact corporations account for over 45 per cent of pressure-group representation in Washington. Much of this representation will take place through professional lobbyists, whose financial strength helps consolidate their influence.

Of course, business groups do not simply lobby collectively. Business interests are by no means homogeneous and there is intense competition between different sets of business interests.

Labour groups

Limits on unions

Trade unions in the United States have never reached the levels of power achieved by their European counterparts. Unions were probably at their most powerful in the 1930s and 1940s when the tide of opinion during the Depression turned in favour of organized labour. The Wagner Act (1935) outlined the unions' right to organize strikes. Nevertheless, during the same period they suffered significant reversals of fortune. The most serious was the Taft-Hartley Act (1947) which outlawed the closed shop.

Decline

Since its high point in 1945 trade union membership has been in decline. Today there are approximately 18 million members of the AFL-CIO – the equivalent of the Trades Union Congress; this represents 20 per cent of the workforce.

Non-ideological

Unions in the United States are relatively non-ideological, preferring to lobby actively on behalf of their members' pay and working conditions rather than work towards a socialist vision of society. They are loosely attached to the Democratic Party but various leaders have at times supported the Republican Party, for example Jackie Presser of the Teamsters Union. Their non-ideological stance helps them to act on behalf of their members, whichever party is in power.

Agriculture groups

America's farm population has fallen consistently over the last 50 years and now the 3 million farmers represent only 3.5 per cent of the working population. Whilst their numbers have fallen so has their influence. For many years the electoral weight of farmers was great; some congressmen were virtually elected on the strength of the farm vote. The electoral importance of farmers has diminished as the population has moved to urban centres and, since the Supreme Court decisions on malapportionment in the 1960s, the boundaries of electoral districts have been redrawn to reflect those movements (see page 149).

The two major farm groups are the American Farm Bureau Federation and the National Farm Union. The former is the larger group, whilst the latter has its support concentrated mainly in the west and midwest. Apart from the main organizations there are smaller bodies, such as the National Milk Producers Federation and the National Livestock Feeders Federation. Some agricultural concerns are sufficiently large to be viewed as businesses in their own right – they are known as **agribusinesses** – and they will campaign for their own interests.

Although their electoral influence has diminished agriculture groups continue to lobby very actively in Washington. The issue of government subsidies to the agricultural community is high on the agenda of these groups, particularly for the National Farm Union.

Professional bodies

As the professions have developed over the last 40 years, so their professional bodies have become more influential. Organizations like the American Bar Association (ABA) and the American Medical Association (AMA) are extremely powerful groups in Washington. The ABA, for example, plays a significant role in the nomination of judges.

AMA

The AMA fought a hard, but ultimately losing, battle in the 1960s against the introduction of Medicare and Medicaid, referring to the proposals as 'socialized medicine'. At the time the association represented 70 per cent of doctors, but since then it has lost some of its influence as members of the medical profession have turned to more specialized organizations to represent their interests. Nevertheless its 271,000 members represent 50 per cent of the 532,000 doctors in the United States and in 1981 and 1982 its political action committee was the biggest spender of all, contributing $1,737,090 to federal candidates.

Other powerful professional groups include the American Federation of Teachers which, virtually single-handedly, persuaded Jimmy Carter to create the Department of Education in 1979 and later prevented Ronald Reagan from dismantling it.

Ideological groups

There are a number of groups which do not act on behalf of economic interest but attempt to protect the rights and interests of a particular section of the population.

The New Right

The New Right is not a single group but a collection of groups all seeking to promote right-wing values as solutions to political, economic and social problems. These groups came to prominence in America in the 1980s during the presidency of Ronald Reagan. Reagan himself was an advocate of many of their policies. More recently, New Right ideas have been seen in the *Contract With America*, the 'manifesto' of the Republican Party in the 1994 mid-term elections.

Economically the New Right advocates a strong private economy with little interference from the government. They believe in the efficacy of the 'free market', unrestrained by government regulation and manipulation. As such the role of government should be to create an advantageous environment for the business with low taxes and limited spending – resulting in a balanced budget.

Many of the groups that make up the New Right are of religious origin. This is most clearly seen in the area of social policy. The New Right is opposed to abortion, pornography and promotes prayer in schools. Well-known figures from this wing of the Republican Party include Jerry Falwell, Pat Buchanan and Pat Robertson.

NAACP

The National Association for the Advancement of Colored People (NAACP) is particularly well known for its work towards enhancing civil rights. Established in 1909 the NAACP chose legal action and lobbying of Congress to further its cause and was the sponsor of the *Brown* v. *Board of Education, Topeka, Kansas* case in 1954.

Other organizations include the National Organization of Women, which has lobbied for greater rights for women and has thrown itself behind the Equal Rights Amendment, and the National Taxpayer Union which favours an end to budget deficit and the approval of a balanced budget amendment.

Conservative Coalition

Although the most well-known ideological groups have traditionally been from the liberal section of the political spectrum in recent years conservative groups have gained greater prominence. Most well known is Pat Robertson's Conservative Coalition, which promotes traditional moral virtues regarding education, abortion, prayer and pornography, as well as a strong, anti-communist foreign policy and free-market economics.

Promotional groups

Although not as large as the interest groups category promotional groups are extremely significant in the American political process. Their importance can be traced back to the 1970s when Watergate and Vietnam created a greater cynicism in the American people and an unwillingness to leave the government to look after the public interest. The nature of the important promotional groups reflect this concern. They include Common Cause, Public Citizen, the National Audubon Society and the Sierra Club.

In view of their objectives such groups are sometimes referred to as **public-interest groups**. They tend to rely on the good offices of individuals who are prepared to give up their time and money to a cause. As an individual's commitment to a public cause is not necessarily as reliable as a commitment to self-interest these groups can suffer from fluctuating membership.

Environmental groups have developed in the 1970s and 1980s as Americans have become more concerned about the world in which they live. Not surprisingly, the development of environmental awareness coincided with relative economic prosperity.

Ralph Nader

Public Citizen is a Ralph Nader organization committed to advancing the cause of the consumer. Nader came to prominence in the 1960s when he played a key role in forcing General Motors to withdraw one of their models, the Corvair, which was considered not road-worthy. Since then Nader has lobbied on behalf of consumers and has created a number of organizations including Congress Watch, which monitors the performance of the people's representatives.

Common Cause also lobbies on behalf of consumers. It is particularly concerned with ethics in government. It has lobbied hard on the issues of election finance and open government.

Pressure-group power

Pressure groups attempt to influence decision-makers in the hope that their favoured policies will be adopted. In order to do so, they must be able to attract the attention of the decision-makers and be able to compete against other groups. The competition between groups can be fierce. How powerful an individual group becomes depends on the nature of the group.

Membership

The most obvious point made about pressure-group membership is that those with many members will be the most influential. Groups that can tap into a large membership are likely to be public-interest groups. Their causes are often able to inspire large-scale support, which can be mobilized to send letters and make telephone calls to members of Congress, to attend mass rallies and demonstrations, and to contribute to the group's funds.

'Outsider' groups

Public-interest groups, however, are often **'outsider' groups**. This means that they do not have strong links with any decision-makers and so rely upon the impact of public opinion in order to achieve the desired effect. Therefore, to an extent, the use of such 'outsider' tactics can be a sign of weakness.

Representation

It may not simply be the size of the membership that affects the influence of some groups. The number of potential members could be just as important. If a group can claim to speak on behalf of a significant proportion of potential members the decision-makers may take it more seriously. The American Medical Association and the range of consumer groups illustrate this point. The AMA represents approximately 50 per cent of the doctors in the United States. This gives its views considerable weight. Consumer groups on the other hand find it almost impossible to recruit such a high proportion of their potential members because 'consumers' are such a nebulous and numerous group.

Finance

Members do not only allow groups to apply pressure to decision-makers they are also the main providers of finance. Private-interest groups often have a significant advantage over public-interest groups in this area. Professional groups have relatively wealthy members who are able to donate generously and corporate interests are able to channel funds from their main business into its Political Action Committee (see page 164). Public-interest groups tend to rely on contributions from their members – rich or poor. Families USA, a public-interest group which lobbies on family issues, relied on contributions from wealthy individuals until it could build up a mailing list of sufficient size (225,000) to finance its operations.

Lobbyists

In modern American politics finance is particularly important as pressure groups use funds to pay professional lobbyists, to contribute funds to election campaigns and to organize media campaigns. Hiring lobbyists to act on behalf of a group is very expensive, anywhere from $5,000 to $30,000 per month. Similarly a quarter-page advertisement in the *Washington Post* costs over $13,000.

Relationship with decision-makers

Pressure groups attempt to foster good relations with decision-makers. Those that build close contacts in some or all of the branches of government are known as **'insider' groups**. Their relationship is sometimes referred to as a **'subsystem'**.

'Subsystems'

Within a 'subsystem', government policy-makers and pressure groups may work closely together. This is known as **corporatism.** When working together the government bodies and pressure groups recognize and accommodate each other's needs; therefore both parties benefit. In some cases this relationship may even result in the pressure group regulating its own area of policy, for example the American Bar association has the right to license lawyers to practise in the United States.

'Issue networks'

The alternative arrangement to a 'subsystem' is an **'issue network'**. This refers to groups emerging on an ad hoc basis to play a part in the decision-making of a particular area. It implies that groups enter and leave a policy area easily in order to propose or to oppose a public policy initiative.

It is sometimes the case that the 'subsystem' and 'issue network' models come into conflict. If new actors enter an area of policy normally dominated by a 'subsystem' the actors with a long-term interest may attempt to block and delay any policy initiatives until outside interest has diminished before reverting to the normal 'subsystem' pattern.

The targets of pressure-group activity

The ability of pressure groups as a whole to wield influence in the political system is determined by the nature of the government. However, 'government' in this case can mean both the political complexion of the government, i.e. whether it is Republican or Democratic, and the characteristics of the governmental system, i.e. whether there is an emphasis on separation of powers and how powerful political parties are within that system.

The complexion of the government

Politics in the United States is not based on ideological differences. The Democratic Party tends to be more liberal than the Republican Party but both are very broad, loose coalitions designed primarily to win election across a politically diverse country. Therefore the ideological compatibility of pressure groups and the executive or the majority party in the House or Senate tends to be less relevant than in Britain. However, at times in the history of the United States differences of political opinion have been important. The trade union movement tended to be looked upon more favourably during the period of the New Deal and relatively badly during Ronald Reagan's presidency.

Comparison

In Britain the degree of influence individual pressure groups wield depends on the ideological leanings of the government as well as of the group itself. During the Labour government (1974–79) the trade union movement was clearly welcomed in government circles as the government put together its Social Contract policies. They could, therefore, be termed 'insider' groups. When Mrs Thatcher's Conservative party assumed power in 1979 the trade unions were immediately consigned to 'outsider' status as they were no longer consulted about government policy. The major determinant of the trade union–government relationship was their ideological compatibility.

The structure of government

Access points

Pressure groups are able to enter the political system via **'access points'**. In effect these are holes in the system which enable groups to gain access to decision-makers.

The American political system is very open and is riddled with access points. The strong separation of powers between state governments and the federal government created two layers of government for groups to target. Within the federal government the separation of powers between executive, legislature and judiciary also creates opportunities for pressure groups.

State v. federal government

State government

At the level of state government, pressure groups are faced with a similar structure to that at federal level. Federal laws are made by state legislatures, all of which, except Nebraska, are bicameral; the executive is controlled by the governor; and laws are applied by the state courts. Each of these institutions offers opportunities for group activity.

Local government

Within states there are additional layers of local government. The Mayors of the cities, local councils and local administrative agencies all have control over their areas of jurisdiction. Again, they present opportunities to pressure groups.

Comparison

The British unitary constitution means that political power is concentrated with central government. Local government has relatively few functions and only as much independence as Parliament chooses to give it. Hence local government in Britain provides a range of access points with regard to issues like town planning but for relatively few other areas.

Many corporations that would seek to influence state or local governments are larger financial concerns than the states themselves. Therefore their potential influence is enormous. Not only are they able to bring their financial wealth to bear on a particular situation but their value to the local community also makes their wishes almost impossible to ignore.

Federal dominance

However, since the New Deal of the 1930s, the federal government has become much more important than state and local governments for many pressure groups. The federal government controls the major government contracts, legislates on all of the key economic and social issues and is therefore a much more valuable target for groups.

Congress

Congress is bicameral but both the Senate and the House of Representatives are powerful and so both represent important targets for pressure-group activity. However, a great deal of congressional business is carried on through its committee system. Standing committees in the House and the Senate have legislative and investigative functions, they are responsible for specific areas of policy and the floor of each house tends to follow the advice of the committees. All of these points make the committees very attractive targets for pressure groups.

Comparison

Although the British Parliament is bicameral the houses do not share equal powers. In the twentieth century the power of the House of Lords has diminished. It has the power to debate and delay legislation but has no power over finance. Therefore many pressure groups consider it of limited value and will concentrate their attentions on the House of Commons.

Sub-committees

Since the adoption of the sub-committee bill of rights in the House in 1973 sub-committee government has been institutionalized. Committees with over twenty members must have at least four sub-committees, each of which has its own staff. Therefore the sub-committees multiply the number of access points for pressure groups.

Hearings

The method congressional committees use to conduct their business is often a hearing. The members of the committee put questions to witnesses in order to determine opinion on issues or legislative proposals. These hearings present ideal opportunities for pressure groups to put their case to members of Congress and many will act as witnesses, giving testimony about their area of expertise.

Lobbyists

A great deal of the 'influence peddling' is not carried out by pressure groups themselves, but by their lobbyists. The number of registered lobbyists increased from 3,420 in 1976 to 8,800 in 1986 but most experts believe that this figure seriously understates the true figure. Perhaps a more accurate estimate is approximately 20,000; or 30 lobbyists for every member of Congress. Lobbyists swarm over Congress to such an extent that the corridor outside the committee room of the House Ways and Means Committee has been nicknamed 'Gucci Gulch', due to the number of well-heeled lobbyists who gather there.

Lobbyists are employed to act as intermediaries between the pressure group and the decision-makers. Traditionally the success of an individual pressure group would be determined by the knowledge that group had of the system and the contacts it was able to build up. Today, this is the lobbyists' area of expertise. They understand the system and know who to contact because most of them are ex-government employees or are ex-politicians themselves. Michael Deaver, ex-deputy chief of staff; Kenneth Duberstein, ex-congressional liaison and Lyn Nofziger, former political liaison, all worked in the Reagan White House but left to put their contacts to good use in the lobbying business.

Comparison

Although political lobbying in Britain is by no means as advanced as it is in the United States it is becoming increasingly important in the political process. Approximately a third of MPs are employed as consultants to lobbying companies or private corporations. Their functions range from posing questions, taking part in debate and initiating legislation law on behalf of their clients.

It is not only American corporations and pressure groups that hire lobbyists. Competition for foreign aid and the goodwill of the American government is now so intense that countries hire lobbyists. In 1986 South Korea was reportedly paying Michael Deaver the sum of $1.5 million to represent it whilst the Reagan White House held inquiries into unfair trade practices.

Limits on lobbying

There are limits on the activities of lobbyists. Bribery of a member of Congress has been an offence since 1909. And since the Federal Regulation of Lobbying Act (1946) individuals and organizations whose 'principal' role is paid lobbying are required to register and to file the amounts of money they spend on the lobbying process. Many groups avoid this by arguing that lobbying is not their 'principal' activity. The Ethics in Government Act (1978) limits the ability of ex-government employees to return to the private sector and begin lobbying their former colleagues, with whom they worked directly. They are not allowed to do so for two years.

Comparison

In Britain lobbying individual members of the House of Commons is of limited value because on so many issues their behaviour will be determined by their party loyalty rather than their own opinions. The result is a House of Commons that is highly organized. A high degree of party discipline reduces the number of access points for pressure groups.

Party discipline

In the United States the level of party loyalty in Congress is low. Members know that their election and re-election depends not on their party but on their own ability to raise finance and the electorate in their states or districts. The candidate-orientation of the system makes members of Congress susceptible to pressure-group influence. Once again, it is the lobbyist who is on hand to help with a candidate's re-election.

PACs

Many pressure groups set up Political Action Committees (PACs) through which they

Political Action Committees

Political Action Committees (PACs) take two forms:

- segregated fund
- non-connected

Segregated fund PACs are attached to their parent body and receive funds from that body. They are not allowed to raise funds from the public. Non-connected PACs are not attached to a particular interest or body and raise money from the public, usually through direct-mailing techniques. The money is then spent on behalf of the candidate in order to avoid the limits imposed on contributions direct to campaigns imposed by the Federal Election Campaign Act of 1974.

contribute to candidates' election campaigns. In 1975 there were 608 PACs; by 1990 that number had risen to over 4500. In 1988 PACs contributed $172 million to candidates. Former Congressman Leon Panetta, now President Clinton's Chief of Staff, commented on this situation in 1986: 'There's a danger that we're putting ourselves on the auction block every election. It's now tough to hear the voices of the citizens in your district. Sometimes the only things you can hear are the loud voices in the three-piece suits carrying a PAC cheque.' In 1986 PACs contributed, on average, 34 per cent of campaign funds for elections to the House.

Incumbents and PACs

Over 75 per cent of PAC finance goes to incumbents. To PACs there is a distinct advantage in **'incumbent politics'**. Once contacts have been made with committee chairs and members it makes little sense for them to be lost at the next election. The large amounts of money they are prepared to spend raises the stake and makes it extremely difficult for challengers to enter the game. Unless, that is, a PAC has decided to 'target' an incumbent with a view to deposing them at the next election. So-called 'attack PACs' channel money to the political opponents of members of Congress they wish to see removed from office.

Obviously an ability to determine elections in this way would be a major cause for concern in any democracy. There are limits on PAC activities. They are allowed to contribute only $5,000 to a candidate's primary campaign and $5,000 to a candidate's election campaign. However, they are allowed to spend indirectly on a candidate's campaign by buying advertising space on their behalf. To an extent their influence in presidential election campaigns has been reduced by the introduction of government funding, which has reduced the necessity of PAC finance and imposes spending restrictions on candidates. In 1984 Walter Mondale refused to accept contributions from PACs, as did Michael Dukakis and Jesse Jackson in 1988. However, in elections to Congress candidates receive a considerable proportion of their funding from PACs. In 1990 PAC money accounted for 21 per cent of funding for candidates for the House and 41 per cent for senatorial candidates.

The executive

The head of the executive branch of government is of limited value in terms of 'access'.

One person, the president, offers few opportunities for pressure groups to have their say. The president's time is short and access to it very restricted.

Bureaucracy

The bureaucracy, on the other hand, is ideal for pressure-group activity. The bureaucracy is divided into a myriad of access points. Departments, independent executive agencies, independent regulatory commissions and the Executive Office of the President are all sub-divided and all have their areas of jurisdiction and responsibility. Every bureau and every official is a potential target for pressure-group influence.

Comparison

In Britain the Parliamentary system combined with the first-past-the-post electoral system means that the party forming government is likely to have an overall majority in the House of Commons. Therefore a great deal of power is concentrated in the hands of the executive. As such it is an attractive target for pressure-group activity but nonetheless difficult to break into because access points are relatively few.

As the prime minister and members of the Cabinet have many calls on their time it makes sense for pressure groups to spend most of their time lobbying civil servants rather than their political masters. It is officials, after all, who advise ministers and implement policy; they therefore have considerable influence.

Appointees

The methods pressure groups choose to employ will depend on the level of the bureaucrat with whom they are dealing. In the case of political appointees the best way to wield influence is for a group to become part of the appointment process. Groups will lobby the administration and the relevant Senate committee very hard in an effort to influence the appointment of key personnel. For example James Watt, who was appointed secretary of the interior in the Reagan administration, had long been an advocate of allowing federally owned land to be exploited by private companies. His appointment was enthusiastically supported by oil, gas and mineral companies. When he came into office he granted contracts for strip-mining on land that had been used as nature reserves and allowed offshore oil rigs to be set up, which often polluted local beaches.

Co-operation

Once in office bureaucrats will be subjected to further pressure-group attention. Groups can offer advice, information and co-operation to bureaucrats. In some cases they may even become part of the decision-making process.

'Clientelistic' relationships

The most notorious pressure group–bureaucracy relationships have been christened **'clientelistic'** because the group and the bureaucrats reinforce each other's goals. The relationship between the Pentagon and the contractors, the military–industrial complex, is the most well-known example. Relationships which extend to include the relevant congressional committees are known as **'iron triangles'**, or 'cosy triangles'. They are said to have an iron grip on public policy-making in their field.

The military–industrial complex

When President Eisenhower left office in 1961 he gave a warning: 'in the councils of government we must guard against the acquisition of unwarranted influence, whether sought or unsought, by the military–industrial complex. The potential for the disastrous rise of misplaced power exists and will persist.'

The symbiotic relationship between the Pentagon and the defence contractors has prospered since 1961. The military are anxious to acquire ever more sophisticated weapons, whilst the defence industry is keen to attract as much business as possible.

The judiciary

Test cases

Judges are often ignored in an analysis of pressure-group activity. However, the power of the Supreme Court to interpret the constitution and therefore to make policy is attractive to pressure groups. They will often finance cases on their route through the lower courts in the hope of bringing a test case before the Supreme Court. Perhaps the best-known example is *Brown* v. *Board of Education, Topeka, Kansas* (1954), which declared racial segregation in schools unconstitutional. The case was sponsored by the National Association for the Advancement of Colored People (NAACP).

The American Civil Liberties Union also backed a case that was brought before the Supreme Court in 1976. This concerned the constitutionality of the Federal Election Campaign Act (1974). In *Buckley* v. *Valeo* (1976) the court ruled that limits on the amounts individuals could spend on their own campaigns was an infringement of freedom of speech.

Comparison

The judiciary in Britain is subjected to relatively little pressure-group activity, as British courts have only limited powers of judicial review and therefore restricted opportunities to influence the political world. Nevertheless pressure groups do use the courts to their advantage. This was clearly illustrated in 1995 when the group Save Our Railways brought a case before the High Court to successfully challenge aspects of the government's rail privatization programme.

The electorate

Indirect lobbying

All of the targets for pressure-group activity described above experience the application of 'direct' pressure. But the weakness of political parties in the United States opens the way for pressure groups to use indirect lobbying, influencing the electorate who in turn will influence their representatives.

TV

Almost 90 million American households own television sets. By using advertising or even sponsoring their own television channel interest groups can speak to families in their own living rooms. Many of the New Right groups, such as the **Christian Coalition**, have their own television channels to preach the message of right-wing morality.

Comparison

Elections and government in the UK are dominated by political parties. Candidates are elected to government due to their party political allegiance and once in Parliament are more likely to pay attention to the views of their party than to public opinion.

Direct mail

Pressure groups will also use direct-mail techniques to influence public opinion. By mass mailing letters to constituents, groups can keep the electorate up to date with the voting record of their member of congress; target particular groups for fundraising appeals: or encourage people to write to their member of Congress encouraging them to take a stand on a particular issue.

Perspectives on pressure-group activity

It should be apparent from the discussion of the methods employed by pressure groups that there is considerable debate surrounding the desirability of pressure-group influence.

'Interest-group liberalism'

To many the ability of pressure groups to manipulate electoral finance, build strong links with bureaucrats and congressional committees, and influence public opinion suggests that they are distorting the national interest in pursuit of their own interests and that the dominance of wealthy groups in this process subverts democracy in favour of elites in society. This view is particularly associated with the political scientist Theodore Lowi and is usually referred to as **interest-group liberalism**. According to this theory the power of groups is so great that the government has given up its right to make difficult decisions and merely responds to the wishes of the key players.

Pluralism

An alternative perspective is **pluralism**. According to this view pressure-group activity is desirable because it allows **participation** in the political process. Of the three main ways of taking part in the political process it is the only remaining channel open to most citizens through which they can achieve real influence; voting, after all, is irregular and only permits the electorate to give a preference for a collection of policies; and joining a political party gives an individual minimal influence because they tend to be oligarchical in their organization. A pressure group can be formed around any issue about which people feel strongly, and the result is competition between pressure groups. Each group will be pursuing its own interests and in so doing, the argument goes, the final policy will be the best possible result for society. As Ed Davis (California state senator) has said: 'About 90 per cent of all legislation is conceived by special interests. It is merchandized by special interests. And probably less than 5 per cent is inspired by governors, by individual legislators, by government itself. You say, "Oh, isn't that evil!" The answer is "hell no, it isn't evil. That's what democracy is all about"' (*Los Angeles Times*, 19 January 1981).

Checks and balances

Finally, the pervasive influence of pressure groups intensifies the system of checks and balances set up by the Founding Fathers. The multitudinous access points throughout the American system allow an equally large number of groups to exercise influence.

Therefore it is extremely difficult for a single group to achieve anything other than a negative objective. A single group by influencing a particular element of the political system can at best thwart the will of other groups. Therefore the influence of pressure groups has given the United States a veto system, preventing positive or responsible action.

Questions

Short questions

1 a What is the 'military–industrial complex'?
b How influential is it in American politics?
(ULEAC, June 1992)

2 a What is the New Right?
b How influential is it today?
(ULEAC, January 1993)

US questions

1 Should the role of Political Action Committees be further restricted by law? (UODLE, June 1992)

2 Critically examine, giving appropriate examples, the role of pressure groups in the US political system. (UCLES, June 1994)

3 Examine the view that US pressure groups and their associated PACs exert greater influence on the executive and judiciary than they do on the legislature. To what extent and in what ways is it desirable for the judicial branch of government to be exposed to demands from pressure groups? (AEB, June 1993)

4 Consider the view that it is not parties or voters but pressure groups which now dominate Congress. (AEB, June 1991)

5 You are an adviser in the office of a US Political Action Committee which is concerned about health and welfare problems and which seeks greater public funding to resolve them; in particular, the PAC wishes to increase support for its ideas in Congress.

What factors must the PAC consider in developing its strategy? What tactics would you advise the PAC to adopt and what are its chances of success? (AEB, June 1992)

6 Is it accurate to say that pressure groups are now more significant than parties in politics? (ULEAC, January 1995)

7 Do pressure groups make a positive or a negative contribution to democracy in America? (ULEAC, June 1994)

Comparative questions

1 Analyse critically the relationships between political parties and interest groups. (Illustrate your answer with reference to at least two countries.) (ULEAC, June 1993)

2 Do interest groups contribute effectively to the processes of government? (Illustrate your answer with reference to at least two countries.) (ULEAC, January 1995)

3 What factors make interest groups effective? (Illustrate your answer with reference to at least two countries.) (ULEAC, June 1994)

4 Examine the view that although pressure groups are supposed to underpin democracy, they effectively overwhelm the political process in the USA and are virtually ignored in the UK. Consider whether there should be more controls on the spending and activities of pressure groups in either country. (AEB, June 1993)

5 To what extent are interest groups now more important than political parties in shaping public policy? (Illustrate your answer with reference to at least two countries.) (ULEAC, January 1994)

Appendix 1

The Declaration of Independence

A DECLARATION by the Representatives of the United States of America in General Congress Assembled July 4, 1776

When, in the course of human events, it becomes necessary for one people to dissolve the political bands which have connected them with another, and to assume, among the powers of the earth, the separate and equal station to which the laws of nature and of nature's God entitle them, a decent respect to the opinions of mankind requires that they should declare the causes which impel them to the separation.

We hold these truths to be self-evident, that all men are created equal; that they are endowed by their Creator with certain inalienable rights; that among these, are life, liberty, and the pursuit of happiness. That, to secure these rights, governments are instituted among men, deriving their just powers from the consent of the governed; that, whenever any form of government becomes destructive of these ends, it is the right of the people to alter or to abolish it, and to institute a new government, laying its foundation on such principles, and organizing its powers in such form, as to them shall seem most likely to effect their safety and happiness. Prudence, indeed, will dictate that governments long established, should not be changed for light and transient causes; and, accordingly, all experience hath shown, that mankind are more disposed to suffer, while evils are sufferable, than to right themselves by abolishing the forms to which they are accustomed. But, when a long train of abuses and usurpations, pursuing invariably the same object, evinces a design to reduce them under absolute despotism, it is their right, it is their duty, to throw off such government and to provide new guards for their future security. Such has been the patient sufferance of these colonies, and such is now the necessity which constrains them to alter their former systems of government. The history of the present King of Great Britain is a history of repeated injuries and usurpations, all having, in direct object, the establishment of an absolute tyranny over these States. To prove this, let facts be submitted to a candid world:

He has refused his assent to laws the most wholesome and necessary for the public good.

He has forbidden his governors to pass laws of immediate and pressing importance, unless suspended in their operation till his assent should be obtained; and, when so suspended, he has utterly neglected to attend to them.

He has refused to pass other laws for the accommodation of large districts of people, unless those people would relinquish the right of representation in the legislature: a right inestimable to them, and formidable to tyrants only.

He has called together legislative bodies at places unusual, uncomfortable, and distant from the depository of their public records, for the sole purpose of fatiguing them into compliance with his measures.

He has dissolved representative houses repeatedly for opposing, with manly firmness, his invasions on the rights of the people.

He has refused, for a long time after such dissolutions, to cause others to be elected; whereby the legislative powers, incapable of annihilation, have returned to the people at large for their exercise; the state remaining, in the meantime, exposed to all the danger of invasion from without, and convulsions within.

He has endeavoured to prevent the population of these States; for that purpose, obstructing the laws for naturalization of foreigners, refusing to pass others to encourage their migration hither, and raising the conditions of new appropriations of lands.

He has obstructed the administration of justice, by refusing his assent to laws for establishing judiciary powers.

He has made judges dependent on his will alone, for the tenure of their offices, and the amount and payment of their salaries.

He has erected a multitude of new offices, and sent hither swarms of officers, to harass our people, and eat out their substance.

He has kept among us, in time of peace, standing armies, without the consent of our legislatures.

He has affected to render the military independent of, and superior to, the civil power.

He has combined, with others, to subject us to a jurisdiction foreign to our Constitution, and unacknowledged by our laws; giving his assent to their acts of pretended legislation:

for quartering large bodies of armed troops among us:
for protecting them by a mock trial, from punishment, for any murders which they should commit on the inhabitants of these States:
for cutting off our trade with all parts of the world:
for imposing taxes on us without our consent:
for depriving us, in many cases, of the benefit of trial by jury:
for transporting us beyond seas to be tried for pretended offenses:
for abolishing the free system of English laws in a neighboring province, establishing therein an arbitrary government, and enlarging its boundaries, so as to render it at once an example and fit instrument for introducing the same absolute rule into these colonies:

for taking away our charters, abolishing our most valuable laws, and altering, fundamentally, the powers of our governments:
for suspending our own legislatures, and declaring themselves invested with power to legislate for us in all cases whatsoever.

He has abdicated government here, by declaring us out of his protection, and waging war against us.

He has plundered our seas, ravaged our coasts, burnt our towns, and destroyed the lives of our people.

He is, at this time, transporting large armies of foreign mercenaries to complete the works of death, desolation, and tyranny, already begun, with circumstances of cruelty and perfidy scarcely paralleled in the most barbarous ages, and totally unworthy of the head of a civilized nation.

He has constrained our fellow citizens, taken captive on the high seas, to bear arms against their country, to become the executioners of their friends, and brethren, or to fall themselves by their hands.

He has excited domestic insurrections amongst us, and has endeavoured to bring on the inhabitants of our frontiers, the merciless Indian savages, whose known rule of warfare is an undistinguished destruction of all ages, sexes, and conditions.

In every stage of these oppressions, we have petitioned for redress, in the most humble terms; our repeated petitions have been answered only by repeated injury. A prince, whose character is thus marked by every act which may define a tyrant, is unfit to be the ruler of a free people.

Nor have we been wanting in attention to our British brethren. We have warned them, from time to time, of attempts made by their legislature to extend an unwarrantable jurisdiction over us. We have reminded them of the circumstances of our emigration and settlement here. We have appealed to their native justice and magnanimity, and we have conjured them, by the ties of our common kindred, to disavow these usurpations, which would inevitably interrupt our connections and correspondence. They, too, have been deaf to the voice of justice and consanguinity. We must, therefore, acquiesce in the necessity which denounces our separation, and hold them, as we hold the rest of mankind, enemies in war, in peace, friends.

We, therefore, the representatives of the United States of America, in general Congress assembled, appealing to the Supreme Judge of the world for the rectitude of our intentions, do, in the name, and by the authority of the good people of these colonies, solemnly publish and declare, that these united colonies are, and of right ought to be, free and independent states: that they are absolved from all allegiance to the British Crown, and that all political connection between them and the state of Great Britain is, and ought to be, totally dissolved; and that, as free and independent states, they have full power to levy war, conclude peace, contract alliances, establish commerce, and to do all other acts and things which independent states may of right do. And, for the support of this declaration, with a firm reliance on the protection of Divine

Providence, we mutually pledge to each other our lives, our fortunes, and our sacred honour.

Appendix 2

Virginia Bill of Rights

Adopted June 12, 1776

A declaration of rights made by the representatives of the good people of Virginia, assembled in full and free convention; which rights do pertain to them and their posterity, as the basis and foundation of government.

Section 1 That all men are by nature equally free and independent, and have certain inherent rights, of which, when they enter into a state of society, they cannot, by any compact, deprive or divest their posterity; namely, the enjoyment of life and liberty, with the means of acquiring and possessing property, and pursuing and obtaining happiness and safety.

Section 2 That all power is vested in, and consequently derived from, the people; that magistrates are their trustees and servants, and at all times amenable to them.

Section 3 That government is, or ought to be, instituted for the common benefit, protection, and security of the people, nation, or community; of all the various modes and forms of government, that is best which is capable of producing the greatest degree of happiness and safety, and is most effectually secured against the danger of maladministration; and that, when any government shall be found inadequate or contrary to these purposes, a majority of the community hath an indubitable, inalienable, and infeasible right to reform, alter, or abolish it, in such manner as shall be judged most conducive to the public weal.

Section 4 That no man, or set of men, are entitled to exclusive or separate emoluments or privileges from the community, but in consideration of public services; which, not being descendible, neither ought the offices of magistrate, legislator, or judge to be hereditary.

Section 5 That the legislative and executive powers of the State should be separate and distinct from the judiciary; and that the members of the two first may be restrained from oppression, by feeling and participating the burdens of the people, they should, at fixed periods, be reduced to a private station, return into that body from which they were originally taken, and the vacancies be supplied by frequent, certain, and regular elections, in which all, or any part of the former members, to be again eligible, or ineligible, as the laws shall direct.

Section 6 That elections of members to serve as representatives of the people in assembly, ought to be free; and that all men, having sufficient evidence of permanent common interest with, and attachment to, the community, have the right of suffrage, and cannot be taxed or deprived of their property for public uses, without their own consent, or that of their representatives so elected, nor bound by any law to which they have not, in like manner, assented, for the public good.

Section 7 That all power of suspending laws, or the execution of laws, by any authority, without consent of the representatives of the people, is injurious to their rights, and ought not to be exercised.

Section 8 That in all capital or criminal prosecutions a man hath a right to demand the cause and nature of his accusation, to be confronted with the accusers and witnesses, to call for evidence in his favour, and to a speedy trial by an impartial jury of twelve men of his vicinage, without whose unanimous consent he cannot be found guilty; nor can he be compelled to give evidence against himself; that no man be deprived of his liberty, except by the law of the land or the judgment of his peers.

Section 9 That excessive bail ought not to be required, nor excessive fines imposed, nor cruel and unusual punishment inflicted.

Section 10 That general warrants, whereby an officer or messenger may be commanded to search suspected places without evidence of a fact committed, or to seize any person or persons not named, or whose offence is not particularly described and supported by evidence, are grievous and oppressive, and ought not to be granted.

Section 11 That in controversies respecting property, and in suits between man and man, the ancient trial by jury is preferable to any other, and ought to be held sacred.

Section 12 That the freedom of the press is one of the great bulwarks of liberty, and can never be restrained but by despotic governments.

Section 13 That a well-regulated militia, composed of the body of the people, trained to arms, is the proper, natural, and safe defence of a free State; that standing armies, in time of peace, should be avoided, as dangerous to liberty; and that in all cases the military should be under strict subordination to, and governed by, the civil power.

Section 14 That the people have a right to uniform government; and, therefore, that no government separate from, or independent of the government of Virginia, ought to be erected or established within the limits thereof.

Section 15 That no free government, or the blessings of liberty, can be preserved to any people, but by a firm adherence to justice, moderation, temperance, frugality, and virtue, and by frequent recurrence to fundamental principles.

Section 16 That religion, or the duty which we owe to our Creator, and the manner of discharging it, can be directed only by reason and conviction, not by force or violence; and therefore all men are equally entitled to the free exercise of religion, according to the dictates of conscience; and that it is the mutual duty of all to practise Christian forbearance, love, and charity towards each other.

Appendix 3

The Constitution of the United States of America

Proposed by Convention September 17, 1787
Effective March 4, 1789

We the People of the United States, in order to form a more perfect Union, establish justice, insure domestic tranquillity, provide for the common defence, promote the general welfare, and secure the blessings of liberty to ourselves and our posterity, do ordain and establish this **constitution** for the United States of America.

Article I

Section 1 All legislative powers herein granted shall be vested in a Congress of the United States, which will consist of a Senate and House of Representatives.

Section 2 The House of Representatives shall be composed of members chosen every second year by the people of the several states, and the Electors in each State shall have the Qualifications requisite for electors of the most numerous branch of the state legislature.

No person shall be a representative who shall not have attained to the age of twenty-five years, and been seven years a citizen of the United States, and who shall not, when elected, be an inhabitant of that state in which he shall be chosen.

Representatives and direct taxes shall be apportioned among the several States which may be included within this Union, according to their respective Numbers, which shall be determined by adding to the whole number of free Persons, including those bound to Service for a term of years, and excluding Indians not taxed, three-fifths of all other persons. The actual enumeration shall be made within three years after the first meeting of the Congress of the United States, and within every subsequent term of ten years, in such manner as they shall by law direct. The number of representatives shall not exceed one for every thirty thousand, but each state shall have at least one representative; and until such enumeration shall be made, the state of New Hampshire shall be entitled to choose three, Massachusetts eight, Rhode-Island and Providence Plantations one, Connecticut five, New York six, New Jersey four, Pennsylvania eight, Delaware one, Maryland six, Virginia ten, North Carolina five, South Carolina five, and Georgia three.

When vacancies happen in the representation from any state, the executive authority thereof shall issue writs of election to fill such vacancies.

The House of Representatives shall choose their speaker and other officers; and shall have the sole power of impeachment.

Section 3 The Senate of the United States shall be composed of two senators from each state, chosen by the legislature thereof, for six years; and each senator shall have one vote.

Immediately after they shall be assembled in consequence of the first election, they shall be divided as equally as may be into three classes. The seats of the senators of the first class shall be vacated at the expiration of the second year, of the second class at the expiration of the fourth year, and of the third class at the expiration of the sixth year, so that one-third may be chosen every second year; and if vacancies happen by resignation, or otherwise, during the recess of the legislature of any state, the executive thereof may make temporary appointments until the next meeting of the legislature, which shall then fill such vacancies.

No person shall be a senator who shall not have attained to the age of thirty years, and been nine years a citizen of the United States, and who shall not, when elected, be an inhabitant of that state for which he shall be chosen.

The vice-president of the United States shall be president of the Senate, but shall have no vote, unless they be equally divided.

The Senate shall choose their other officers, and also a president pro tempore, in the absence of the vice-president, or when he shall exercise the office of the president of the United States.

The Senate shall have the sole power to try all impeachments. When sitting for that purpose they shall be on oath or affirmation. When the president of the United States is tried, the chief justice shall preside: and no person shall be convicted without the concurrence of two-thirds of the members present.

Judgement in cases of impeachment shall not extend further than to removal from office, and disqualification to hold and enjoy any office of honour, trust, or profit under the United States: but the party convicted shall nevertheless be liable and subject to indictment, trial, judgment, and punishment, according to law.

Section 4 The times, places and manner of holding elections for senators and representatives, shall be prescribed in each state by the legislature thereof; but the Congress may at any time by law make or alter such regulations, except as to the places of choosing senators.

The Congress shall assemble at least once in every year, and such meeting shall be on the first Monday in December, unless they shall by law appoint a different day.

Section 5 Each house shall be the judge of the elections, returns and qualifications of its own members, and a majority of each shall constitute a quorum to do business; but a smaller number may adjourn from day to day, and may be authorized to compel the attendance of absent members, in such manner, and under such penalties, as each house may provide.

Each house may determine the rules of its proceedings, punish its members for disorderly behaviour, and, with the concurrence of two-thirds, expel a member.

Each house shall keep a journal of its proceedings, and from time to time publish the same, excepting such parts as may in their judgment require secrecy; and the yeas and nays of the members of either house on any question shall, at the desire of one-fifth of those present, be entered on the journal.

Neither house, during the session of Congress, shall, without the consent of the other, adjourn for more than three days, nor to any other place than that in which the two houses shall be sitting.

Section 6 The senators and representatives shall receive a compensation for their services, to be ascertained by law, and paid out of the Treasury of the United States. They shall in all cases, except treason, felony, and breach of the peace, be privileged from arrest during their attendance at the session of their respective houses, and in going to and returning from the same; and for any speech or debate in either house, they shall not be questioned in any other place.

No senator or representative shall, during the time for which he was elected, be appointed to any civil office under the authority of the United States, which shall have been created, or the emoluments whereof shall have been increased, during such time; and no person holding any office under the United States shall be a member of either house during his continuance in office.

Section 7 All bills for raising revenue shall originate in the House of Representatives; but the Senate may propose or concur with amendments as on other bills.

Every bill which shall have passed the House of Representatives and the Senate, shall, before it become a law, be presented to the president of the United States; if he approve he shall sign it, but if not he shall return it, with his objections, to that house in which it shall have originated, who shall enter the objections at large on their journal, and proceed to reconsider it. If after such reconsideration two-thirds of that house shall agree to pass the bill, it shall be sent, together with the objections, to the other house, by which it shall likewise be reconsidered, and if approved by two-thirds of that house, it shall become a law. But in all such cases the votes of both houses shall be determined by yeas and nays, and the names of the persons voting for and against the bill shall be entered on the journal of each house respectively. If any bill shall not be returned by the president within ten days (Sundays excepted) after it shall have been presented to him, the same shall be a law, in like manner as if he had signed it, unless the Congress by their adjournment, prevent its return, in which case it shall not be a law.

Every order, resolution, or vote to which the concurrence of the Senate and House of Representatives may be necessary (except on a question of adjournment) shall be presented to the president of the United States; and before the same shall take effect, shall be approved by him, or being disapproved by him, shall be repassed by two-thirds of the Senate and House of Representatives, according to the rules and limitations prescribed in the case of a bill.

Section 8 The Congress shall have power to lay and collect taxes, duties, imposts and excises, to pay the debts and provide for the common defence and general welfare of the United States; but all duties, and excises shall be uniform throughout the United States;

to borrow money on the credit of the United States;

to regulate commerce with foreign nations, and among the several states, and with the Indian tribes;

to establish an uniform rule of naturalization, and uniform laws on the subject of bankruptcies throughout the United States;

to coin money, regulate the value thereof, and of foreign coin, and fix the standard of weights and measures;

to provide for the punishment of counterfeiting the securities and current coin of the United States;

to establish post offices and post roads;

to promote the progress of science and useful arts, by securing for limited times to authors and inventors the exclusive right to their respective writings and discoveries;

to constitute tribunals inferior to the Supreme Court;

to define and punish piracies and felonies committed on the high seas, and offences against the law of nations;

to declare war, grant letters of marque and reprisal, and make rules concerning captures on land and water;

to raise and support armies, but no appropriation of money to that use shall be for a longer term than two years;

to provide and maintain a navy;

to make rules for the government and regulation of the land and naval forces;

to provide for calling forth the militia to execute the laws of the union, suppress insurrections and repel invasions;

to provide for organizing, arming, and disciplining the militia, and for governing such part of them as may be employed in service of the United States, reserving to the states respectively, the appointment of the officers, and the authority of training the militia according to the discipline prescribed by Congress;

to exercise exclusive legislation in all cases whatsoever, over such district (not exceeding ten miles square) as may, by cession of particular states, and the acceptance of Congress, become the seat of the government of the United States, and to exercise like authority over all places purchased by the consent of the legislature of the state in which the same will be, for the erection of forts, magazines, arsenals, dockyards, and other needful building; and

to make all laws which shall be necessary and proper for carrying into execution the foregoing powers, and all other powers vested by this constitution in the government of the United States, or in any department or officer thereof.

Section 9 The migration or importation of such persons as any of the states now existing shall think proper to admit, shall not be prohibited by the Congress prior to the year one thousand eight hundred and eight, but a tax or duty may be imposed on such importation, not exceeding ten dollars for each person.

The privilege of the writ of habeas corpus shall not be suspended, unless when in cases of rebellion or invasion the public safety may require it.

No bill of attainder or ex post facto law shall be passed.

No capitation, or other direct, tax shall be laid unless in proportion to the census or enumeration herein before directed to be taken.

No tax or duty shall be laid on articles exported from any state.

No preference shall be given by any regulation of commerce or revenue to the ports of one state over those of another: nor shall vessels bound to, or from, one state, be obliged to enter, clear, or pay duties in another.

No money shall be drawn from the Treasury, but in consequence of appropriations made by law; and a regular statement and account of the receipts and expenditures of all public money shall be published from time to time.

No title of nobility shall be granted by the United States: and no person holding any office of profit or trust under them, shall, without the consent of the Congress, accept of any present, emolument, office, or title, of any kind whatever, from any king, prince, or foreign state.

Section 10 No state shall enter into any treaty, alliance, or confederation; grant letters of marque and reprisal; coin money; emit bills of credit; make any thing but gold and silver coin a tender in payment of debts; pass any bill attainder, ex post facto law, or law impairing the obligation of contracts, or grant any title of nobility.

No state shall, without the consent of the Congress, lay any imposts or duties on imports or exports, except what may be absolutely necessary for executing its inspection laws; and the net produce of all duties and imposts, laid by any state on imports or exports, shall be for the use of the Treasury of the United States; and all such laws shall be subject to the revision and control of the Congress.

No state shall, without the consent of Congress, lay any duty of tonnage, keep troops, or ships of war in time of peace, enter into any agreement or compact with another state, or with a foreign power, or engage in war, unless actually invaded, or in such imminent danger as will not admit of delay.

Article II

Section 1 The executive power shall be vested in a president of the United States of America. He shall hold his office during the term of four years, and, together with the vice-president, chosen for the same term, be elected, as follows:

Each state shall appoint, in such manner as the legislature thereof may direct, a number of electors, equal to the whole number of senators and representatives to which the state may be entitled in the Congress: but no senator or representative, or person holding an office of trust or profit under the United States, shall be appointed an elector.

The electors shall meet in their respective states, and vote by ballot for two persons, of whom one at least shall not be an inhabitant of the same state with themselves. And they shall make a list of all the persons voted for, and of the number of votes for each; which list they shall sign and certify, and transmit sealed to the seat of the government of the United States, directed to the president of the Senate. The president of the Senate shall, in the presence of the Senate and House of Representatives, open all the certificates, and the votes shall then be counted. The person having the greatest number of votes shall be the president, if such number be a majority of the whole number of electors appointed; and if there be more than one who have such majority, and have an equal number of votes, then the House of Representatives shall immediately choose by ballot one of them for president; and if no person have a majority, then from the five highest on the list the said house shall in like manner choose the president. But in choosing the president, the votes shall be taken by states, the representation from each state having one vote; a quorum for this purpose shall consist of a member or members from two-thirds of the states, and a majority of all the states shall be necessary to a choice. In every case, after the choice of the president, the person having the greatest number of votes of the electors shall be the vice-president. But if there should remain two or more who have equal votes, the Senate shall choose from them by ballot the vice-president.

The Congress may determine the time of choosing the electors, and the day on which they shall give their votes; which day shall be the same throughout the United States.

No person except a natural-born citizen, or a citizen of the United States, at the time of the adoption of this constitution, shall be eligible to the office of president; neither shall any person be eligible to that office who shall not have attained to the age of thirty-five years, and been fourteen years a resident within the United States.

In case of the removal of the president from office, or of his death, resignation, or inability to discharge the powers and duties of the said office, the same shall devolve on the vice-president, and the Congress may by law provide for the case of removal, death, resignation, or inability, both of the president and vice-president, declaring what officer shall then act as president, and such officer shall act accordingly, until the disability be removed or a president shall be elected.

The president shall, at stated times, receive for his services a compensation, which shall neither be increased nor diminished during the period for which he shall have been elected, and he shall not receive within that period any other emolument from the United States, or any of them.

Before he enter on the execution of his office, he shall take the following oath or affirmation: 'I do solemnly swear (or affirm) that I will faithfully execute the office of president of the United States, and will, to the best of my ability, preserve, protect, and defend the constitution of the United States.'

Section 2 The president shall be commander in chief of the army and navy of the United States, and of the militia of the several states, when called into the actual service of the United States; he may require the opinion, in writing, of the principal officer in each of the executive departments, upon any subject relating to the duties of their respective offices, and he shall have power to grant reprieves and pardons for offences against the United States, except in cases of impeachment.

He shall have power, by and with advice and consent of the Senate, to make treaties, provided two-thirds of the senators present concur; and he shall nominate, and by and with the advice and consent of the Senate, shall appoint ambassadors, other public ministers and consuls, judges of the Supreme Court, and all other officers of the United States, whose appointments are not herein otherwise provided for, and which shall be established by law: but the Congress may by law vest the appointment of such inferior officers, as they think proper, in the president alone, in the courts of law, or in the heads of departments.

The president shall have power to fill up all vacancies that may happen during the recess of the Senate, by granting commissions which shall expire at the end of their next session.

Section 3 He shall from time to time give to the Congress information of the state of the Union, and recommend to their consideration such measures as he shall judge necessary and expedient; he may, on extraordinary occasions, convene both houses, or either of them, and in case of disagreement between them, with respect to the time of adjournment, he may adjourn them to such time as he shall think proper; he shall receive ambassadors and other public ministers; he shall take care that the laws be faithfully executed, and shall commission all the officers of the United States.

Section 4 The president, vice-president and all civil officers of the United States, shall be removed from office on impeachment for, and conviction of, treason, bribery, or other high crimes and misdemeanours.

Article III

Section 1 The judicial power of the United States, shall be vested in one Supreme Court, and in such inferior courts as the Congress may from time to time ordain and establish. The judges, both of the Supreme and inferior courts, shall hold their offices during good behaviour, and shall, at stated times, receive for their services, a compensation, which shall not be diminished during their continuance in office.

Section 2 The judicial power shall extend to all cases, in law and equity, arising under this constitution, the laws of the United States, and treaties made, or which shall be made, under their authority; to all cases affecting ambassadors, other public ministers and consuls; to all cases of admiralty and maritime jurisdiction; to controversies to which the United States shall be a party; to controversies between two or more states; between a state and citizens of another state; between citizens of different states; between citizens of the same state claiming lands under grants of different states, and between a state, or the citizens thereof, and foreign states, citizens or subjects.

In all cases affecting ambassadors, other public ministers and consuls, and those in which a state shall be party, the Supreme Court shall have original jurisdiction. In all the other cases before mentioned, the Supreme Court shall have appellate jurisdiction, both as to law and fact, with such exceptions, and under such regulations as the Congress shall make.

The trial of all crimes, except in cases of impeachment, shall be by jury; and such trial shall be held in the state where the said crimes shall have been committed; but when not committed within any state, the trial shall be at such place or places as the Congress may by law have directed.

Section 3 Treason against the United States, shall consist only in levying war against them, or in adhering to their enemies, giving them aid and comfort. No person shall be convicted of treason unless on the testimony of two witnesses to the same overt act, or on confession in open court.

The Congress shall have power to declare the punishment of treason, but no attainder of treason shall work corruption of blood, or forfeiture except during the life of the person attained.

Article IV

Section 1 Full faith and credit shall be given in each state to the public acts, records, and judicial proceedings of every other state. And the Congress may by general laws prescribe the manner in which such acts, records and proceedings shall be proved, and the effect thereof.

Section 2 The citizens of each state shall be entitled to all privileges and immunities of citizens in the several states.

A person charged in any state with treason, felony, or other crime, who shall flee from justice, and be found in another state, shall on demand of the executive authority of the state from which he fled, be delivered up, to be removed to the state having jurisdiction of the crime.

No person held to service or labour in one state, under the laws thereof, escaping into another, shall, in consequence of any law or regulation therein, be discharged from such service or labour, but shall be delivered up on claim of the party to whom such service or labour may be due.

Section 3 New states may be admitted by the Congress into this Union; but no new state shall be formed by the junction of two or more states, or parts of states, without the consent of the legislatures of the states concerned as well as of the Congress.

The Congress shall have power to dispose of and make all needful rules and regulations respecting the territory or other property belonging to the United States; and nothing in this constitution shall be so construed as to prejudice any claims of the United States or of any particular state.

Section 4 The United States shall guarantee to every state in this Union a republican form of government, and shall protect each of them against invasion; and on application of the legislature, or of the executive (when the legislature cannot be convened) against domestic violence.

Article V

The Congress, whenever two-thirds of both houses shall deem it necessary, shall propose amendments to this constitution, or, on the application of the legislatures of two-thirds of the several states, shall call a convention for proposing amendments, which, in either case, shall be valid to all intents and purposes, as part of this constitution, when ratified by the legislatures of three-fourths of the several states, or by conventions in three-fourths thereof, as the one or the other mode of ratification may be proposed by the Congress; provided that no amendment which may be made prior to the year one thousand eight hundred and eight shall in any manner affect the first and fourth clauses in the ninth section of the first article; and that no state, without its consent, shall be deprived of its equal suffrage in the Senate.

Article VI

All debts contracted and engagements entered into, before the adoption of this constitution, shall be as valid against the United States under this constitution, as under the confederation.

This constitution, and the laws of the United States which shall be made in pursuance thereof; and all treaties made, or which shall be made, under the authority of the United States, shall be the supreme law of the land; and the judges in every state shall be bound thereby, any thing in the constitution or laws of any state to the contrary notwithstanding.

The senators and representatives before mentioned, and the members of the several state legislatures, and all executive and judicial officers, both of the United States and of the several states, shall be bound by oath or affirmation to support this constitution; but no religious test shall ever be required as a qualification to any office or public trust under the United States.

Article VII

The ratification of the conventions of nine states shall be sufficient for the establishment of this constitution between the states so ratifying the same.

Done in convention by the unanimous consent of the states present the seventeenth day of September in the year of our Lord one thousand seven hundred and eighty-seven, and of the independence of the United States of America the twelfth. In witness whereof we have hereunto subscribed our names.

Articles in addition to, and amendment of, the constitution of the United States of America, proposed by Congress, and ratified by the legislatures of the several states, pursuant to the fifth article of the original constitution.

[The first ten amendments went into effect in 1791.]

Amendment 1

Congress shall make no law respecting an establishment of religion, or prohibiting the free exercise thereof; or abridging the freedom of speech, or of the press; or the right of the people peaceably to assemble, and to petition the Government for a redress of grievances.

Amendment II

A well-regulated militia, being necessary to the security of a free state, the right of the people to keep and bear arms shall not be infringed.

Amendment III

No soldier shall, in time of peace, be quartered in any house, without the consent of the owner, nor in time of war, but in a manner to be prescribed by law.

Amendment IV

The right of the people to be secure in their persons, houses, papers, and effects, against unreasonable searches and seizures, shall not be violated, and no warrants shall issue, but upon probable cause, supported by oath or affirmation, and particularly describing the place to be searched, and the persons or things to be seized.

Amendment V

No person shall be held to answer for a capital or otherwise infamous crime, unless on a presentment or indictment of a grand jury, except in cases arising in the land or naval forces, or in the militia, when in actual service in time of war or public danger; nor shall any person be subject for the same offence to be twice put in jeopardy of life or limb; nor shall be compelled in any criminal case to be a witness against himself, nor be deprived of life, liberty, or property, without due process of law; nor shall private property be taken for public use, without just compensation.

Amendment VI

In all criminal prosecutions, the accused shall enjoy the right to a speedy and public trial, by an impartial jury of the state and district wherein the crime shall have been committed, which district shall have been previously ascertained by law, and to be informed of the nature and cause of the accusation; to be confronted with the witnesses against him; to have compulsory process for obtaining witnesses in his favour, and to have the assistance of counsel for defence.

Amendment VII

In suits at common law where the value in controversy shall exceed twenty dollars, the right of trial by jury, shall be preserved, and no fact tried by a jury shall be otherwise re-examined in any court of the United States, than according to the rules of the common law.

Amendment VIII

Excessive bail shall not be required, nor excessive fines imposed, nor cruel and unusual punishments inflicted.

Amendment IX

The enumeration in the constitution, of certain rights, shall not be construed to deny or disparage others retained by the people.

Amendment X

The powers not delegated to the United States by the constitution, nor prohibited by it to the states, are reserved to the states respectively, or to the people.

Amendment XI (1798)

The judicial power of the United States shall not be construed to extend to any suit in law or equity, commenced or prosecuted against one of the United States by citizens of another state, or by citizens or subjects of any foreign state.

Amendment XII (1804)

The electors shall meet in their respective states and vote by ballot for president and vice-president, one of whom, at least, shall not be an inhabitant of the same state with themselves; they shall name in their ballots the person voted for as president, and in distinct ballots the person voted for as vice-president, and they shall make distinct lists of all persons voted for as president, and of all persons voted for as vice-president, and of the number of votes for each, which lists they shall sign and certify, and transmit sealed to the seat of the government of the United States, directed to the president of the Senate; the president of the Senate shall, in the presence of the Senate and House of Representatives, open all the certificates and the votes shall then be counted; the person having the greatest number of votes for president, shall be the president, if such number be a majority of the whole number of electors appointed; and if no person have such majority, then from the persons having the highest numbers not exceeding three on the list of those voted for as president, the House of Representatives shall choose immediately, by ballot, the president. But in choosing the president, the votes shall be taken by states, the representation from each state having one vote; a quorum for this purpose shall consist of a member or members from two-thirds of the states, and a majority of all the states shall be necessary to a choice. And if the House of Representatives shall not choose a president whenever the right of choice shall devolve upon them, before the fourth day of March next following, then the vice-president shall act as president, as in the case of the death or other constitutional disability of the president. The person having the greatest number of votes as vice-president, shall be the vice-president, if such number be a majority of the whole number of electors appointed, and if no person have a majority, then from the two highest numbers on the list, the Senate shall choose the vice-president; a quorum for the purpose shall consist of two-thirds of the whole number of senators, and a majority of the whole number shall be necessary to a choice. But no person constitutionally ineligible to the office of president shall be eligible to that of vice-president of the United States.

Amendment XII (1865)

Section 1 Neither slavery nor involuntary servitude, except as a punishment for crime whereof the party shall have been duly convicted, shall exist within the United States, or any place subject to their jurisdiction.

Section 2 Congress shall have power to enforce this article by appropriate legislation.

Amendment XIV (1868)

Section 1 All persons born or naturalized in the United States, and subject to the jurisdiction thereof, are citizens of the United States and of the state wherein they reside. No state shall make or enforce any law which shall abridge the privileges or immunities of citizens of the United States; nor shall any state deprive any person of life, liberty, or property, without due process of law; nor deny to any person within its jurisdiction the equal protection of the laws.

Section 2 Representatives shall be apportioned among the several states according to their respective numbers, counting the whole number of persons in each state, excluding Indians not taxed. But when the right to vote at any election for the choice of electors for president and vice-president of the United States, representatives in Congress, the executive and judicial officers of a state, or the members of the legislature thereof, is denied to any of the male inhabitants of such state, being twenty-one years of age, and citizens of the United States, or in any way abridged, except for participation in rebellion, or other crime, the basis of representation therein shall be reduced in the proportion which the number of such male citizens shall bear to the whole number of male citizens twenty-one years of age in such state.

Section 3 No person shall be a senator or representative in Congress, or elector of president and vice-president, or hold any office, civil or military, under the United States, or under any state, who, having previously taken an oath, as a member of Congress, or as an officer of the United States, shall have engaged in insurrection or rebellion against the same, or given aid or comfort to the enemies thereof. But Congress may by a vote of two-thirds of each house, remove such disability.

Section 4 The validity of the public debt of the United States, authorized by law, including debts incurred for payment of pensions and bounties for services in suppressing insurrection or rebellion, shall not be questioned. But neither the United States nor any state shall assume or pay any debt or obligation incurred in aid of insurrection or rebellion against the United States, or any claim for the loss or emancipation of any slave; but all such debts, obligations, and claims shall be held illegal and void.

Section 5 The Congress shall have the power to enforce, by appropriate legislation, the provisions of this article.

Amendment XV (1870)

Section 1 The right of citizens of the United States to vote shall not be denied or abridged by the United States or by any state on account of race, colour, or previous condition of servitude.

Section 2 The Congress shall have power to enforce this article by appropriate legislation.

Amendment XVI (1913)

The Congress shall have power to lay and collect taxes on incomes, from whatever source derived, without apportionment among the several states, and without regard to any census or enumeration.

Amendment XVII (1913)

The Senate of the United States shall be composed of two senators from each state, elected by the people thereof, for six years; and each senator shall have one vote. The electors in each state shall have the qualifications requisite for electors of the most numerous branch of the state legislatures.

When vacancies happen in the representation of any state in the Senate, the executive authority of such state shall issue writs of election to fill such vacancies: *Provided,* that legislature of any state may empower the executive thereof to make temporary appointments until the people fill the vacancies by election as the legislature may direct.

This amendment shall not be so construed as to affect the election or term of any senator chosen before it becomes valid as part of the constitution.

Amendment XVIII (1919)

Section 1 After one year from the ratification of this article the manufacture, sale, or transportation of intoxicating liquors within, the importation thereof into, or the exportation thereof from the United States and all territory subject to the jurisdiction thereof for beverage purposes is hereby prohibited.

Section 2 The Congress and the several states shall have concurrent power to enforce this article by appropriate legislation.

Section 3 This article shall be inoperative unless it shall have been ratified as an amendment to the constitution by the legislatures of the several states, as provided in the constitution, within seven years from the date of the submission hereof to the states by the Congress.

Amendment XIX (1920)

The right of citizens of the United States to vote shall not be denied or abridged by the United States or by any state on account of sex.

Congress shall have power to enforce this article by appropriate legislation.

Amendment XX (1933)

Section 1 The terms of the president and vice-president shall end at noon on the 20th day of January, and the terms of senators and representatives at noon on the 3rd day of

January, of the years in which such terms would have ended if this article had not been ratified; and the terms of their successors shall then begin.

Section 2 The Congress shall assemble at least once in every year, and such meeting shall begin at noon on the 3rd day of January, unless they shall by law appoint a different day.

Section 3 If, at the time fixed for the beginning of the term of the president, the president elect shall have died, the vice-president elect shall become president. If a president shall not have been chosen before the time fixed for the beginning of his term, or if the president elect shall have failed to qualify, then the vice-president elect shall act as president until a president shall have qualified; and the Congress may by law provide for the case wherein neither a president elect nor a vice-president elect shall have qualified, declaring who shall then act as president, or the manner in which one who is to act shall be selected, and such person shall act accordingly until a president or vice-president shall have qualified.

Section 4 The Congress may by law provide for the case of the death of any of the persons from whom the House of Representatives may choose a president whenever the right of choice shall have devolved upon them, and for the case of the death of any of the persons from whom the Senate may choose a vice-president whenever the right of choice shall have devolved upon them.

Section 5 Sections 1 and 2 shall take effect on the 15th day of October following the ratification of this article.

Section 6 This article shall be inoperative unless it shall have been ratified as an amendment to the constitution by the legislatures of three-fourths of the several states within seven years from the date of its submission.

Amendment XXI (1933)

Section 1 The eighteenth article of amendment to the constitution of the United States is hereby repealed.

Section 2 The transportation or importation into any state, territory, or possession of the United States for delivery or use therein of intoxicating liquors, in violation of the laws thereof, is hereby prohibited.

Section 3 This article shall be inoperative unless it shall have been ratified as an amendment to the constitution by conventions in the several states, as provided in the constitution within seven years from the date of the submission hereof to the states by the Congress.

Amendment XXII (1951)

Section 1 No person shall be elected to the office of the president more than twice, and no person who has held the office of president, or acted as president, for more than two years of a term to which some other person was elected president shall be elected to the office of the president more than once.

But this article shall not apply to any person holding the office of president when this article was proposed by the Congress, and shall not prevent any person who may be holding the office of president, or acting as president, during the term within which this article becomes operative from holding the office of president or acting as president during the remainder of such term.

Section 2 This article shall be inoperative unless it shall have been ratified as an amendment to the constitution by the legislatures of three-fourths of the several states within seven years from the date of its submission to the states by the Congress.

Amendment XXIII (1961)

Section 1 The district constituting the seat of government of the United States shall appoint in such manner as the Congress may direct:

A number of electors of president and vice-president equal to the whole number of senators and representatives in Congress to which the district would be entitled if it were a state, but in no event more than the least populous state; they shall be in addition to those appointed by the states, but they shall be considered, for the purposes of the election of president and vice-president, to be electors appointed by a state; and they shall meet in the district and perform such duties as provided by the twelfth article of amendment.

Section 2 The Congress shall have power to enforce this article by appropriate legislation.

Amendment XXIV (1964)

Section 1 The right of citizens of the United States to vote in any primary or other election for president or vice-president, for electors for president or vice-president, or for senator or representative in Congress, shall not be denied or abridged by the United States or any other state by reason of failure to pay any poll tax or other tax.

Section 2 The Congress shall have the power to enforce this article by appropriate legislation.

Amendment XXV (1967)

Section 1 In case of the removal of the president from office or of his death or resignation, the vice-president shall become president.

Section 2 Whenever there is a vacancy in the office of the vice-president, the president shall nominate a vice-president who shall take office upon confirmation by a majority vote of both houses of Congress.

Section 3 Whenever the president transmits to the president pro tempore of the Senate and the speaker of the House of Representatives his written declaration that he is unable to discharge the powers and duties of his office, and until he transmits to them a written declaration to the contrary, such powers and duties shall be discharged by the vice-president as acting president.

Section 4 Whenever the vice-president and a majority of either the principal officers of the executive departments or of such other body as Congress may by law provide, transmit to the president pro tempore of the senate and the speaker of the House of

Representatives their written declaration that the president is unable to discharge the powers and duties of his office, the vice-president shall immediately assume the powers and duties of the office as acting president.

Thereafter, when the president transmits to the president pro tempore of the Senate and the speaker of the House of Representatives his written declaration that no inability exists, he shall resume the powers and duties of his office unless the vice-president and a majority of either the principal officers of the executive departments or of such other body as Congress may by law provide, transmit within four days to the president pro tempore of the Senate and the speaker of the House of Representatives their written declaration that the president is unable to discharge the powers and duties of his office. Thereupon Congress shall decide the issue, assembling within forty-eight hours for that purpose if not in session. If the Congress, within twenty-one days after receipt of the latter written declaration, or, if Congress is not in session, within twenty-one days after Congress is required to assemble, determines by two-thirds vote of both houses that the president is unable to discharge the powers and duties of his office, the vice-president shall continue to discharge the same as acting president; otherwise, the president shall resume the powers and duties of his office.

Amendment XXVI (1971)

Section 1 The right of citizens of the United States, who are eighteen years of age or older, to vote shall not be denied or abridged by the United States or by any state on account of age.

Section 2 The Congress shall have the power to enforce this article by appropriate legislation.

Amendment XXVII (1992)

No law, varying the compensation for the service of the Senate and Representatives, shall take effect, until an election of Representatives shall have intervened.

Sources

Stephen Ambrose, *Nixon*, vols 1, 2, 3, Simon & Schuster, 1991

Christopher Bailey, *The US Congress*, Blackwell, 1989

Hugh Brogan, *The Pelican History of the United States of America*, Penguin, 1986, © Longman, 1985 (*Longman History of the Unites States of America*)

Walter Dean Burnham, *Critical Elections and the Mainsprings of American Politics*, Norton, 1970

Archibald Cox, *The Court and the Constitution*, Houghton Mifflin, 1987

Marcus Cunliffe, *The Presidency*, Houghton Mifflin Co., 1972

Philip John Davies and Fredric A Waldstein (eds), *Political Issues in America Today*, Manchester University Press, 1987

R V Denenberg, *Understanding American Politics*, Fontana, 1992

Federalist Papers, The Mentor, © The New American Library of World Literature, 1961

Eric Goldman, *The Tragedy of Lyndon Johnson*, Knopf, 1968

Alan Grant, *The American Political Process*, Dartmouth, 1991

Doris Kearns, *Lyndon Johnson and the American Dream*, Harper & Row, 1976

Thomas Mann, *Elections and Change in Congress*, American Enterprise Institute, 1981

Joe McGinniss, *The Selling of the President*, Trident Press, 1969

Stephen B Oates, *With Malice toward none, The Life of Abraham Lincoln*, George Allen & Unwin, 1977

Gilian Peele, Christopher J Bailey, Bruce Cain and Guy Peters, *Developments in American Politics*, Macmillan, 1994

Arthur Schlesinger Jr, *The Cycles of American History*, Penguin, 1989

Jay M Shafritz, *Dictionary of American Politics*, HarperCollins, 1993

Malcom Shaw, *Roosevelt to Reagan, The Development of the Modern Presidency*, Hurst, 1987

Hedrick Smith, *The Power Game*, Collins, 1988

Peter Woll, *American Government: Readings and Cases*, Little, Brown & Co, 1981

Peter Woll and E Zimmerman, *American Government*, McGraw Hill, 1992

Index

abortion, 150–1
'access points', 161
Adams, John Quincy, 10
advice, 115
advisory primaries, 49
agribusinesses, 156
agriculture, 20, 156–7
'alphabet agencies', 106
AMA *see* American Medical Association
ambassadors, 88
18th Amendment, prohibition, 19
amendments
  antifederalists, 34
  Founding Fathers, 34
Amendments I–XXVII, 185–91
American expansion, 12–15
American Medical Association (AMA), 157, 159
American Revolution, 6
anti-communism, 22
antifederalism, 31, 34
appeals, 140–1
appellate courts, 152
appointees, 165
appointments, 86
appropriations committee, 133
Article I, 176–80
Article II, 85, 180–2
Article III, 182–3
Article IV, 183–4
Article V, 184
Article VI, 184
Article VII, 184
Articles of Confederation, 29–31
Articles of Constitution, 176–84
authorization committee, 133

'backlash' effect, 99
balanced budget, 135
balances, checks, 122, 144, 167–8
battles, 7
bi-partisan, 110
bicameral, 38, 122–3, 162
'big government', 106
Bill of Rights, 35
  Virginia, 30, 174–5
bills, 35, 124
binding primaries, 49
black judges, 142, 143
Black Panthers, 24
block grants, 43
bloody Kansas, 14
Board of Supervisors, 38
Boston Tea Party, 6
bribery, 163
Britain, power comparison, 39
British constitution, 32
broad messages, 55
brokered conventions, 52
Brown case, 23
Brownlow Committee, 111
budget committee, 133
budget deficit, 134–5
Budget and Impoundment Control Act (1974), 134, 136
budgetary procedure, Congress, 133
budgets
  federal, 106
  president, 87
bureaucracy, 85–6, 114
  co-operation, 165
  origins, 105–6
  pressure groups, 165
business groups, 155–6
  lobbying, 155
buying an image, 59

cabinet, 104–5, 107–8
California primaries, 50
Calvinists, 2
campaign finance, British comparison, 61
campaigns
  candidate-orientated, 93
  expenses, 50
  finance, 60, 77–8
  organization, 77–8
  pressures, 50
  simple messages, 55
candidate-led policy, 78
candidate-orientated, 76, 93, 128
candidates, incumbent, 51
capitalism, 83–4
Capitol Compact, 79–80
Career Service Reform Act (1978), 108–10
Carolinas, 3
Carter, Jimmy, 73, 78
case initiation, 152

'catch-all' parties, 71–2, 78, 127
categorical grants, 43
caucuses, 48, 49
cause groups, 155
CEA *see* Council of Economic Advisors
centralization, 99
certiorari writ, 140
charisma, 93
checks/balances, 122, 167–8
  Supreme Court, 144
chief diplomat, 88
chief executives, powers, 85–6
Chief Justice, 142
chief legislator, 86, 126
chief of staff, 95
choreography, 52–3
Christian Coalition, 166
city, 38
civil liberties, 148–51
civil rights
  Earl Warren, 146
  legislation 1960s, 24
  National Association for the Advancement of Colored People, 19
  post war, 22–3
  Truman, 23
civil service, Pendleton Act 1883, 79
Civil War, 17
  cause, 40
  ending, 16
  map, 16
  seeds, 12–14
class, 73
Clay, Henry, 10
clientelism, 117
'clientelistic' relationships, 165
Clinton administration, 95
Clinton, Bill, coalition-building, 94
closed primaries, 48
co-operation, 165
co-operative federalism, 41–3
co-ordination, executive branch, 114–20
coalition, 69
coalition-building, Clinton, 94
'coat-tails' effect, 92
codification, 28
Cold War, 22
colonies
  protest, 5–6
  taxation, 7
commander-in-chief, 88–9
commerce clause, 40
committee appointments, 129
committee system, 131–3
Committee to Re-elect the President (CREEP), 77–8
communism, 22, 83–4
Compromise, Great, 31
concurrent jurisdiction, 42
concurrent powers, 39
Confederacy, formation, 16
Confederation, Articles, 29–31
conference committees, 124, 131
conflicts, 113, 115
Congress, 121–38
  attitude, 136
  budgets, 133
  committee system, 131–3
  constitution, 122–3
  control, 92–3
  finances, 126, 133–6
  functions, 123–6
  independence, 126
  information, 130–1
  inter-relationships, 126
  investigations, 125
  judicial reviews, 145–6
  legislation, 125
  party loyalty, 81
  performance, 126–36
  pressure groups, 162–4
congressional authority, 98
congressional campaigns, 63
congressional elections, 62–7
  1994, 64
  finance, 63–5
  incumbency, 65–6
  primaries, 63
congressional oversight, 118–19
congressional reform, 97
congressional veto, 99
Connecticut Compromise, 31
1980s conservatism, 151
Conservative Coalition, 158
conservative opposition, Roosevelt, 21–2
conservatives, 73
constitution, 28–36, 176–91
  amendments, 35
  British comparison, 34
  changing, 34–6
  Congress, 122–3
  dispute resolution, 32–6
  elections, 33
  executive power, 31
  interpretation, 144
  judicial interpretation, 36
  judiciary, 31
  limits, 152
  ratification, 34
  Supreme Court, 33

constitutional constraints, 89–92, 98–9
constitutional convention, 28–9, 30–1
constitutional courts, checks/balances, 144
constitutional powers, 85–9
constitutionalism, 152
constitutions, definition, 28
Continental Association, 6
Continental Congress, 6
Contract With America, 80–1
contribution rules, campaign finance, 60
control, Congress, 92–3
corporatism, 160
'cosy triangles', 165
Council of Economic Advisors (CEA), 113
counties, 48, 75
'court packing', 144
Crash, The, 20
creative federalism, 42
CREEP *see* Committee to Re-elect the President
cycles, 97

daily news, 59–60
'Daisy Girl', 56
'100 days', 96–7
de facto, 24, 147
de jure, 24, 147
1984 debate, 59
Debs, Eugene, 18–19
decision-making, 140, 160
Declaration of Independence, 6, 7, 170–3
declining population, Georgia, 3
Defense, Department of, organization, 109
deficits, 134–5
delegates, 128, 130
  national party conference, 48
  number in state, 61
democracy, 33–4
  economic motives, 33
Democratic divisions, 70
  Vietnamization, 27
Democratic Party
  1968 national convention, 52
  Clinton, 70
  proportional representation, 49
  success, 65
democratic principle, elections, 46–7
Democratic reforms, 77
Democratic-Republicans, party system, 69
denied powers, Federal, 39
departments, 107–10
  creation, 105
Depression
  1920s, 19–20
  federal aid, 22
  presidents, 96

direct mail, 167
discipline, weak parties, 93
discontented settlers, 2
dispute resolution, constitution, 32–6
divisions, 115
Dixiecrats, 70
Doctrine of Nullification, 11
domestic focus, 90
domestic/foreign policy, 89–90
Douglas, Stephen A, 14
  Lincoln, 15
'dream ticket', 54
Dred Scott Case (1857), 14, 145
dual federalism, 40–1

Earl Warren, 146
early settlers, 1
economic circumstances, presidents, 96–7
economic climate 1970s, 155
economic collapse, 1920s, 20
economic power, 83–4
economic reform, 19
economics, 22, 33
economy
  Jacksonian democracy, 11
  New England, 3
Eisenhower, President DD, 87, 95
election campaigns, 54–60
  British comparison, 54–5, 56
  geography, 55
  styles, 56–60
election debates, 57
election messages, regional variations, 55–6
elections, 46–67
  1824, 10–11
  1994, 65–6
  constitution, 33
  democratic principle, 46–7
  finance, 50–1
  non-partisan, 38
  number, 46–7
  raising funds, 50–1
  results, 91
  spending limits, 50
electoral college, 54, 61–2
  1992 election, 59
  Founding Fathers, 33
electoral districts, malapportionment, 149
electoral role, 76
electoral success, 90–2
electorate, pressure groups, 166–7
employees, 106–7
enforcement, 152
English colonies, 2–3
  imperial administration, 5–6

English expansion, 3–4
enumerated powers, federal, 38–9
EOP *see* Executive Office of the President
Equal Rights Amendment (ERA), proposed, 35
ERA *see* Equal Rights Amendment
'era of good feelings', 10–11
ethics, 163
executive
  judicial reviews, 146
  pressure groups, 164–5
executive branch, 104–5
  co-ordination, 114–20
Executive Office of the President (EXOP or EOP), 111–13, 115
executive power, government, 31
executive privilege, 101
EXOP *see* Executive Office of the President
expansion, 105–6

factions, 68
faithless voters, 61
FECA *see* Federal Election Campaign Act; Federal Election Campaign Finance Act (1972)
federal administration, 105–20
  British comparison, 107
  budget, 106
  growth, 106–7
  structure, 107–10
federal aid, 22
federal budgets, 87
federal bureaucracy, 104–20
federal Courts, 140–1
federal dominance, 162
Federal Election Campaign Act (FECA), 60, 63–4
Federal Election Campaign Finance Act (FECA), 78
federal government
  intervention, 41–2
  limits, 30
  power, 122
  v. state, 161
federal powers, 9, 38–9
Federal Reserve Board, 111
federal spending, 42
federal-state relationship, 39–40
federalism, 30, 37–45
  antifederalism, 31
  creative, 42
foundations, 8–10
Federalist, The, 68
Federalists, party system, 69
figureheads, 90
filibuster, 124

finance
  elections, 50–1
  Perot, 72
  pressure groups, 159
  Republicans, 65
financial control, Congress, 126
financial powers, Congress, 133–6
flexible funding, 43
foreign policy, 89–90
Founding Fathers, 32, 33
  amendments, 34
  electoral college, 33
  presidents, 84–5
France
  early settlers, 1–2
  North America, 3
fratricidal strife, 53
free states, new, 13
Freedom of Information Act (1966), 130–1
'frontlash' effect, 99
fundraising, 50–1, 79

Georgia, 3, 29
gerrymandering, 149
Gingrich, Newt, 80
Gompers, Samuel, 18–19
Gore, Albert, 54
governing role, 78
government
  branches, 29
  legislature, 85
government complexion, 160
government intervention, 106
government offices, allocation, 79
government role, 73
government structure, 37–8, 126–7
governors, 38
grant-in-aid programme, 42
Great Compromise, 31
Great Society, 24–7, 42–3, 106
Gulf of Tonkin, 25, 27

Hamilton, Alexander, 8
  economic strategies, 9
head of State, 88
hearings, 162
House of Representatives
  composition, 123
  democracy, 33

identity, national, 32
ideological groups, 157–8
IEAs *see* Independent Executive Agencies
immigration, 13, 18
impeachment, 100, 127

'imperial presidency', 99–101
'imperilled presidency', 101
implementation, 115
'impotent presidency', 101
incumbent candidates, 51
'incumbent politics', 164
independence, 126, 170–3
Independence Party, 72
Independent Executive Agencies (IEAs), 110
Independent Regulatory Commissions (IRCs), 110–11
independent voters, 56, 76–7
indirect lobbying, 166
indirect voting, 61
industry, 18, 166
information, 130–1
inherent powers, 39
'insider' groups, 160
inter-relationships, 126
'interest-group liberalism', 167
interest groups, 154
Interstate Commerce Commission, 19
investigations, 125
Iran-Contra affair, 101
IRCs *see* Independent Regulatory Commissions
'iron triangles', 118, 165
'issue networks', 160

Jackson, Andrew, 10, 11
Jacksonian democracy, 11–12
Jefferson, Thomas, 7, 9
Johnson, President Lyndon B
  Congress, 94
  'credibility gap', 96
  Great Society, 24–7, 43
Johnston, General Joseph E, 17
judicial activism, 146
judicial appointees, 141
judicial decisions, 141
judicial independence, 141–4
judicial interpretation, 36
judicial power, 89
judicial restraint, 150
judicial reviews, 9, 144–51
judiciary, 31, 140
  political influence, 142–3
  pressure groups, 166

Kennedy, John F, 84
Keynesian economics, 106
King, Martin Luther, 23, 24
Kissinger, Henry, 113
Ku Klux Klan, 17

labour groups, 156
laws, 5, 6
'layer-cake' federalism, 41
leadership, 22
league of states, 30
Lee, General Robert E, 17
legislature
  bicameral, 122–3
  Congress, 121, 125
  government, 85
  New Deal, 21
  organization, 78
  State, 38
  veto powers, 118–19
legitimation, 125
liberalism, 73, 167
liberty, constitution, 32
Lincoln, Abraham, 15
  Douglas, Stephen A, 14
line-item vetoes, 38
'lobby fodder', 121
lobbying, 94, 95, 116, 133
  business groups, 155
  Congress, 162–3
  finance, 159
  limits, 163
local government, 38, 74, 161
log-rolling, 94
long-term influence, 89
loose constructionists, 150
Louisiana Purchase, 12

McCulloch v. Maryland, 146
machine politics, 75
Madison, James, 9, 68, 145–6
malapportionment, 149
Malcolm X, 24
mandatory primaries, 49
'marble-cake' federalism, 44
Marbury v. Madison, 145–6
marginal states, 55
marking up, 124, 131
Marshall, John, 145
Marshall Court, 40, 146
Maryland v. McCulloch, 146
mass party, 69
mechanization, early twentieth-century, 18
media
  attention, 84
  events, 52–3
  relations, 95–6
  spotlight, 90
Medicaid, 106
Medicare, 106
membership, 159
mercantilism, 5

'mercantilist' campaigns, 57
meritocracy, 104
Mexico, war, 13
mid-term elections, 63, 65–6
Midwest primaries, 50
'militarist' campaigns, 56–7
military-industrial complex, 117, 166
mini-bureaucracy, 115
minority groups, 149–50
Missouri Compromise, 13–14
  Taney, 14
modern conventions, 52
modern era, 87
monarchical powers, 99
monarchs, 33
Monroe, James, 10

NAACP *see* National Association for the Advancement of Colored People
Nader, Ralph, 158
NAM *see* National Association of Manufacturers
National Association for the Advancement of Colored People (NAACP), 19, 157–8, 166
National Association of Manufacturers (NAM), 155–6
national committees, 75
national convention 1964, 53
national convention 1968, 52
national convention 1972, 52
national convention 1992, 53
national conventions, 50, 51
national debt, Hamilton, 8–9
national economy (1816–19), 10
national identity, 32
National Performance Review, 116
national security advisers, 113
National Security Council (NSC), 113
national supremacy, 40
negative advertising, 55–6
negative campaigning, 55, 56
negative power, 130
neutrality, 105, 108
Neutrality Acts, 88
new century, 17–18
new constitution, 8
New Deal, 20–2
  big government, 106
  coalition, 70
  legislature, 21
  opposition, 41
New Democrats, 73–4
New England, 3
New Federalism, 43–4
New Hampshire primary, 50
New Jersey plan, 31
New Right, 157
new states, free, 13
new world, 1
1920s,The
  Depression, 19–20
  prosperity, 20
Nixon, Richard, 22
  Court nominees, 143
  grants, 43
  'imperial presidency', 99–100
  Kissinger, 113
  media relations, 96
nominations, 47, 76–7
non-connected Political Action Committees, 164
non-partisan, elections, 38
North America, supremacy, 3–5
North American Free Trade Agreement, Clinton, 74
NSC *see* National Security Council

Office of Management and Budget (OMB), 112–13
'Olive Branch' message, 7
OMB *see* Office of Management and Budget
open primaries, 48
organized labour, early twentieth-century, 18
original intent, 150
original jurisdiction, 140
O'Sullivan, John L, 13
outsiders, 50, 159
over-production, 1920s, 20
'overshoot and collapse', 101
ownership, 4

pacific states, 13
PACs *see* Political Action Committees
participation, 167
party
  bosses, 75
  competition, 73–4
  discipline, 78, 127, 163
  fightback, 79–81
  reform, 75–6
  structures, 74–6
  system, 69–70
  units, 75
  unity, 53
  whips, 128
party discipline, Congress, 129, 130
passing a bill, 124
peaceful resistance, 23–4
Pendleton Act 1883, 79, 108
permanence, 105, 141

Perot, Ross, 71, 72
personal staff, 77
personalities, 93–5
persuasion, 94, 115
'picket fence' federalism, 44
'pigeon-holed' bills, 124
Planned Parenthood, 151
'plumbers, the', 100–1
pluralism, 167
pocket veto, 87, 124
policy, 51, 78–9
Political Action Committees (PACs), 51, 60, 64, 163–4
political appointees, 110, 116–18
political circumstances, 96–7
political decisions, 141
political parties, 68–82
  definition, 69
  functions, 76–9
politicization, 142–3
popular sovereignty, 14, 29
population growth, 12–13
Populist Party, 71
'pork-barrel' legislation, 130
post-Revolution, 30
post-World War II
  leadership, 22
  prosperity, 22
post-Vietnam, 27
potent forces, 85
power
  democratic transfer, 9
  too much/too little, 101–2
powers
  chief executives', 85–6
  division, 32–3
  federal government, 122
  presidential, 32–3
  separation, 32–3, 122, 146
  state governments', 38–9
  Supreme Court, 144–51
PR *see* proportional representation
precincts, 48, 74
prerogative powers, 98
presidency, 83–103
President, control of departments, 90
President pro tempore, 129
President of the Senate, 129
presidential candidates, 51–2
presidential checks, 86
presidential elections, 47, 47–62
  1992, 58
presidential experience, 93–5
presidential image, 84
presidential influence, Supreme Court, 89
presidential perceptions, 83–4
presidential veto, 86–7
presidents, 91
pressure groups, 154–69
  Congress, 162–4
  decision-making, 160
  Executive, 164
  finance, 159
  perspectives, 167–8
  power, 159–60
  targets, 160
primaries, 48, 77
  advice, 49
  congressional elections, 63
  organization/finance, 77
primary dominance, 49
primary season, 47–51
  British comparison, 47–8
  finance, 50–1
  structure, 49–50
primus inter pares, 105
private-interest groups, 155
professional bodies, 157
Progressive Party, 71
progressive reform, 19
prohibition, 19
promotional groups, 155, 158
proportional representation (PR), 49
prosperity, 1920s, 20
public-interest groups, 158
Puritans, 2

Quakers, 2
quality, 130
quantity, 130
Quayle, Dan, 54

race, 149
raising funds, 50–1, 79
ratification, 31, 34
re-election uncertainties, 51
Reagan, Ronald, 44
  Court nominees, 143
  freedom, 73
  White House Office, 112
Reaganomics, 134
reconstructions, Civil War, 16–17
regional primaries, 50
Rehnquist Court, 148
reorganization, 115
'reports', 131–2
representation, 123–5, 129–30, 159
Republican National Committee (RNC), 79
Republican Party
  Kansas-Nebraska Act, 14
  primary dominance, 49

Republicans
advantage, 65
agenda, 81
difficulties, 92
party system, 69
reserved powers, 39
respect, 152
'resurgent Congress', 97, 136
revenue, 5, 43, 133
Revolution, American, 6–8
'revolving door', 116
right-to-life, 151
rights of accused, 148
RNC *see* Republican National Committee
Roosevelt, Franklin D, 20–2
media relations, 96
'rule', 124
rule of law, 141

Sandford v. Dred Scott (1857), 145
scrutiny, 125
secession, southern states, 15
Second Continental Congress, 7
sectional groups, 155
segregated fund, 164
segregation
equal, 41
peaceful resistance, 23–4
select committees, 132
self-restraint, 150
Senate
block, 81
composition, 125
democracy, 33
majority leader, 129
prestige, 123
ratification, 105, 142
Senior Executive Service, 110
seniority rule, 80, 129
separation of powers, 84–5
settlers, 3
shaping the message, 55–6
Sherman, General William T, Civil War, 17
single ideology, 73
size, 114
Court, 143
slavery, 145
1700s, 3
Civil War, 16
Dred Scott Case, 14
Mississippi, 13
white backlash, 16
social circumstances, 96–7
social welfare, 106
'soft money', 60
'solid south', 70
'sound bites', 60
South Carolina, secession, 15
Southern Strategy, 70
southern withdrawal, 15–16
Spain, 1
SPC *see* Steering and Policy Committee
Speaker of the House, 124, 128
'spin doctors', 60, 96
split-ticket voting, 92
'spoils system', 108
staff, 95, 130
standing committees, 131
'stars', 84
state delegates, 30
state governments
functions, 38–9
judicial reviews, 146
powers, 38–9
v. federal, 161
state judiciary, 38
state parties, 75
state powers
democracy, 33
federal, 39
state structure, 38
state of the Union, 86–7
state's rights, Civil War, 16
statutory agencies, 111
Steering and Policy Committee (SPC), 132
strict constructionists, 41, 150
structure, 161
sub-committees, 133, 162
'subsystems', 160
suburban voters, 74
sunshine rules, 131, 132
Super Tuesday, 49–50
'superdelegates', 77
supremacy, North America, 3–5
Supreme Court, 139–53
accused rights, 148
affirmative action, 147
checks/balances, 144
composition, 142
constitution, 33
limitations, 152
malapportionment, 149
national supremacy, 40
power, 144–51
presidential influence, 89
rights of accused, 148
size, 143
social composition, 143
supremacy, 146
'swaps', 44

symbiosis, 117

Taney Court, 14
taxation, colonies, 7
test cases, 166
Tet Offensive, 26
third parties, 71–3
Thomas, Clarence, 143
'toe the party line', 92
topocracy, 44
trade unions, 18, 156
transient parties, 71
transport systems, inland, 10
Treaty of Ghent (1814), 10
Truman, President HS, 23
TV, 57, 166
twentieth century, 17–18
Tyler, John, 12

Union, 15–16
unions (trade unions), 18, 156
unitary states, 39

vetoes, 38, 86, 118
vice-presidents, 53–4
Viet Cong, 26
Vietnam
  Johnson, 25–7
  Kennedy, 24–5
  troops' withdrawal, 27
Vietnamization, democratic divisions, 27
Virginia
  Bill of Rights, 174–5
  English colonies, 2
  plan, 30–1
voter loyalty, 56–7, 76–7
voting rights, 19

war powers, 89, 98
War Powers Act (1973), 98–9, 136
wards, 48, 75
wars
  1812, 9–10
  Independence, 7–8
  Mexico, 13
  Pacific states, 13
Watergate, 87, 112
weak party discipline, 93
Whigs, 11–12, 69
white backlash, 16
White House Office (WHO), 112
winner-take-all (WTA), 48–9, 72
winning candidates, 61–2
winning delegates, 48
women, 19, 35
world role, 88
World War II, 22, 88
writ of certiorari, 140
WTA *see* winner-take-all